Ergo

Thinking Critically and Writing Logically

Sheila Cooper
San Francisco State University

Rosemary Patton
San Francisco State University

HarperCollins*CollegePublishers*

Senior Acquisitions Editor: Jane Kinney
Developmental Editor: Susan Messer
Project Coordination and Text Design: PC&F, Inc.
Cover Design: Kay Petronio
Photo Researcher: Diane Peterson
Production/Manufacturing: Michael Weinstein/Paula Keller
Compositor: PC&F, Inc.
Printer and Binder: R. R. Donnelley & Sons Company
Cover Printer: The Lehigh Press, Inc.

For permission to use copyrighted material, grateful acknowledgment is made to the copyright holders on pp. 233–234, which are hereby made part of this copyright page.

ERGO: THINKING CRITICALLY AND WRITING LOGICALLY

Copyright © 1993 by Sheila Cooper and Rosemary Patton

Library of Congress Cataloging-in-Publication Data

Patton, Rosemary.
    Ergo : thinking critically and writing logically / Rosemary
  Patton, Sheila Cooper.
      p.   cm.
  Includes index.
  ISBN 0-06-500264-4 (student edition) ISBN 0-06-500265-2 (instructor's edition)
    1. English language—Rhetoric. 2. Critical thinking. 3. Logic.
I. Cooper, Sheila. II. Title.
PE1408.P27 1993
808'.042—dc20
                                                              92-24997
                                                                CIP

93 94 95 9 8 7 6 5 4 3 2

He who will not reason, is a bigot; he who cannot, is a fool; and he who dares not, is a slave.

—Lord Byron

A mind that is stretched to a new idea never returns to its original dimension.

—Oliver Wendell Holmes

The vital habits of democracy: the ability to follow an argument, grasp the point of view of another, expand the boundaries of understanding, debate the alternative purposes that might be pursued.

—John Dewey

Contents

Preface

We have designed our book so that it can be used as the central text in a course that combines critical thinking and writing or in a course in written argumentation. But we also see its potential as an ancillary text in an introduction to critical thinking with an emphasis on logic, and in a variety of composition classes where argument and critical thinking are components. In some writing classes, sections on introductory logic may not be appropriate. And in a logic-based critical thinking class, no one could cover all the writing instruction. Ideally, the text could be used in a two-semester sequence combining critical thinking and writing.

In any case, we assume that *Ergo: Thinking Critically and Writing Logically* will be most effective in classes where the students have already completed an introductory composition course. However, with more advanced writers, or if further writing instruction is added, the text could serve in a freshman writing class. As you can see, how you choose to use *Ergo* will depend on the emphasis you and your course require.

The text reflects the sequence in which first our course, Writing Logically, and then *Ergo* itself have evolved. But the sequence of chapters can be altered and sections of a chapter used in conjunction with other chapters according to a particular instructor's preference. Where we think it helpful, we have given cross-references to other chapters. You will notice that the ten chapters are not balanced in terms of length; while more chapters emphasize reasoning strategies, those which concentrate on writing instruction (Chapters 4 and 10 in particular) are considerably longer. Sections of these two chapters may be used in conjunction with assignments in other chapters.

We have included a number of the collaborative activities to encourage an interactive approach to learning and hope these will serve as suggestions for how to present some of the material. Most of the writing assignments and exercises could, in fact, be approached collaboratively, even where we have not explicitly included directions. We know that not all students will be familiar with some of the terms we use in directions for exercises and writing assignments, but we assume that those who choose our text will elaborate instruction as they find it necessary. In some exercises we have asterisked (*) selected items and provided a list of possible answers at the end of the text.

We owe many debts of gratitude. We are grateful to our students over the past decade, a few of whom are represented here and to whom we dedicate this text. They have helped us test, shape, and reflect upon the material in *Ergo* and, with their enthusiasm and their questions, inspired us to grow with them in the rewarding enterprise of thinking critically and writing logically. We are equally indebted to our colleagues in the English Department at San Francisco State who have nurtured us as writing teachers. Special thanks go to William Robinson, whose perceptive, intelligent, and innovative approaches to teaching writing inform our efforts in every chapter. Additional appreciation goes to Jo Keroes, a friend and mentor who has encouraged us at every step along the way, and to Gray Patton for his patient support during the long hours when all thought, critical and otherwise, threatened to fade. Our closing words of gratitiude go to Michael Cooper for his unflagging enthusiasm for *Ergo* and tireless commitment to keeping our computers compatible.

We have learned much from those who participate each year in the International Conference on Critical Thinking & Educational Reform, conducted by the Center for Critical Thinking and Moral Critique at Sonoma State University. We are also grateful to the Research and Professional Development Committee at San Francisco State, who granted one of us assigned time to work on this text in 1990. And, we owe much to the persistent enthusiasm of our editor, Jane Kinney, and to Susan Messer, our developmental editor who helped us revise *Ergo* into a better book.

Finally, we are both grateful and astonished that our friendship has survived, even flourished, during this long and critical collaboration.

Sheila Cooper
Rosemary Patton

Chapter
1

Thinking and Writing— A Critical Connection

It is doubtful whether a man [or woman?] ever brings his faculties to bear with their full force on a subject until he writes upon it.

—Cicero

*F*or more than two thousand years, thinkers and writers have commented on the close relationship between thinking and writing. It would hardly seem debatable that to write well we need to think clearly. And the evidence is strong for concluding that writing about our ideas can help to clarify them. Taking this notion a step further, many would argue that the act of writing can create ideas, can lead writers to discover what they think. Language, according to many scholars, gives birth to thought, and written language provides a way to refine our thoughts since, unlike speech, it can be manipulated until it accurately reflects our thinking.

THINKING MADE VISIBLE

Consider writing then as thinking made visible, as thinking in slow motion, a process whereby we can inspect and reflect upon what we are thinking about. As novelist E. M. Forster put it, "How can I tell what I think till I see what I've said?" Roger Traynor, a former Chief Justice of the California Supreme Court, agreed when he spoke of writing and the law:

> I have not found a better test for the solution of a case than in its articulation in *writing,* which is *thinking at its hardest.*

Writing and thinking, when taken seriously, are not easy—a reality which led painter and critic Sir Joshua Reynolds to comment, "There is no expedient to which we will not resort to avoid the real labor of thinking." And many writers have groaned over the pain of writing. New York writer Fran Lebowitz takes an extreme position on the subject: "Writing is torture. It is very hard work. It's not coal mining, but it's work."

WRITING IS NATURE'S WAY OF LETTING YOU KNOW HOW SLOPPY YOUR THINKING IS.

THE POWER OF WRITING PERSUASIVELY

But, while writing and thinking may be difficult, mastery and success in both can be well worth the effort. We live in an increasingly complex society where clear writing is often essential. If we are not able to articulate a request, a complaint, or an endorsement in precise, forceful language, we may find ourselves settling for less than we need or deserve, or giving to others the right to impose their decisions on us. If we can't write a persuasive application, the job or graduate school position may go to someone else. Linguist Robin Lakoff in her book *Talking Power,* puts it this way:

> In a meritocracy such as ours, we believe that those who best demonstrate the ability to think and persuade should have the lion's share of power. Articulateness according to the rules goes a long way; and its possessors are assumed to possess intelligence and virtue as inseparable concomitants. People who say things right, who plead their cases well, will be listened to and their suggestions acted upon. They will make the money, win the offices, find love, get all the goodies their society has to give.

OUR MULTICULTURAL SOCIETY

It should be noted, however, that in a multicultural society such as ours, there are those who question our singular admiration for persuasive rhetoric, who look to less confrontational means of exploring issues and resolving differences. Seen through the eyes of a Japanese visitor, Yoshimi Ishikawa, who came here at age 18 and spent two years working and observing, the United States is a surprisingly violent nation. In his book, *Strawberry Road,* he claims that "the violent impression that America makes on foreigners is a result not just of its high crime rate but also of the one-sided nature of conversation here." But he too concludes that "the power to persuade and be eloquent are weapons one needs to survive in America." Whether a virtue or a weapon, the power of persuasion is seen as an asset in America today.

As you will discover in *Ergo: Thinking Critically and Writing Logically,* we are inclined to share both Lakoff and Ishikawa's views and recognize that if we are to embrace the multiplicity of views represented in our culture we must avoid dogmatic, one-sided advocacy.

CRITICAL THINKING

If, as we maintain, there is a strong relationship between thinking clearly and writing well—if one skill strengthens the other—then integrating the two as a course of study makes sense. But what do we mean by "thinking clearly"? Poets and engineers, marketing experts and philosophers would find any number of differing applications for such a broad term. For our purposes we have found it helpful to narrow our focus and concentrate on the phrase *critical thinking*. This term has assumed a central position in both academic and public life, and is variously defined today.

EXERCISE 1A

Defining Critical Thinking

Before you read further in this chapter, we would like you to put this book aside, take a piece of paper and write a few sentences discussing what you think the phrase *critical thinking* means. If you do this in class, you may want to compare notes with other students.

Critical Thinking as Self-Defense

In most contexts today the term critical thinking means censorious or fault-finding, but it comes to us from the Greek *kriticos* and Latin *criticus* meaning able to discern or separate. It is this sense of critical that we have in mind—discerning or discriminating; thought characterized by careful analysis and judgment. As former student Denise Selleck put it: "Thinking critically is the ability to understand a concept fully, taking in different sides of an issue or idea while not being swayed by the propaganda or other fraudulent methods used to promote it." She recognizes the importance of an open mind and the element of self-defense implicit in critical thinking. In particular, the media and advertising, with which we are confronted daily, require the rigorous application of critical thinking if we want to be protected adequately from false claims, questionable judgments, and deceptive arguments.

Take, for example, food packaging. Until recently, little scrutiny was given to extravagant and often deliberately misleading information about the fat content of many foods. Only the most discerning shopper could figure out where the truth lay when a frozen dinner was advertised on the front of the package as being 91 percent fat free (in weight), while the fine print on the back revealed it to be 20 percent fat free (in content). Similar deception has surrounded the word *light*, an undefined term used indiscriminately to suggest that a product is low in calories and healthy. (You will find more on definition and the precise use of language in Chapter 10.) We cannot be vigilant enough in our efforts to defend ourselves from those who would manipulate us, all too often for their personal gain.

EXERCISE 1B

Interpreting an Advertisement

In the fall of 1989 and winter of 1990, the Philip Morris Companies, makers of cigarettes and other products, ran what were called by *Newsweek* the "Smokeless Cigarette" ads, a series showing celebrated public figures endorsing the Bill of Rights. Nowhere did the actual product, cigarettes, appear—either in print or image.

These ads were designed for people like you—literate adults. The creators of such ads expect you to apply limited critical thinking at one level—to make the necessary connections—but to suspend such thinking at a crucial point.

For an interesting exercise in critical thinking, go to your library, look through copies of *Time, Newsweek, U.S. News and World Report*, or major newspapers from that period, and locate one or two examples of these ads, make a copy, and check how prepared you are to respond to such ads by answering the following questions.

1. What factual information do you need in order to understand the ad?
2. What feature of the Bill of Rights does Philip Morris want you to infer?
3. What product are they promoting?
4. What conclusion do they want to leave you with?
5. How successful would you predict the ad to be?
6. Do you feel manipulated by the ad? If so, why?

If you are unable to find these ads, you may want to examine some current advertisements which promote controversial products, bring samples to class, and work together figuring out what effects the advertiser hopes to achieve and how you, as a consumer, respond. Why do you think the Philip Morris Company refused to grant permission for us to reprint their Bill of Rights ads here?

An Open Mind

Another definition of critical thinking that also captures the spirit we hope to foster in this book comes from Richard Paul of Sonoma State University: "The disposition to think clearly and accurately in order to be fair." Like student

Denise Selleck, Paul suggests the importance of developing an open mind, of listening attentively to the views of others.

EXERCISE 1C

Evaluating Your Own Critical Thinking

Try a little self-analysis.

1. List two ideas, beliefs you are sure of, about which you wouldn't change your opinion.
2. Which would require support if you were to persuade someone else?
3. List two beliefs you hold dear but which you could, with new evidence, change your position on.
4. List one statement made recently by a generally respected person—a political figure, celebrity, or teacher, for example—that you would not challenge.
5. List one such statement you would challenge.

After answering these questions, rate yourself according to the following checklist to discover how closely your critical thinking conforms to Paul's definition:

Do you automatically dismiss positions opposed to your own?

Do you take your own beliefs for granted without recognizing the need for support?

Do you deny that your beliefs could change?

Do you accept public information without question?

Do you always assume that your intuition is sufficiently reliable, requiring no further rational deliberation?

Discuss with a classmate or a group of classmates your responses to this self-analysis and compare notes on your willingness to listen to opposing views.

At this point, you may feel overwhelmed or ill-equipped to respond to all the questions in exercises B and C. But it is our intention that as you work your way through this text you will be able to address such issues with confidence.

Profile of a Critical Thinker

If we examine the implications of Denise Selleck and Richard Paul's definitions and the questions above, we can begin to formulate a profile of how a critical thinker might behave. <u>Critical thinkers question their own beliefs as</u> <u>well as those of others, formulate well-reasoned arguments to support their</u> <u>beliefs, recognize the possibility of change in their beliefs, and express their</u> <u>beliefs in clear, coherent language.</u> As a consequence, they stand a better chance of being both fair and reliable in the conclusions they reach and the actions they take, and will find themselves better protected from those who seek to take advantage of them.

Is this all there is to it? Obviously not. The creative imagination adds another dimension to the concept of critical thinking. We don't see a sharp line drawn between reason and imagination, but rather an interplay between the two. A daydreamer is just as capable of thinking critically as is a rational pragmatist. Metaphor can play as important a role in argument as it does in poetry. Writer Zora Neale Hurston, in her autobiography *Dust Tracks on a Road*, remembers the persuasive power of a mentor's argument for honesty: "Truth is a letter from courage." The image contributes to the argument.

Our theory of critical thinking welcomes originality, encourages personal opinion, and considers paradox and ambiguity to be central to thinking well, reflecting the world as we know it. Sometimes a successful critical thinker must be able to hold two or more opposing views on an issue at once. For example, raising tuition at your college could be the only way to ensure current levels of instruction. But, paradoxically, doing so could mean that you and other students would be unable to stay in school. Reconciling such conflicts, thinking through the issues to discover alternatives, can represent a difficult but important accomplishment of critical thinking.

EXERCISE 1D

Using Intuition and Reason to Make Decisions

1. Write a paragraph or two about a decision you made on the basis of intuition.
2. Write a paragraph or two describing a dilemma you have faced in which either choice would have both compelling advantages and disadvantages.

AUDIENCE AND PURPOSE

A major distinction between writing outside the classroom and writing for a class lies in the audience to whom we write, what novelist and essayist Virginia Woolf refers to as "the face beneath the page." Job-related writing tasks, for example, include a designated audience and a real purpose. An employee may write to a superior requesting a raise or to another company proposing a cooperative venture. Readers of a newspaper often express their opinions in persuasive letters to the editor, and many a college student has depended on familiarity with the audience and careful manipulation of circumstance to explain a poor grade to parents. But in a class, students are asked to write papers for the teacher to critique and grade, usually with no specified purpose beyond successfully completing an assignment. Teachers cannot remove themselves from the role of ultimate audience, but for most of the major writing assignments in this text we have suggested an additional audience to lend some authenticity to each project. You will find that the task of thinking through a potential audience and purpose for your writing will extend the critical thinking component of many assignments.

 ## WRITING ASSIGNMENT 1

Considering Your Audience

Choose any public issue that disturbs you—be it small or large, campus, community, or cosmic—and write *two* short papers (one-and-a-half to two pages *each*) expressing your concern.

1. In the first version, direct your writing to someone connected to, perhaps responsible for, the problem you are concerned about. Your purpose here is to communicate your concern or displeasure and possibly persuade the person responsible to take appropriate action.
2. In the second version, address an individual who is in no way connected to the problem you are disturbed about. Your purpose here is to explain the situation, to inform your reader of something he may know nothing about and is not in a position to change.

Number the two papers at the top and clearly identify each audience.

WHAT YOU CAN EXPECT FROM THIS BOOK

In this book we explore a variety of strategies for expanding both writing and thinking skills, emphasizing the symbiotic relationship between them. We propose no formulas, no quick solutions. Rather, we view the development of each as a process which can take different turns for different people. Reflecting our views on this diversity, writing assignments throughout this book aim to avoid rigid adherence to form. Contrary to the advice of many writing texts, essays in real life are not limited to prescribed numbers of paragraphs or a required sequence of parts. Essays, whether explanatory or persuasive, should be designed to communicate a writer's ideas in such a way that the writer's purpose is clear and logical and satisfies the needs of a particular audience. And obviously, while there may be advantages in one approach to thinking over another, there is no one right way to think.

The Sequence

We begin, in Chapter 2, with reading critically and making inferences, essential tasks for the analysis and construction of arguments to come. You will start writing immediately, in this first chapter, but before we ask you to build your own fully developed arguments in Chapter 4, you will practice, in Chapter 3, recognizing and analyzing argument structure. As you cover the rhetoric of argument and prepare the longer writing assignments in Chapter 4, you will reinforce reasoning by continuing to look to logic—both formal and informal—in Chapters 5 through 9. Logic, from the Greek word *logos*, which means both "word" and "reason" (no accident, perhaps), can be defined as the branch of philosophy that studies the consistency of arguments. In Chapter 10, "Language and Meaning," we address writing issues again.

Collaborative Approaches

With your instructor, you can work out collaborative approaches to many exercises and writing assignments. You will find that the more opportunities you have to work with classmates the clearer your thinking is likely to become, and the more likely it will be that the assignments will reflect the writing and problem solving you will encounter in the working world, where we must often work on projects in collaboration with others. (This text, written by two authors, represents an example of such a collaboration.)

Sharpening Sentence Skills

Throughout many of the chapters, you will find practice in sentence building skills, simple review for some of you, new strategies for others. Ideas tend to travel in sentences, and the greater the fluency of your sentences, the better equipped you will be to express complex reasoning in cohesive, logical prose. This is not a handbook of grammar and usage, but is, rather, a carefully sequenced selection of rhetorical strategies selected to complement particular topics and issues. The logical relationships between ideas in a sentence as well as approaches to the composing process come early, in Chapters 2, 3, and 4. Some refinements come later: parallelism, particularly important in persuasive writing, in Chapter 7; sentence development with appositives, and sentence focus with concrete subjects and active verbs, in Chapter 10. These sentence skills also may be addressed on an individual basis, not necessarily in the sequence given here.

AVOIDING SEXIST LANGUAGE

In recent decades we have become increasingly aware of how inadequate English is when we need to make specific gender references. We find no problem when we know a person's name, but often we need to refer to indi-

"You'll just love the way he handles."

viduals in a more general way. Consider our references to a writer or a student in this text. You will notice that we alternate between female and male designations—in even-numbered chapters, she/her/hers, in odd-numbered, he/him/his. This reflects not arbitrary choice but one of the ways writers today resolve the problem posed by the lack of a gender neutral pronoun for the third person singular.

But this deficiency in our language reflects more than a simple inconvenience. The way we use language—the choices we make, the emphasis we place—suggests a broad range of personal and community attitudes, conscious and subliminal. A world described only in terms of masculine references assumes a world dominated by men. It is not surprising, therefore, that as women began to share the public worlds of business, politics, medicine, art, and sport, the universal masculine referents presented a bruising contradiction and a linguistic dilemma for writers and public speakers.

Not so many years ago, readers were content to let the masculine pronouns stand for all humanity. No longer. While some traditionalists still prefer the familiar surface of prose uncluttered by the complications to which revision of pronouns leads, a growing majority is no longer willing to accept a discourse that renders females invisible.

Attempts to invent a new singular pronoun comparable to the helpful plural "they" to solve this problem have so far failed. In the meantime we are left with a number of choices. We must choose carefully on the basis of audience, purpose, circumstance, context, and ultimately, personal inclination, all the time recognizing the implications of our choice.

Often we can use a plural noun to which the all-purpose plural pronoun—they, their, them—refers:

Writers need to be aware of *their* audience when choosing language.

But when the noun we are referring to is singular, we have various choices, many of which may displease some readers:

Each writer must consider the audience when revising *his or her* [*his/her*] paper.

First, *he/she* [*she/he, s/he*] must decide how much background information the particular audience will need.

First, *he* must decide how much background information the particular audience will need. [This represents the traditional use of "he" as a referent for both males and females.]

First, *she* must decide how much background information the particular audience will need. [This choice redresses centuries of exclusion.]

Or we can sometimes drop the pronoun:

Each writer must consider the audience when revising a paper. [A simplification of ". . . when revising his/her paper."]

Many readers object to the awkwardness that multiple pronouns create in the flow of a sentence. Others are offended by the implicit sexism of relying exclusively on the third person masculine pronoun [he, him, his].

Usage is changing, slowly, to allow *they/them/their* to refer to grammatically singular nouns and particularly to the pronoun "everyone," a practice which has been standard in spoken English.

Everyone should remember to include opposing views in *their* written arguments.

Almost *everyone* knows someone, often someone in *their* own family, who is addicted to drugs.

In the meantime, the point is to be sensitive to the audience and aware of the power of language, while at the same time representing issues and events accurately and observing conventions of written English as closely as possible.

ENJOYING THE CHALLENGE OF THINKING AND WRITING

In his poem "The Four Quartets," T. S. Eliot writes of the "intolerable wrestle / With words and meaning." But before you conclude that this whole enterprise is to be a bleak struggle, let us assure you that our goal is quite the contrary. Systematic thinking can be an exciting adventure. Polishing your prose to convey your ideas precisely can be enormously satisfying. Writer Isaac Asimov expresses such an outlook well:

> Thinking is the activity I love best, and writing to me is simply thinking through my fingers.

Our expectations are broad and flexible. What we ask is that you reflect on your ideas, support your opinions, and practice writing about them with care. We hope to foster fair and independent thinking, a capacity for empathy, and the ability to advocate your own ideas logically and fluently.

 ## WRITING ASSIGNMENT 2

Your Writing

Write an essay in which you discuss your writing experiences, in school and out—how you feel about writing, what you consider your strengths and weaknesses as a writer, your ideas on the value of learning to write well, and any other thoughts you have about yourself as a writer.

Audience   Your primary audience for this assignment is your instructor, but you as the writer will also be an audience as you write your way to an understanding of your attitude toward writing.

Purpose   To inform your instructor about your writing experiences and to gain insight into your individual writing process.

Chapter
2

Inference

Question

What do you infer from this cartoon?

Answer

As the evidence suggests, the joke is on the snake whose attempt to bite the man is thwarted by the man's wooden leg. Though we do not see the snake strike the wooden leg, we see its crumpled fangs and the man's footprints. On the basis of these observations we infer what must have happened. But it is important to note that we do not see the snake strike; instead, we see evidence which indicates that this is the case. We make an inference.

WHAT IS AN INFERENCE?

An inference is a conclusion about the unknown made on the basis of the known. We see a car beside us on the freeway with several old and new dents; we infer that the driver must be a very bad one. A close friend hasn't called in several weeks and doesn't return our calls when we leave messages; we infer that she is angry with us. Much of our thinking, whether about casual observations or personal relationships, involves making inferences.

How Reliable Is an Inference?

There is an enormous range in the reliability of inferences; some inferences are quite credible, but inferences based on very little evidence or on evidence which may support many different interpretations should be treated with skepticism. Indeed, the strength of an inference can be tested by the number of different explanations we can draw from the same set of facts. The greater the number of possible interpretations, the less reliable the inference.

In the cartoon, given the footprints and the snake's extended fangs, we cannot arrive at any other inferences but that the snake bit the wooden leg and that by extension, the usual pattern of pain inflicted is reversed. But the inferences drawn in the other two cases are not as reliable. The driver of the dented car may not be the owner: she may have borrowed the car from a friend, or she may own the car but have recently bought it "as is." Our friend may not have called us for a number of reasons: a heavy work schedule, three term papers, a family crisis. She may not have received our messages. These alternate explanations weaken the reliability of the original inferences. Clearly, the more evidence we have to support our inferences and the fewer interpretations possible, the more we can trust in their accuracy.

The language of inference
The verbs *to infer* and *to imply* are often confused, but they can be readily distinguished.

to imply: To suggest, indicate indirectly, hint, intimate. What a writer, speaker, action, or object conveys.

to infer: To arrive at a conclusion by reasoning from facts or evidence. What a reader, listener, or observer determines or concludes.

A writer, speaker, action, or object implies something, and readers, listeners, or observers infer what that something is. A final distinction: Only *people* can make inferences; *anything* can imply meaning.

EXERCISE 2A

Interpreting a Cartoon

Quickly determine the message the following cartoon implies. What inferences do you draw from the evidence given? After writing a short response, compare your interpretation with others in the class. Are they the same?

WHAT IS A FACT?

We make inferences based on our own observations or on the observations of others as they are presented to us through speech or print. These observations often consist of facts, information that can be verified. There are footprints in the sand. There are dents in the car. You have not spoken to your friend in several weeks. Our own observations attest to the truth of these claims. But often we are dependent on others' observations about people, places, and events which we cannot directly observe. Take for example the claim that the last American troops left Vietnam on March 29, 1973. Few of us observed this action firsthand, but those who did reported it, and we trust the veracity of their reports. Books, newspapers, magazines, and television programs are filled with reports—facts—giving us information about the world that we are unable to gain from direct observation. If we doubt the truth of these claims, we usually can turn to other sources to verify or discredit them. Facts come in a vast array of forms—statistics, names, events—and are distinguished by their ability to be verified. Confusions tend to grow less from the facts themselves, more from the inferences we make based on a given set of facts. It is important, however, as we discuss later in other chapters, to think critically about our sources, including our own observations, in order to understand possible biases.

WHAT IS A JUDGMENT?

When we infer that the snake struck the wooden leg, we laugh but are unlikely to express approval or disapproval of the snake's action. On the other hand, when we infer that the woman in the car in front of us is a poor driver, we express disapproval of her driving skills; we make a judgment, in this case a statement of disapproval. Or, when we infer from a friend's volunteer work with the homeless that she is an admirable person, we express our approval, make a favorable judgment. A judgment is also an inference, but while many inferences are free of positive or negative connotation, such as "I think it's going to rain," a judgment will always express the writer or speaker's approval or disapproval.

EXERCISE 2B

Distinguishing between Facts, Inferences, and Judgments

Determine whether the following statements are *facts* (reports), *inferences*, or *judgments* and explain your reasoning. Note that some may include more than one, and some may be open to interpretation.

> *Example:* I heard on the morning news that the city subway system has ground to a halt this morning; many students will arrive late for class.
>
> "I heard on the morning news that the city subway system has ground to a halt this morning": *fact.* I did hear it and the information can be verified.
>
> "Many students will arrive late for class": *inference.* This is a conclusion drawn from the information about the breakdown of the subway.

*1. The death penalty should be abolished.

2. For sale: lovely three-bedroom house in forest setting, easy commute, a bargain at $325,000.

*3. In the 1960s the Space Program had a much larger budget than the Defense Department; in the 1980s the reverse was true.

4. Arnold has a drinking problem.

5. Walter Clemmons, reviewing *You Must Remember This*, states that "Joyce Carol Oates' 17th novel is one of her most powerful."

6. After I took Richard Simmons' Vitamin Pills, the boss gave me a raise. Those pills sure did the trick.

7. Commuter—one who spends his life
   In riding to and from his wife;
   A man who shaves and takes a train
   And then rides back to shave again.

   —E. B. White

THE FAR SIDE By GARY LARSON

"Oh, what a cute little Siamese. ... Is he friendly?"

Failure to draw logical inferences can sometimes be dangerous.

EXERCISE 2C

Drawing Logical Inferences

Draw inferences from the following statements and evaluate the relative reliability of your inferences.

[The first three statements are taken from a survey comparing the college freshmen of 1986 to the college freshmen of 1966.]

1. This year's college freshmen smoke less than previous classes (down from 17 to 9 percent).
2. College students today consider being "very well off" a top personal goal (up from 44 to 71 percent).
3. The college freshmen of 1986 had higher high school grades than their predecessors of 20 years ago, but need more remedial help, according

to a study done for the American Council on Education by the Higher Education Research Institute of UCLA.

4. In 1988, 35 percent of high school athletes were girls, compared to only 7 percent in 1972. Similarly, women accounted for one-third of all college athletes in 1988, according to the NCAA.

EXERCISE 2D

Solving Riddles

Use your inferential skills to solve these riddles by English poet John Cotton.

1.
Insubstantial I can fill lives,
Cathedrals, worlds.
I can haunt islands,
Raise passions
Or calm the madness of kings.
I've even fed the affectionate.
I can't be touched or seen,
But I can be noted.

2.
We are a crystal zoo,
Wielders of fortunes,
The top of our professions.
Like hard silver nails
Hammered into the dark
We make charts for mariners.

3.
I reveal your secrets.
I am your morning enemy,
Though I give reassurance of presence.
I can be magic,
or the judge in beauty contests.
Count Dracula has no use for me.
When you leave
I am left to my own reflections.

4.
My tensions and pressures
Are precise if transitory.
Iridescent, I can float
And catch small rainbows.
Beauties luxuriate in me.

I can inhabit ovens
Or sparkle in bottles.
I am filled with that
Which surrounds me.

5.
Containing nothing
I can bind people forever,
Or just hold a finger.
Without end or beginning
I go on to appear in fields,
Ensnare enemies,
Or in another guise
Carry in the air
Messages from tower to tower.

6.
Silent I invade cities,
Blur edges, confuse travellers,
My thumb smudging the light.
I drift from rivers
To loiter in early morning fields,
Until Constable Sun
Moves me on.

—John Cotton, *Times Literary Supplement*

APPLICATION TO WRITING

Achieving a Balance Between Inference and Facts

We need to distinguish inferences, facts, and judgments from one another in order to evaluate as fairly as possible the events in our world. Whether these events are personal or global, we need to be able to distinguish between facts, verifiable information that we can rely on, and inferences and judgments, which may or may not be reliable.

We also need to evaluate the reliability of our own inferences. Are there other interpretations of the facts? Have we considered all other possible interpretations? Do we need more information before drawing a conclusion? These are useful thinking skills which we need to practice, but how do these skills relate to writing? To answer that question, read the following paragraph and distinguish between statements of fact and inference.

Members of Congress work very hard. Indeed, the average member of Congress works 70 to 80 hours a week on public business, ranging from committee hearings to floor debate to meetings with constituents. The workweek is usually seven days, four or five in Washington and the weekend back in the district—a nomadic existence that strains family life and physical well-being. During their district work periods they meet with individuals, visit senior-citizen homes or community centers, respond to large amounts of mail and read reports on significant issues facing their districts.

—*adapted from "Don't Be Beastly to Congress" by Norman J. Ornstein*

This paragraph contains two inferences; the other statements are factual, capable of verification. Notice that the facts support and convince us of the inferences. After reading this paragraph we believe that members of Congress do, indeed, work very hard and lead stressful lives, claims or inferences which in turn support the writer's thesis [not stated here] that members of Congress are justified in asking for larger salaries.

INFERENCES	FACTS
Members of Congress work very hard.	Indeed, the average member of Congress works 70 to 80 hours a week on public business, ranging from committee hearings to floor debate to meetings with constituents.
. . . a nomadic existence that strains family life, physical well-being.	The workweek is usually seven days, four or five in Washington and the weekend back in the district. . . .
	During their district work periods they meet with individuals, visit senior-citizen homes or community centers, respond to large amounts of mail and read reports on significant issues facing their districts.

Facts Only

Most expository writing consists of this blend of inference and fact with the one supporting the other. If you were to write a paper consisting only of facts it would be of no interest to the reader because reading facts which lead nowhere, which fail to support a conclusion, is like reading the telephone book. Jeff Jarvis, a book reviewer for *The New York Times Book Review*, comments on the dangers of this kind of writing:

Objectivity, in some quarters, means just the facts, ma'am—names, dates and quotations dumped from a notebook onto the page. But facts alone, without perspective, do not tell a story. Facts alone, without a conclusion to hold them together, seem unglued. Facts alone force writers to use awkward transitions, unbending formats or simple chronologies to fend off disorganization.

A facts-only approach can also have serious consequences in our schools' textbooks. A recent report on public education cites such facts-only textbooks as one of the causes of students' lack of interest and poor achievement.

Elementary school children are stuck with insipid books that "belabor what is obvious" even to first graders. At the high school level, history—or "social studies"—texts are crammed with facts but omit human motivations or any sense of what events really meant.

Deputy chairman John Agresto of the National Endowment of the Humanities said that "at the end of each chapter, I could imagine any student saying, 'So what?'"

Keep the danger of a facts-only approach in mind when you are assigned a research paper. Do not assume that teachers are looking exclusively for well-documented facts; they also want to see what you make of the data, what conclusions you draw, what criticisms and recommendations you offer. Do not fall into the trap of one eager young college freshman, Charles Renfrew, who, proud of his photographic memory, expected high praise from a distinguished philosophy professor for a paper on Descartes. He suffered disappointment but learned a lasting lesson when he read the comment: "Too much Descartes, not enough Renfrew." A photographic memory for factual information can be an asset, but your own inferences and judgments fully explained are also important.

Selecting facts

Equally important when considering the facts you use in your papers is your selection of which facts to include and which to omit. When we omit relevant facts we may be reflecting personal, political, or cultural biases, and in the process distorting "reality." The omission of certain facts from accounts of historical events can have serious consequences, in small ways and large. Audre Lorde in her book, *Zami: A New Spelling of My Name* (1982), illustrates this point eloquently.

I had spent four years at Hunter High School, with the most academically advanced and intellectually accurate education available for "preparing young women for college and career." I had been taught by some of the most highly considered historians in the country. Yet, I had never once heard the name mentioned of the first man to fall in the American revolution [Crispus Attucks], nor even been told that he was a Negro. What did that mean about the history I had learned?

Lorde is illustrating what others in recent decades have been noting. Harvey Wasserman's *History of the United States* and Frances Fitzgerald's

America Revised: History School Books in the Twentieth Century, for example, explore the ways in which historians, through a systematic selection process, have distorted history.

Inferences Only

It is possible to err in another direction as well; a paper consisting only of inferences and judgments would bore and antagonize the reader as she searches for the basis of our claims, the facts to support our opinions. If our writing is to be logical, convincing and interesting, we must draw inferences and support them with relevant facts.

WRITING ASSIGNMENT 3

Analyzing a Recent Inference

Write a paragraph about a recent inference you've made. Consider what facts the inference was based on and why you made it, whether the inference was logical given the facts that led to it, whether you think others might have made a different inference from the same data, and why they might have done so. Whether you do this exercise spontaneously in class or with more time for reflection at home, check your analysis with one classmate or a small group with whom you exchange and discuss your responses.

Audience   Yourself and other members of the class.

Purpose   To think critically about your own thinking.

WRITING ASSIGNMENT 4

Making Inferences about Fiction

Read the short story, *Hostess,* by Donald Mangum, and write a response (about one page) based on the inferences you make about the narrator. Include the facts on which these inferences are based and an explanation of why you made such inferences.

Audience   Assume that your audience has also read the story; your classmates represent an appropriate audience.

Purpose   To reveal the narrator's character.

Hostess

My husband was promoted to crew chief, and with the raise we moved into a double-wide, just up the drive. Half the park came to the house-warming. Well, Meg drank herself to tears and holed up in the toilet, poor thing. "Meg? Hon?" I said from the hall. "You going to live?" She groaned something. It was seeing R.L. with that tramp down in 18 that made her do this to herself. Now there was a whole line of beer drinkers doing the rain dance out in the hall, this being a single-bath unit. I was the hostess, and I had to do something. "Sweetheart," I said, knocking. "I'm going to put you a bowl on the floor in the utility room." The rest of the trailer was carpeted.

Dale, my husband, was in the kitchen with an egg in his hand, squeezing it for all he was worth. Veins stuck out everywhere on his arm. Paul and Eric were laughing. "What's going on in here?" I said.

Dale stopped squeezing and breathed. "I got to admit," he said, "I never knew that about eggs." I could have kicked him when he handed Paul five dollars. I found the bowl I was after, plus a blanket, and took care of Meg.

Then Hank and Boyce almost got into a fight over a remark Hank made about somebody named Linda. They had already squared off out-side when it came out that Hank was talking about a Linda *Stillman,* when Boyce thought he meant a Linda *Faye.* Well, by that time every-body was ready for something, so the guys agreed to arm-wrestle. Hank won, but only because Boyce started laughing when Kathy Sueanne sat in Jason's supper and Jason got madder than Kathy Sueanne did because there wasn't any more potato salad left.

You won't believe who showed up then. R.L.! Said he was looking for Meg. "You think she wants to see you, R.L.?" I said. "After what you did to her with that trash Elaine?" So he said he'd only kissed Elaine a couple of times. "Or not even that," he said. "She was the one kissed *me.*"

"You know what you can kiss," I said. He stood there looking like some dog you'd just hauled off and kicked for no good reason. "Well, come on," I said, taking him by the shirt. I led him to the utility room to show him the condition he'd driven his darling to. I'm here to say, when R.L. saw that precious thing curled up in front of the hot-water heater he sank to his knees in shame. I just closed the door.

Back in the den, there was this Australian kangaroo giving birth on the television. The little baby kangaroo, which looked sort of like an anchovy with legs, had just made it out of its mama and was crawling around looking for her pouch. The man on the show said it had about ten minutes to get in there and find a teat or it would die. He said a lot of them don't make it. I got so wrought up watching that trembly little fellow that I started cheering him on. So did everyone else. Well, to everyone's relief, the little thing made it. Then Gus wanted to know why everyone over there always called each other Mike. Nobody had any idea.

Eric ate a whole bunch of dried cat food before figuring out what it was and that somebody had put it in the party dish as a joke. He tried to act like it didn't bother him, but he didn't stay too long after that. Melinda went out to her car for cigarettes, and a yellow jacket stung her behind the knee, so when she came in howling, Rod slapped this big wad of chewed tobacco on the spot to draw out the poison, which made her howl even louder, till I washed it off and applied meat tenderizer and let her go lie in the guest bed for awhile.

That's when something strange happened. The phone started ringing, and I ran back to get it in Dale's and my bedroom, which was the closest to quiet in the trailer. I answered and just got this hollow sound at first, like you get with a bad connection over long-distance.

There was a mumble, then a woman's voice said, "She's gone." I didn't recognize the voice, but I was sure what "gone" meant by the way she said it. It meant someone had died. Then she said—and she almost screamed it—"Someone should have been here. Why weren't you and Clarence here?"

Now, I don't know a soul in this world named Clarence, and this was clearly a case of the wrong number. "Ma'am," I said as gently as I knew how.

"You'll have to talk louder," she said. "I can hardly hear you."

I curled my hand around my lips and the mouthpiece and said, "Ma'am, you have dialled the wrong number."

"Oh, God, I'm sorry," she said. "Oh dear God." And here is the strange thing. The woman did not hang up. She just kept saying "Dear God" and crying.

I sat there listening to that woman and to all the happy noise coming from everywhere in the trailer and through the window from outside, and when she finally brought it down to a sniffle I said, "Honey, who was it that passed away?"

"My sister," she said. "My sister, Beatrice." And it was like saying the name started her to sobbing again.

"And none of your people are there?" I said.

"Just me," she said.

"Sweetheart, you listen to me," I said, trying to close the window for more quiet. Sweet Christ, I thought. Dear sweet Christ in Heaven. "Are you listening, angel? You should not be alone right now. You understand what I'm telling you?" I said, "Now, I am right here."

—Donald Mangum

WRITING ASSIGNMENT 5

Reconstructing the Lost Tribe

Every language is also a special way of looking at the world and interpreting experience. Concealed in the structure of language are a whole set of unconscious assumptions about the world and the life in it.

—Clyde Kluckhohn

With the above quotation in mind, imagine that a previously unknown civilization has been discovered and that linguistic anthropologists, after observing the civilization for a while, have delineated the following characteristics about the society's language:

Three words for terrain, designating "absolutely flat," "rolling," and "slightly hilly."

No word for ocean.

Dozens of terms for grains, including eight for wheat alone.

Several words for children, some of which translate as "wise small one," "innocent leader," and "little stargazer."

Seven terms to describe the stages of life up to puberty, only one term to describe life from puberty to death.

The word for sex translates as "to plant a wise one."

Terms for woman are synonymous with "wife and mother."

Terms for man are synonymous with "husband and father."

Twenty words for book.

No words for violent conflict or war.

Nine words for artist.

Terms for praise translate as "peacemaker" and "conciliator."

While there are words for cow, pig, calf, and sheep, there are no terms for beef, pork, veal, leather, or mutton.

Several words for precipitation, most translating as "rain," only one meaning "snow."

Several words for leader but all are plural.

Four words meaning theater.

The topic   Write an essay in which you characterize the society that uses this language.

As you analyze the characteristics of the language you will be reconstructing a culture. Obviously, because the data are very limited, you will have to make a few educated guesses and qualify conclusions carefully. ("Perhaps," "possibly," "one might conclude," "the evidence suggests," and similar hedges will be useful.)

The approach

Examine and group the data; look for patterns

Draw inferences, depending only on the data given.

Cite evidence to support these inferences—be sure to base all your conclusions on the linguistic evidence provided. Do not draw inferences which you don't support with specific examples. Be sure to use all the data.

Explain your line of reasoning—how and why the data lead to the inferences you have made.

Don't simply write a narration or description based on the information. A narrative or story will only *imply* the conclusions you have arrived at from examining the data. This can be enjoyable to write and entertaining to read, and certainly requires critical thinking, as does all good fiction. But your purpose here is *to explain* why you have made the inferences you have and to back up your inferences with facts drawn from the language list.

Consider giving a name to this tribe to help focus your sentences.

Audience and Purpose   You have a wide range of possibilities here; we leave the choice to you. Your paper may assume the form of a report, scholarly or simply informative, directed to any audience you choose. It may be a letter to a personal friend or fictional colleague. It may be a traditional essay for an audience unfamiliar with the assignment, explaining what the language tells us about the people who use or used it. What is crucial for success is that you, as the reporter-writer, assume that *you have not seen this tribe and have no first-hand evidence of it. You will also assume that your reader does not have a copy of this assignment;* it is up to you to cite all the specific evidence (the terms given in the list) to justify your inferences.

In Chapter 4, we discuss at some length strategies for approaching a writing task and the stages that contribute to a successful writing process. You may find it helpful to look ahead to the "Writing as a Process" section of that chapter.

SUMMARY

In order to interpret the world around us and write effectively about it, we need to be able to distinguish facts, inferences, and judgments from one another and to evaluate the reliability of our inferences.

In written exposition and argument, it is important to achieve a balance between fact and inference, to support our inferences with facts and reasoning.

The way a community uses language can both reflect and shape its culture and social organization.

KEY TERMS

Facts information that can be verified.
Inference a conclusion about something we don't know based on what we do know.
Judgment an inference that expresses either approval or disapproval.

Chapter
3

The Structure of Argument

You always hurt the one you love!

*I*n logic, an argument is not a fight but a rational piece of discourse, written or spoken, which attempts to persuade the reader or listener to believe something. For instance, we can attempt to persuade others to believe that off-shore drilling will harm the environment or that a vote for a particular candidate will insure a better city government. Though many arguments are concerned with political issues, arguments are not limited to such topics. We can argue about books, movies, restaurants, and cars, to name just a few of the possibilities. Whenever we want to convince someone else of the "rightness" of our position by offering reasons for that position, we are presenting an argument.

PREMISES AND CONCLUSIONS

The structure of all arguments, no matter what the subject, consists of two components: **premises** and **conclusions.** The **conclusion** is the key assertion which the other assertions support. These other assertions are the **premises,** reasons which support the conclusion. For example:

> Because a child born with ancephaly (a developmental disorder that prevents the brain from forming) has no capacity for mental functioning, and because there are infants in desperate need of organ transplants, the organs of such a child should be harvested.

In this example, the conclusion—that the ancephalic child's organs should be harvested—is supported by two premises: that such a child has no capacity for mental functioning and that there are infants in desperate need of organ transplants. For a group of assertions to be an argument, the passage must contain both these elements—a conclusion and at least one premise.

> Look at the following letter to the editor of a news magazine:

> I was horrified to read "Corporate Mind Control" and learn that some companies are training employees in New Age thinking, which is a blend of the occult, Eastern religions and a smattering of Christianity. What they're dealing with is dangerous—Krone Training will be disastrous to the company and the employee.

This writer thinks that she has written an argument against Krone Training, but her letter consists of a conclusion only, which is in essence that Krone Training is not a good idea. Because she fails to include any premises in support of her conclusion, she fails to present an argument and fails to convince anyone who did not already share her belief that Krone Training is "dangerous" and "disastrous." A conclusion repeated in different words may look like an argument but shouldn't deceive a careful reader. (See Chapter 9 for more on deceptive arguments.) Formulate a premise that would transform the letter into an argument.

PREMISE AND CONCLUSION INDICATORS

In order to evaluate the strength of an argument, we need to understand its structure, to distinguish between its premises and conclusion. **Indicator words,** conjunctions and other transitions which indicate logical relationships between ideas, often help us to make this distinction. Notice the radical change in meaning which results from the reversal of two clauses joined by the indicator word "because":

> I didn't drink because I had problems. I had problems because I drank.

> —*Writer Barnaby Conrad*

The use of indicator words in argument is especially important since they indicate which assertions are being offered as premises and which as conclusions. For example:

Because former Cincinnati Reds manager Pete Rose violated organized baseball's rules against gambling, the decision to deny him admittance to the Hall of Fame was just.

or

Former Cincinnati Reds manager Pete Rose violated organized baseball's rule against gambling, *so* the decision to deny him admittance to the Hall of Fame was just.

In the first example, "because" indicates a premise, a reason in support of the conclusion that the decision to deny Rose admittance to the Hall of Fame was just. In the second example, "so" indicates the conclusion.

"Because" and "since" are two of the most common premise indicators while "so," "therefore," "thus," "hence," and "consequently" are among the most common conclusion indicators.

conclusion because *premise*

premise therefore *conclusion*

Special note: "and" as well as "but" often connect premises.

STANDARD FORM

With the help of indicator words, we can analyze the structure of an argument and then put it into **standard form.** An argument in standard form is an argument reduced to its essence, its premises and conclusion. In other words, it is an outline of the argument. In the previous argument on infant organ transplants, each premise is indicated by the "because" that introduces it, the conclusion then following from these two premises. In standard form, the argument looks like this:

Premise 1   A child born with ancephaly has no capacity for mental functioning.
Premise 2   There are infants in desperate need of organ transplants.
∴ The organs of such a child should be harvested.

Note: ∴ is a symbol in logic meaning "therefore."

Read this argument about the enforcement of seat belt laws.

Even though we now have a mandatory seat belt law, 33 percent of the state's motorists do not use seat belts on freeways and 48 percent don't use them on surface streets. This disregard for the law results in part from present requirements which permit a citation only after the motorist is halted for some other violation.

This law should be changed. Officers should be able to stop and cite a motorist solely for not wearing a safety belt because this strengthening of enforcement regulations would save lives.

The state's Office of Traffic Safety has reported that compliance with seat belt laws is 13 percent to 17 percent higher in states with primary enforcement than in states like ours with secondary enforcement. And it follows, according to statistics quoted in a report by a major newspaper's economics editor, Vlae Kershner, that traffic deaths are 8 percent to 9 percent lower in the primary enforcement states. Therefore, primary enforcement would save about 300 lives a year in our state, where some 3,500 people die in traffic accidents annually.

Though this argument is three paragraphs long, in standard form it can be reduced to two sentences:

Premise 1   Statistics show that primary enforcement of safety belt laws saves lives.
∴ Officers should be able to stop and cite a motorist solely for not wearing a safety belt.

The first paragraph provides the reader with necessary background information since the writer can't assume that readers will know the specifics of the current seat belt law or the percentage of people who observe it.

The second paragraph contains the conclusion and the premise which supports it, as indicated by the placement of "because."

The third paragraph contains premise support—factual documentation in support of the inference that strengthening enforcement regulations would save lives.

The conclusion of this argument—that officers should be able to stop and cite motorists for not wearing seat belts—is also an inference, a judgment. Indeed, all conclusions are inferences. If they were facts we would not need to supply premises to support them; we would simply verify them by checking the source. In this argument, the one premise is also an inference, one we would be inclined to accept since it is so well supported with facts based on a comparison between states with secondary enforcement of seat belt laws and states with primary enforcement.

Examine this argument:

San Francisco Giants fans have long argued that the city should build a downtown baseball stadium. If the city doesn't build a new stadium the team may leave, and a major city deserves a major league team. Furthermore, the summer weather in downtown San Francisco is superior to that at Candlestick Park, the present site, and access for San Franciscans would be greatly improved.

In this example, four separate premises are offered for the conclusion.

Premise 1   If the City doesn't build a new stadium, the team may leave.
Premise 2   A major city deserves a major league team.

Premise 3   Summer weather in downtown San Francisco is superior to that at Candlestick Park.

Premise 4   Access for San Franciscans would be greatly improved.

∴ The city should build a downtown baseball stadium.

EXERCISE 3A

Reducing Simple Arguments to Standard Form

Put each of the following arguments into standard form by first circling the indicator words, and then identifying the conclusion and lastly the premises. List the premises, numbering each separate statement, and write the conclusion using the symbol ∴. Leave out indicator words as well as words that connect the premises, such as "and" or "but," since standard form identifies premises and conclusions, but write each premise and the conclusion as a complete sentence.

Example: All politicians make promises they can't keep, and Jerry is nothing if not a politician. He will, therefore, make promises he can't keep.

1. All politicians make promises they can't keep.
2. Jerry is a politician.
   ∴ He will make promises he can't keep.

*1. Because hunting an endangered species is forbidden and the bald eagle is an endangered species, it follows that hunting bald eagles is prohibited.

*2. Abortion raises important moral questions, for abortion involves both a woman's right to privacy and the question of when life begins, and anything that involves personal rights and the onset of life raises serious moral questions.

3. Many biologists and gynecologists argue that life does not begin at conception. And the Supreme Court ruled in 1973 that to restrict a woman's right to have an abortion violates her right to privacy. These two facts lead us to believe that abortion should remain a woman's choice.

4. Capital punishment is not justified for the reason that, with capital punishment, an innocent person might be executed, and no practice which might kill innocent people is justified.

5. Because some killers are beyond rehabilitation, society should have the right to execute those convicted of first degree murder. More uniform implementation of the death penalty may serve as a deterrent, and victims' families are entitled to appropriate vengeance. Furthermore, the costs of maintaining a prisoner for life are too great, and no state guarantees that life imprisonment means no parole.

6. In his celebrated work "On Liberty," a defense of freedom of speech, John Stuart Mill argues that "power can be rightfully exercised over

any member of a civilized community" only in order to "prevent harm to others." Because he maintains that no opinion, no matter how disagreeable, can inflict harm, it follows that we don't have the right to suppress opinion.

7. In spite of all the controversy, we didn't need the new movie rating NC-17 as we did not need the X rating before it. The R rating already protects children, and any further restriction of choice violates our freedom of expression guaranteed under the First Amendment. And as critics pointed out, the R-rated "Sheltering Sky" was more sexually explicit than the NC-17-rated "Henry and June," so the distinction between the two ratings appears to be unclear as well as unnecessary.

8. S. Frederick Starr, President of Oberlin College, argues in a controversial *New York Times* column that "colleges and universities should explore the possibility of a three-year baccalaureate." He claims that "higher education, private and public, is too expensive" with costs having risen 4.4 percent faster than inflation over a decade. He believes that a three-year degree would automatically reduce the cost to families and taxpayers by one quarter, and would provide several concrete educational benefits as well.

EXERCISE 3B

Reducing an Editorial to Standard Form

Put the argument presented in the following editorial into standard form.

Solves Surplus Problem

To the Editor:

　　At last, someone else—Elizabeth Joseph (Op-Ed, May 23)—has put into words what I have been silently thinking for some time: Polygamy makes good sense. **1**

Nurit Karlin

Ms. Joseph writes from the perspective of a wife. I write **2**
from the perspective of a divorced working mother. How
much more advantageous it would be for me to be part of a
household such as Ms. Joseph describes, rather than to be
juggling my many roles alone.

If polygamy were legal, the problem—and I see it as a **3**
problem—of the surplus of extra women would disappear
rapidly. No matter how many polemics there may be in favor
of the free and single life style, a divorced woman can feel
extra in today's society, more so if she has children, which
can isolate her from a full social life. How much easier to
share the burdens—and the jobs.

When more women can rediscover the joys of sisterhood **4**
and co-wifehood (which are as old as the Bible), and over-
come residual jealousy as a response to this type of situation, I
think our society will have advanced considerably.

Frieda Brodsky
Brooklyn, May 23, 1991

DIAGRAMMING ARGUMENTS

Another way to analyze the structure of an argument is to diagram it. When we
put an argument into standard form, we reduce it to its premises and conclusions, emphasizing major points while ignoring statements which serve as
premise support. But when we diagram an argument, we sketch it to illustrate

the logical relationship between all assertions (claims of fact or opinion) regardless of their function, and reveal the logical direction in which ideas flow.

First, every assertion in the passage must be numbered according to simple chronology. The first assertion is #1, the second is #2, and so on. Here it is necessary to point out that a sentence may contain more than one assertion. Take for example: "Because the flag is a symbol of our country, no one should be allowed to burn it." This is one sentence but it asserts two ideas. So, if we were to number this sentence in order to diagram it, "the flag is a symbol of our country" would receive a #1, and "no one should be allowed to burn it" would receive a #2.

After numbering the assertions in the argument, place the number of the conclusion (whether that number turns out to be #1 or #3 or #7) at the bottom of the diagram. Then finish the diagram by connecting the numbers of the remaining assertions to the conclusion using arrows. These arrows symbolize a "therefore" relationship between the assertions they connect. To test the accuracy of the diagram, read "therefore" for each arrow as you follow its downward direction. Or, substitute "because" for the arrows, reading from the conclusion upward. The following example illustrates the process.

(1) The state's Office of Traffic Safety has reported that compliance with seat belt laws is 13 percent to 17 percent higher in states with primary enforcement than in states with secondary enforcement. And (2) it follows, according to statistics quoted in a report by *Chronicle* economics editor Vlae Kershner, that traffic deaths are 8 percent to 9 percent lower in the primary enforcement states. Therefore, (3) primary enforcement would save about 300 lives a year in our state, where some 3,500 people die in traffic accidents annually.

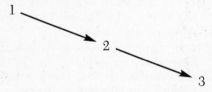

This diagram illustrates a *serial argument*—each assertion supports the one which follows it.

Argument diagrams can reflect several different relationships between premises in addition to the serial example above. Illustrations of these relationships follow.

A *convergent argument*—the premises support the conclusion (converge on the conclusion) separately, each providing a different, unrelated reason.

(1) Cats are clean animals, and (2) they also provide quiet companionship. Furthermore, (3) they do not require nearly as much care as dogs do. (4) I think they make wonderful pets.

A *linked argument*—two premises are interdependent, together providing support for a conclusion.

(1) Linda is now in law school, and (2) we all know that lawyers are more concerned with making money than with justice, so (3) I assume that Linda will soon be more concerned with money than with what's right.

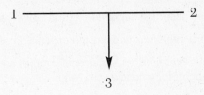

Note that in a linked argument the assertions support the conclusion only if they are joined. In the example above, the assertion that Linda is in law school does not support the conclusion that she will care more about money than justice. But when that assertion is linked to the generalization about lawyers, the connection to the conclusion is clear.

A *divergent argument*—a set of premises leading to two (or more) separate conclusions.

(1) Destroying the flag, a symbol of freedom, does not destroy the thing it represents. Indeed, (2) this freedom gains strength from our tolerance of dissent. Therefore, (3) an individual should not be prosecuted for expressing his political views by burning the flag, and (4) a constitutional amendment prohibiting such an act is not needed.

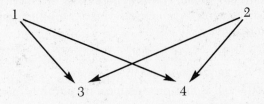

Any *combination* of these four patterns is possible; one conclusion, for example, could be supported by both a serial sequence of premises and one or more convergent premises.

An example:

(1) Supreme Court deliberations should be televised. (2) Similar coverage of proceedings in the House and Senate has proved enormously success-ful. And (3) the American public would become more informed, (4) which would in turn lead to their being more politically active.

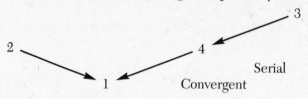

---

serial argument: each assertion supports the one which follows it.

convergent argument: premises support the conclusion separately.

linked argument: two premises (or occasionally more) are interdependent, together providing support for a conclusion.

divergent argument: a set of premises leading to two (or more) separate conclusions.

Distinguishing among the different ways premises and conclusions inter-relate can help clarify the precise logic of arguments. If time and space allow, you will find diagramming even more useful if you write out (in abbreviated form) each assertion in place of the numbers illustrated in the diagrams above.

EXERCISE 3C

Diagramming Arguments

Following the steps outlined above, diagram these six arguments and identify the type of relationship (serial, convergent, linked, divergent) that your dia-gram reveals. You can agree in your class whether to use numbers or written assertions in your diagrams.

*1. Always wear a helmet when bicycling in the city since motorists often do not see you and so accidents are common.

2. Since a bottle bill would provide incentives to return rather than dis-card bottles and cans, such a bill would reduce the public litter which seems to grow worse each day. Our state should enact and enforce a bottle bill.

*3. We all know that jogging is beneficial physically, but it also relieves stress. This indicates that it is an effective remedy for depression. Hence you should jog on a regular basis.

4. If you are drunk, then you should refrain from driving. It is wrong to risk innocent people's lives, and drunk drivers certainly pose this threat.

5. Since the Mayor is giving the project her strong support, and private investors have agreed to pay 50 percent of the cost, it is clear that the proposed waterfront development will be built. So the opposition should surrender gracefully, and the contractors should submit their bids.

6. The student union building is ugly and uncomfortable. The preponderance of cement makes the building appear cold and gray both inside and out. Many of the rooms lack windows so that one is left staring at the cement wall. The chairs are generally cheap and uncomfortable. The poor lighting makes studying difficult, and the terrible acoustics make conversations almost impossible. We should sue the architect.

AMBIGUOUS ARGUMENT STRUCTURE

Sometimes, the precise direction of an argument seems ambiguous; what is offered as conclusion and what is meant as supporting premise can be unclear. In such cases, it is important to look for what is most reasonable to believe, to give *the benefit of the doubt.* Try each assertion as the conclusion and see if the premises provide logical support for it, beginning with what seems most likely to be the intended conclusion.

Closely allied with the benefit of the doubt is the ancient methodological principle known as *Occam's razor.* Named for William of Occam, the most influential philosopher of fourteenth-century Europe (immortalized a few years ago as William of Baskerville in Umberto Ecco's novel, *The Name of the Rose*), this principle advocates economy in argument. As William of Occam put it, "What can be done with fewer assumptions is done in vain with more." Convoluted arguments, often those that sound the most impressive, can be difficult to unravel and rarely advance good reasoning. The ultimate question, however, when constructing an argument is always: What is enough? In the words of Tony Morrison, in her novel *Beloved,* "Everything depends on knowing how much, and good is knowing when to stop." But in most cases, our readers require more detailed support than we, as the advocates of a position, are likely to think necessary.

APPLICATION TO WRITING

Argument Structure and Logical Essay Organization

When we diagram arguments or put them into standard form, we ask critical questions: Is this assertion the conclusion we are being led to believe? Or is it a premise supporting the conclusion? Or does it support another premise? Asking and answering questions such as these sharpens our analytical skills. But these two methods of analyzing argument structure also have specific applications to writing.

Standard form can provide an outline of the argument, an excellent aid in essay organization, one you can use either to plan your essay or to revise it. Such an outline states the thesis of the essay—the conclusion of the argument—and each premise signals a new point to be developed.

At some stage in your writing process (see more on this subject in Chapter 4), you will find it useful to analyze your argument to determine the relationships between the premises. If you can see that you have a convergent argument—none of the premises relates to the others but each supports the conclusion directly—then you know that the order in which you present the premises in your paper may not be very significant. But if, on the other hand, you discover that there is a serial relationship between some or all of the premises, or that two of the premises are linked, then you must arrange the paragraphs and provide transitions between them in a manner which shows this relationship.

If you have thought out your argument very carefully before you start writing, you will find that putting it in standard form can lead to a good working outline from which to proceed. Or you may find that you can impose standard form or diagram your argument only when you have done some writing. (Remember writing's power to actually generate ideas.) This kind of outlining is particularly helpful in the revision stage of your paper. Diagramming should be limited to your key premises and conclusion or to individual paragraphs. You don't want diagramming to interfere with your writing process. But an understanding of how premises relate to the conclusion can be helpful to you as a writer and to your readers.

EXERCISE 3D

Analyzing Essay Structure

Look back to the first paper you wrote for Writing Assignment 1, in Chapter 1. See how successfully you can write the central argument in standard form and then diagram it. If you have difficulty imposing standard form on the argument, try sketching a sequence of premises that *would* lead logically to the conclusion you wanted to present in that paper and then write your revised sequence in standard form. (For guidance, look back to the argument on seat belt enforcement earlier in this chapter.) Now try a diagram of the argument. You will be working with the central premises and conclusion only, not all the supporting arguments for each premise. Diagramming extended complex arguments can be difficult, so don't be disturbed if your lines of reasoning fail to conform to a perfect diagram.

Logical Relationships Between Ideas—Indicator Words

Indicator words (conjunctions and other transitions) are especially important in written argument because the strength of an argument is in part dependent on the clarity of the relationships between the premises and the conclusion. But their use is not limited to argument. Whether we are describing our Aunt Frances or telling of our narrow escape from an avalanche, these words are essential to conveying a logical sequence of thought. If logical connections are missing, the reader cannot follow the line of reasoning and will either stop reading or supply his own connections which may not be the ones intended.

Not all, but many indicator words fall into three categories: coordinating conjunctions, subordinating conjunctions, and major transitions (often referred to as transitional or conjunctive adverbs in grammar texts).

JOINING CHART

Logical relationship	Coordinating conjunctions	Subordinating conjunctions	Major transitions
Addition	and		also moreover
Contrast and Concession	but yet	while whereas although though even though	however on the other hand
Cause	for	because since as	
Result Effect	so and so	so that in that in order that	therefore thus hence consequently
Condition		if unless provided that	

Note that while the list of coordinating conjunctions is complete, the other two lists are partial, featuring only the most common indicator words from both categories.

Many of these words mean almost the same thing; they express the same logical connections between the ideas they join. For example, "but," "although," and "however" all express contrast, so we can join the following two ideas with any one of the three, and arrive at a similar, if not identical, meaning.

I love foreign films, *but* I have difficulty with subtitles.

I love foreign films *although* I have difficulty with subtitles.

I love foreign films; *however,* I have difficulty with subtitles.

Choice of Indicator Words

So what determines our choice? Notice that the two sentences joined by "but" and "although" are less formal in tone than the sentences joined by "however." We often find transition words such as "however," "moreover," "hence," and "consequently" in formal documents—legal briefs and contracts. In less formal writing these transition words can be distracting, and so the best writers use them sparingly. Try an "And" or a "But" instead of "Moreover" or "However" to open a sentence and save the major transitions for extra emphasis.

On those occasions when we use transition words, it can often be effective for fluency to embed them within the clause rather than begin with them. For example:

Zoe loves foreign films and rarely sees American made movies; *however,* her roommate prefers American gangster films. ["However" begins the clause.]

Zoe loves foreign films and rarely sees American made movies; her roommate, *however,* prefers American gangster films. ["However" is embedded within the clause.]

A Review: Punctuation of Indicator Words

Coordinating conjunctions—put a comma before the conjunction when it joins two independent clauses unless the clauses are quite short.

The homeless are creating and living in unsanitary conditions all over America, so cities must provide housing for them.

Subordinating conjunctions—introductory subordinate clauses [clauses which begin with a subordinating conjunction] are usually followed by a comma.

Although the homeless are creating and living in unsanitary conditions all over America, cities are not providing needed housing.

When a subordinate clause follows the main clause, the comma is usually omitted.

Cities are not providing needed housing *even though* the homeless are creating and living in unsanitary conditions all over America.

Major transitions—transitional words and phrases, because they do not join sentences but only connect ideas, should be preceded by a semicolon or a period when they come between two clauses.

The homeless are creating and living in unsanitary conditions all over America; *therefore,* cities must provide adequate housing for them.

If in the example above a comma rather than the semicolon preceded "therefore," many readers would consider it a run-together sentence or comma splice.

When a major transition is embedded within a clause, it is usually set off with commas.

The homeless are creating and living in unsanitary conditions all over America; cities, *therefore,* must provide adequate housing for them.

EXERCISE 3E

Joining Sentences for Logic and Fluency

Make this disjointed argument cohesive and logical by joining sentences with appropriate indicator words. You don't need to change the sequence of sentences.

Obstetricians perform too many caesareans. They can schedule deliveries for their own convenience. They can avoid sleepless nights and canceled parties. They resort to caesareans in any difficult delivery to protect themselves against malpractice suits. Caesareans involve larger fees and hospital bills than normal deliveries. Caesarean patients spend about twice as many days in the hospital as other mothers.

The National Institutes of Health confirmed that doctors were performing many unnecessary caesarean sections. They suggested ways to reduce their use. The recommendation was widely publicized. The obstetricians apparently failed to take note. In 1980, the operation was performed in 16.5 percent of United States' births. In 1987, 24.7 percent of the births were Caesareans.

HIDDEN ASSUMPTIONS IN ARGUMENT

Even when arguments appear to be well supported with premises and, where necessary, logical relationships are signaled with indicator words, many real-life arguments come to us incomplete, depending on **hidden assumptions**, unstated premises and conclusions. Sometimes a missing premise or conclusion will be so obvious that we don't even recognize that it is unstated.

The burglar had dark hair, so Tracey certainly wasn't the burglar.
[Missing premise: Tracey does not have dark hair.]

Ken is lazy and lazy people don't last long around here.
[Missing conclusion: Ken won't last long around here.]

Since I've sworn to put up with my tired VW until I can afford a BMW, I must resign myself to the bug for a while longer.
[Missing premise: I can't afford a BMW now.]

Filling in the omitted assumptions here would seem unnecessarily pedantic or even insulting to our intelligence.

Literature, by its nature elliptical, depends on the reader to make plausible assumptions:

Yon Cassius has a lean and hungry look; such men are dangerous.

— *Shakespeare, Julius Caesar*

Shakespeare assumes his audience will automatically make the connection—Cassius is a dangerous man. But not all missing assumptions are as obvious or as acceptable. At the heart of critical thinking lies the ability to discern what a writer or speaker leaves **implicit**—unsaid—between the lines of what he has made **explicit**—what he has clearly stated.

Dangers of Hidden Assumptions

Examine this seemingly straightforward argument:

John is Lisa's father, so clearly he is obligated to support her.

What's missing here? All fathers are obligated to support their daughters (or their children). But would everyone find this premise acceptable under all conditions? Probably not. What about the age factor? What about special circumstances: Lisa's mother has ample means while John is penniless and terminally ill? Or Lisa was legally adopted by another family, John being her birth father?

The danger with such incomplete arguments (sometimes called by their Greek name, **enthymemes**) lies in more than one direction. A writer may leave his readers to supply their own assumptions, which may or may not coincide with those of the writer. If the issue is controversial, the risks of distorting an argument increase. Or, writers may deliberately conceal assumptions to hide an unsound, often misleading argument. Watch for these in advertising and politics. If you are on the alert for such deceptions, you are better able to evaluate what you read and hear and thus protect your own interests.

Two examples of misleading arguments:

1. A few years ago a major bank promoted its IRAs (Individual Retirement Accounts) with the following list of reasons for preferring their bank: their IRAs were tax deductible, provided safety, and would yield high interest. The implication: *their* IRAs were a superior investment. The reality: IRAs (at that time) were superior investments, but in fact *most* banks offered the same advantages. The concealed premise—their bank was offering a unique service—while a helpful sales device, was false. The suppressed premise, or tacit assumption, looks quite different when it is exposed and made explicit. The bank knew better than to risk a challenge to such a claim.

2. Echoing the arguments of the National Physicians for Social Responsibility and some public school districts, the Board of Education of a prominent Archdiocese refused to participate in a federal civil defense program that taught ways of preparing for nuclear war. They objected to instructions for teachers and students which recommended that "if there should be a nuclear flash, especially if you feel the warmth from it, take cover instantly in the best place you can find. If no cover is available, simply lie down on the ground and curl up." Their objections were leveled not at the specific suggestions but at the underlying unstated assumption: that nuclear war is survivable. In the words of the Board: "To teach children that nuclear war is a survivable disaster is to teach them that nuclear war is an acceptable political or moral option."

Hidden Assumptions and Standard Form

To help sort out the stated and unstated assertions in an argument, it can be illuminating to write out the argument in standard form. This means including the important hidden assumptions so the complete argument is before you and putting brackets around these assumptions to distinguish them from stated premises and conclusions.

Examples:

1. Harold is a politician so he's looking out for himself.

    a. [All politicians look out for themselves.]
    b. Harold is a politician.
    ∴ Harold is looking out for himself.

2. Products made from natural ingredients promote good health, so you should buy Brand X breads.

a. Products made from natural ingredients promote good health.
b. [Brand X breads are made from natural ingredients.]
∴ You should buy Brand X breads.

3. Products made from natural ingredients promote good health, and Brand X breads are made from natural ingredients.

a. Products made from natural ingredients promote good health.
b. Brand X breads are made from natural ingredients.
∴ [You should buy Brand X breads.]

EXERCISE 3F

Identifying Hidden Assumptions

A. The following arguments are missing either a premise or a conclusion. Put them into standard form, adding the implicit premise or conclusion; then place brackets around the missing assumptions you have inserted. A word to the wise: As with all argument analysis, find the conclusion first and then look for what is offered in its support.

*1. Maggie is a musician, so she won't understand the business end of the partnership.
2. Those who exercise regularly increase their chances of living into old age, so we can expect to see Anna around for a very long time.
3. I never see Loretta without a book; she must be highly intelligent.
4. Having become so central a part of our culture, television cannot be without its redeeming features.
5. Who shall give this woman in marriage?
6. **CONVICTED:** U.S. Petty Officer 3/c **Mitchell T. Garraway, Jr.;** of premeditated murder in the stabbing of a superior officer; in Newport, R.I., Jan 30., 1986. The military court must now decide his sentence; its options include the death penalty. The last execution carried out by the Navy took place in 1849. (*Newsweek*)
7. From a letter to the *Sacramento Bee* after an article reporting that a nursing mother had been evicted from a downtown department store cafeteria (Thanks to Perry Weddle of Sacramento State University for this one.):

It was inhumane to deny this woman the right to nurse her baby in the cafeteria because she was simply performing a natural bodily function. (Where will this argument take you once you supply the suppressed assumption?)

B. The following article appeared in the news section of the Durham, North Carolina *Herald-Sun* (July 12, 1991). Read it carefully and supply the hidden assumption(s) the paper seems to be leading us to.

Edward Kennedy Jr. discloses treatment
for alcohol abuse

WASHINGTON (AP) — Sen. Edward Kennedy's 29-year-old son said Thursday he spent three weeks in a Hartford, Conn. alcohol treatment center.

"At times, life has presented me with some difficult challenges and I am doing my best to face up to them," said Edward M. Kennedy, Jr., who lost his right leg to cancer when he was 12.

"I have spent the last three weeks in an alcohol treatment program at the Institute of Living in Hartford," he said.

"My decision to seek help was based on my belief that continued use of alcohol is impairing my ability to achieve the goals I care about," he said.

William Kennedy Smith, the senator's nephew, is charged with rape in connection with an alleged sexual assault on March 30 at the family's Palm Beach, Fla. compound.

C. Find one advertisement or political cartoon in print journalism which clearly depends for its message on one or more unstated assumptions. Clip or photocopy the ad, write out the principal argument including the missing assertions, and bring it to class to discuss with classmates.

Political innuendo

Sometimes politicians, seeking strategies for damaging their opponents without risking a libel suit, can slander with **innuendo,** indirect derogatory remarks which are implicit rather than explicit. Their bias often lurks in such hidden or subtly veiled suggestions.

EXERCISE 3G

Recognizing Innuendo

In June 1989, the Republican National Committee, referring to the newly elected Democratic Speaker of the House, issued a three-page memorandum titled "Tom Foley: Out of the Liberal Closet." The memo went on to compare Foley's voting record with that of Representative Barney Frank, Democrat of Massachusetts, openly homosexual, who was described in the memo as "the ultra-liberal representative from Massachusetts."

1. What inference does the Republican National Committee want you to draw about Speaker of the House Tom Foley? What facts suggest this conclusion? Are there additional inferences to be drawn from linking these two names?

2. In a newspaper or magazine article, find an example of a writer leading you to a judgment. State the unstated assumption and the evidence that led you to recognize such an assumption.

APPLICATION TO WRITING

Hidden Assumptions—Audience Awareness

As stated above, politicians and advertisers may deliberately suppress assumptions in order to manipulate the public. We will assume that we as careful writers do not share this goal and would not deliberately leave important assumptions unstated. At the same time, we don't want to bore our readers by spelling out unnecessary details. How do we determine what material to include, what to leave out?

George Lakoff and Mark Johnson, in their book *Metaphors We Live By*, point out that meaning is often dependent on context. They offer the following sentence as an example.

We need new sources of energy.

This assertion means one thing to a group of oil executives and quite another to an environmental group. The executives may assume the writer is referring to more offshore drilling, while the environmentalists may think the writer is referring to greater development of solar or other alternate sources of energy.

As writers we must consider our audience very carefully and understand the purpose for which we are writing. We will make choices about which assumptions must be made explicit according to our knowledge of the reader. Are we writing for an audience predisposed to agree with us, or one which is opposed to our point of view? Are we writing for readers who are knowledgeable about the subject or ignorant? The answers to these questions help us to determine what material to include and what to omit.

EXERCISE 3H

Identifying Your Reader

A common feature of many publications today is a section called "Personals." *The Nation* and *The New York Review of Books* (both probably in your library), and many local periodicals, including some campus papers, carry "Personals." What follows are four such ads, two from women who advertised in *Focus*, a public television magazine; and two from men who advertised in *The Daily Californian*, the University of California at Berkeley student newspaper.

Form four groups and choose one of the following ads to analyze and respond to together.

From *The Daily Californian*

MALE UCB student, 25, 6' 1", interested in music, religion, literature, psychedelics, nature etc. seeks Lithuanian woman with beautiful soul—witty, pretty, intellectual, virtuous—for fun, friendship, maybe more.

ENGLISH/MUSIC major, 25, would like to meet witty, intellectual, attractive female (pref. math/physics/other science major) for concerts, foreign films & after dinner activities.

From *Focus*

Sensual Blue-eyed Blonde, successful entrepreneur, 30, 5'4" who is attractive, well travelled, well read, and has a great sense of humor, seeks a spiritual, self aware (single white male, 30--45), 5'10" or taller, who is worldly but grounded, successful but sensitive, healthy but not fanatical and open to pursuing a long-term commitment. Note and photo appreciated.

Pretty Woman, International travel, Ivy education, health career, would like to meet professional man, 35-50, for tennis, dancing, bear hugs and possible first-time family. Photo appreciated.

Your aim is to understand the writer of the ad who will then become the audience for your response. Read the ad of your choice carefully. What kind of person is the writer? What can you infer about his or her character, personality, and values? What does the publication he or she chose to advertise in reveal about the writer? Read between the lines; what hidden assumptions are buried there?

After completing your analysis, as a group write a brief response informed by your knowledge of the writer of the ad. If time permits, reading these responses to the class might be entertaining.

WRITING ASSIGNMENT 6

A Letter of Application

Now, turn to the classified ads in any newspaper, select a job, and write a letter of application (a one-page cover letter). You will need to consider your audience very carefully in order to create a profile of your reader and a response which will appeal to him. Instead of a job in the classifieds, you may prefer to select an internship or a job on campus for this application.

Audience A person who will be evaluating you for a position you particularly want.

Purpose To present yourself as a desirable and qualified applicant for the position.

SUMMARY

In logic, the word argument has a special meaning, referring to rational discourse composed of premises and a conclusion rather than to a fight. It is useful to be able to recognize premises and conclusions in order to fully understand what an argument is proposing. Expressing arguments in standard form and diagramming the logical relationships between assertions in an argument are two helpful strategies for understanding arguments.

Understanding the structure of arguments can be useful to writers when considering the organization of their written arguments.

The logical connections between assertions in argument can be signaled by indicator words (conjunctions and phrases) to promote a logical flow of prose and ideas.

Arguments are frequently presented with some of the premises or the conclusion implied rather than stated. Sometimes such hidden assumptions are obvious, but in some instances they can be misleading and need to be made explicit. Recognizing hidden assumptions in argument is an important part of critical thinking.

KEY TERMS

Argument a rational piece of discourse, written or spoken, which attempts to persuade the reader or listener to believe something. Composed of at least one premise in support of a conclusion.

Conclusion the key assertion in an argument, the statement which the other assertions support; the point one hopes to make when presenting an argument.

Premise a reason which supports the conclusion in an argument.

Indicator words words or phrases which indicate, or signal, the logical relationship between assertions in an argument. "Therefore" and its synonyms signal a conclusion; "because" and its synonyms signal a premise.

Standard form an argument reduced to its essence, its principal premises and conclusion listed in simple outline form with premises numbered and conclusion stated at the end.

Argument diagram a sketch of an argument in which all assertions are numbered in order and then laid out in a diagram with arrows connecting them to the conclusion to illustrate the precise logical relationship between assertions.

Hidden assumptions missing, unstated premises and conclusions in arguments; assertions that are necessary to recognize in order to fully understand an argument.

Explicit clearly stated, distinctly expressed.

Implicit suggested so as to be understood but not plainly expressed.

Enthymeme an argument in which a premise or conclusion is implied rather than stated.

Innuendo an indirect remark or reference, usually implying something derogatory.

Chapter
4

Written Argument

If the cultivation of understanding consists in one thing more than in another, it is surely in learning the grounds of one's own opinions.

—John Stuart Mill

*I*n the previous chapter, we focused on the structure of argument, distinguishing between premises and conclusions and reducing arguments to these two basic components. But how do we generate these premises and conclusions? How do we begin to write an argument? Where do we begin when faced with any writing assignment?

FORMULATING A WRITTEN ARGUMENT— WRITING AS A PROCESS

In a panic about just this problem, many writers turn to the five paragraph essay format—introduction, three supporting paragraphs, and conclusion— and choose material which will easily fit into this preconceived mold. Writers rely on this formula because they fear that without it they will produce an incoherent essay. They assume that if they follow it, their writing will at least be organized. Student writers must learn to let go of this "safety net" because even though it may save them from anxiety and a disorganized essay, it can also determine the content of the essay; if an idea does not fit easily into the mold, the writer must discard it. This rigid structure prevents writers from exploring their topic, from following thoughts which may lead to interesting insights, and from allowing the material, the content, to find the shape which best suits it.

The most common misconception that student writers have is that a good writer is one who sits at her desk and produces in one sitting a polished, mechanically correct, cohesive piece of writing. If they are unable to do this, they conclude that they cannot write, and approach all writing tasks with dread and apprehension. As a first step toward improving their writing, students must discard this myth and replace it with a realistic picture of how writers write. Hemingway, in Paris in the 1920s writing his first collection of short stories, *In Our Time*, spent whole mornings on single paragraphs. Gustave Flaubert, the famous French author of *Madame Bovary*, would spend a day finding "le mot juste," the right word. While no one expects students, whose goal is to produce a competent essay rather than a literary masterpiece, to spend this kind of time on their writing, students must realize that writing is a complex intellectual act, that it involves many separate tasks, and that the mind is simply not able to handle all of these tasks at once. It is an unrealistic expectation that it should.

As writer Henry Miller saw it, "Writing, like life itself, is a voyage of discovery." Let's look at the distinct tasks involved in the act of writing an essay, in this voyage of discovery:

generating ideas

focusing a topic

establishing a thesis

organizing the essay

organizing paragraphs

providing transitions between sentences and paragraphs

polishing sentences for fluency

choosing appropriate diction (word choice)

correcting grammar, usage, spelling, and punctuation

And of course each of these tasks could be broken down further. What is the solution to this problem, this mental overload that writing forces on us? The answer is that it must be done in stages.

Writing is a *process* that breaks down into roughly three stages—creating, shaping, and correcting. A common error students make is to focus their energy on what should be the last stage (correcting) at the beginning, when the focus should be on the creative stage of the writing process. The effect of this misplaced attention is to inhibit *creative thinking*. It is essential that the writer give ample time to the first stage, to generating ideas, to following impulsive thoughts even if they may initially appear unrelated or irrelevant. At this stage a writer must allow herself to experience confusion, to be comfortable with chaos; she must learn to trust the writing process, to realize that out of this chaos a logical train of thought will gradually emerge. Most important of all, writers must learn to suspend all criticism as they explore their topic and their thinking.

Strategies for Generating Ideas

Two concrete methods for beginning this exploration are brainstorming and freewriting, one or both of which you may already be familiar with.

To **brainstorm**, simply put the topic of the writing assignment at the top of a blank piece of paper. Then jot down words or phrases that come to mind as you think about this topic—as many words as possible even if you are not sure they relate directly to the topic. After brainstorming, look at your list, circling ideas which you want to develop, drawing lines through those that are decidedly unrelated or uninteresting, and drawing arrows or making lists of ideas that are connected to one another. At this point you should be able to go on to the next stage, organizing your essay either by writing an outline or by simply listing main points that you want to develop into paragraphs. Brainstorming is particularly effective with two or more people.

In **freewriting**, you once again begin by writing your topic on a blank sheet, but instead of jotting down words and phrases, you write continuously, using sentences. These sentences do not have to be mechanically correct, nor do they have to be connected. The only rule of freewriting is that you may not stop writing; you may not put down your pen or leave the keyboard for a set length of time. After freewriting for five to ten minutes if writing by hand, or longer if using a typewriter or computer, read over your freewriting, circling ideas that you find interesting or insightful. Now you may do another freewriting on the idea or ideas you have circled, or you may try to formulate a thesis or to list ideas you want to develop.

Both of these methods have two things in common. They are relatively painless ways to begin the writing process, and they allow you to circumvent your own worst enemy, your self-criticism, the voice that says, "That's not right," "That's not what I mean," "This doesn't make sense." Critical evaluation of your writing is necessary but inappropriate and self-defeating if you are critical at the beginning. In addition, freewriting may offer surprising access to ideas you never knew you had.

The First Draft

After exploring your topic in this way, you will have a sense of what you want to say and will be ready for a first draft. When you complete this draft, you can reshape it, adding and deleting ideas, refining your thesis, polishing sentences for fluency, and finally writing another draft. Zora Neale Hurston described the process as "rubbing your paragraphs with a soft cloth."

The Time to be Critical

The time to be critical arrives when you have a complete draft. Now is the time to read with a critical mind, trusting your instinct that if a word, a sentence, or a passage seems unclear or awkward to you, your reader will most likely stumble over the same word, sentence, or passage. Finally you will be ready to check your spelling (in the dictionary or with a computer program), and your punctuation (in an English handbook); to read your essay aloud or to a friend, always ready to write another draft if it becomes necessary.

Teacher and writer Donald Murray in an essay on revision entitled "The Maker's Eye," points out a key difference between student writers and professional writers:

> When students complete a first draft, they consider the job of writing done—and their teachers too often agree. When professional writers complete a first draft, they usually feel that they are at the start of the writing process. When a draft is completed, the job of writing can begin.

Every stage in the writing process is important, and each must be given its due. To slight one is to limit the success of the final product. There are exceptions of course. Some writers, for example, are able to compress some of these steps, to generate and organize ideas before ever putting pen to paper. But for most of us, successful writing results from an extended writing process that is continually recursive.

A caution: The danger in the way we have described the writing process is that we make it seem as though it progresses in three neat steps, that it proceeds in a linear fashion from prewriting to writing to rewriting and correcting. In fact, this process is messy. You may be editing the final draft when you decide to add a completely new paragraph, an idea that didn't exist in any of the previous drafts. Nevertheless, if you realize that writing involves many separate tasks, that it is chaotic and unpredictable, you will not be defeated before you begin by criticizing yourself for having to do what all writers do—struggle to find your way, to express your thoughts so that you and your reader understand them.

In the following poem, Richard Wilbur describes this struggle.

THE WRITER

In her room at the prow of the house
Where light breaks, and the windows are tossed with linden,
My daughter is writing a story.

I pause in the stairwell, hearing
From her shut door a commotion of typewriter-keys
Like a chain hauled over a gunwale.

Young as she is, the stuff
Of her life is a great cargo, and some of it heavy:
I wish her a lucky passage.

But now it is she who pauses,
As if to reject my thought and its easy figure.
A stillness greatens, in which

The whole house seems to be thinking,
And then she is at it again with a bunched clamor
Of strokes, and again is silent.

I remember the dazed starling
Which was trapped in that very room, two years ago;
How we stole in, lifted a sash

And retreated, not to affright it;
And how for a helpless hour, through the crack of the door,
We watched the sleek, wild, dark

And iridescent creature
Batter against the brilliance, drop like a glove
To the hard floor, or the desk-top,

And wait then, humped and bloody,
For the wits to try it again; and how our spirits
Rose when, suddenly sure,

It lifted off from a chair-back,
Beating a smooth course for the right window
And clearing the sill of the world.

It is always a matter, my darling,
Of life or death, as I had forgotten. I wish
What I wished you before, but harder.

EXERCISE 4A

Describing Your Writing Process

Consider this poem for a few minutes. What two things does Wilbur compare the writing process to? What do these metaphors say about his view of the writing process? Identify and explain a metaphor that describes your own writing process.

Metaphors, figures of speech containing an implied comparison, can provide a vivid means of probing and revealing ideas. The creative thinking we do when we compare one thing to another can lead to new understanding. When we think creatively about our writing process, we are likely to *see* our writing in fresh and instructive ways.

One Writer's Process

Let us add to Wilbur's poem a description of the writing process which produced the opening pages of this chapter.

Day 1:

I spent two hours at the computer writing on the topic, "Writing as a process." During this freewriting, my goal was to say everything I could think of on this subject that was important for students to know. Most of the paragraphs were focused on one point, but there were no transitions between sentences and paragraphs and most of the sentences were only an approximation of the ideas I was trying to express. As I typed, I jotted down ideas which I wanted to include but which at the moment were interrupting the idea I was currently working on. I gave no thought to punctuation or spelling. Getting ideas on paper was my top priority.

Day 2:

I printed a copy of the three pages of freewriting I had done the previous day, and spent three hours revising: eliminating, adding, and moving passages; providing transitions and rephrasing most of the sentences.

Day 3:

I spent one hour polishing my sentences but made no major additions or deletions in the content.

Day 4:

I spent one last hour on a final review of my sentences, revising only a few of them. I checked my spelling with the help of a computer program which indeed turned up several misspellings.

As you can see, it took a total of seven hours to write three single-spaced typed pages which will take most readers ten minutes to read. And I still was not finished. The next step was to give this draft to my co-author, who made further revisions. As Donald Murray notes in his essay on revision, "Most readers underestimate the amount of rewriting it usually takes to produce spontaneous reading." But we can take heart from novelist Kurt Vonnegut: "This is what I find most encouraging about the writing trades: They allow mediocre people who are patient and industrious to revise their stupidity, to edit themselves into something like intelligence."

Focusing Your Topic

Having illustrated the major steps of the writing process, we now return to an early step, focusing and refining the topic. At one time or another, we have all been part of heated political discussions between friends or family members.

Grandfather states that taxes are too high under the new administration. Cousin Susan points out that corporations do not pay their fair share, while Dad shouts that the government funds too many social programs and allows too many foreigners to immigrate to this country. These discussions are often discursive and unsatisfying because they are not focused on one clear and precise **question at issue**.

For an argument to be successful, one person does not necessarily have to defeat another; one point of view does not have to be proven superior to another. An argument can also be considered successful if it opens a line of communication between people and allows them to consider—with respect—points of view other than their own. But if an argument is to establish such a worthwhile exchange, it must focus first on a single issue and then on a particular question at issue.

The issue   An **issue** is any topic of concern and controversy. Not all topics are issues since many topics are not controversial. Pet care, for instance, is a topic but not an issue; laboratory testing of animals, on the other hand, is an issue. In the hypothetical family discussion above four issues are raised: taxes, the new administration, immigration, and government–funded social programs. No wonder such a discussion is fragmented and deteriorates into people shouting unsupported claims at one another.

The question at issue   Whether we choose our own issue or are assigned one, the next step is to choose one **question at issue**—a particular aspect of the issue under consideration. Abortion, for instance, is an issue which contains many questions at issue.

Should abortion remain legal?

Should the government fund abortions for poor women?

Should a man have the right to prevent a woman from aborting their (or, some might argue, her) fetus?

Should minors be required to obtain parental permission in order to have an abortion?

When does life begin?

A writer who does not focus on one and only one question at issue risks producing a disorganized essay, one that will be difficult to follow since the readers will not be sure they understand the point the writer is arguing. Writing on the contested law that minors must obtain parental permission in order to have an abortion, one student kept drifting away from that question at issue to another: Is abortion immoral? Since both her questions at issue were part of the same issue, abortion, and hence related, she was unaware that her paper was going in two different directions. The result was a disorganized, disjointed essay. In order to avoid this pitfall, visualize the issue as a circle and the various questions at issue as x's within that circle.

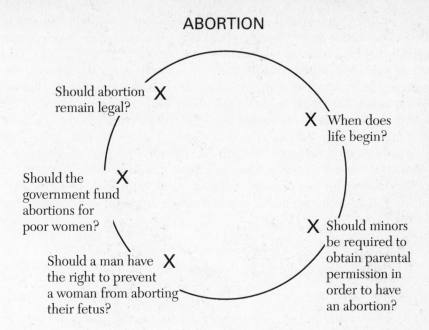

ABORTION

Should abortion remain legal? X

X When does life begin?

Should the government fund abortions for poor women? X

X Should minors be required to obtain parental permission in order to have an abortion?

Should a man have the right to prevent a woman from aborting their fetus? X

The thesis The final step in establishing the focus of an essay is determining the **thesis**. While the issue and question at issue state, respectively, the subject and focus of the paper, they are neutral statements; they do not reveal the writer's opinion nor should they. To encourage objective analysis, the question at issue should be expressed in neutral rather than biased or emotionally charged language. The thesis, however, states the writer's position, her response to the question at issue.

When we begin a paper we may not know our position. We may need to learn more about the question at issue through research before arriving at a conclusion. But if our question at issue is clear and precise, we can proceed without a definite thesis or with only a tentative one since the writing process itself will help us to arrive at one.

And we don't necessarily have to arrive at a "yes" or "no" response to the question at issue. For example, if the question at issue is whether or not school administrators should have the right to censor student newspapers, our response may not be an unequivocal yes or no but a qualified response:

> School administrators should not have the right to censor student newspapers unless an article is libelous.

After completing the necessary research and examining various points of view, we may still be unable to reach a final conclusion. In this case, the thesis of the paper may be an evaluation of these various points of view with a tentative stand based on the unfolding of future events. [See Writing Assignment 9 on page 81.]

In essays by professional writers, the thesis is sometimes indirectly stated; it may be implicit rather than explicit. For instance, writer Sheila Koran argues in an essay that gay and lesbian couples should have the same legal spousal rights as married couples. She never directly states this thesis as she describes the life she lives with her mate, a life like any other family's, but the point is clearly made; the reader is never confused about the purpose of the essay. In general, the more experienced the writer, the more she is able to write a focused essay without an explicit thesis.

Another option we have when writing a thesis is to decide whether or not it should be "closed" or "open." An open thesis states the writer's opinion but not the reasons for her opinion. A closed thesis includes both the writer's opinion and all of the reasons or premises which support this conclusion. For example:

An "open" thesis:

Capital punishment should be abolished.

A "closed" thesis:

Because capital punishment violates our moral code, costs the state an exorbitant amount of money in trial costs, ignores the risk of mistaken verdicts, and is not an effective deterrent, it should be abolished.

A compromise:

Capital punishment raises serious moral, economic, and practical questions, the nature of which suggests that capital punishment should be abolished.

Which thesis statement is better or more correct? It is a matter of choice, the writer's choice. Some writers fear that the closed thesis will not capture the reader's interest, believing that if all the reasons for the conclusion are given in the thesis, the reader's curiosity will not be aroused. On the other hand, a writer may prefer the greater clarity of the "closed" thesis, for herself and her readers. In any case, even if a writer chooses the open thesis approach, at some point in the process she should be just as clear about the reasons for her position as the writer who chooses the closed thesis.

As a general guideline to assist you in deciding the most suitable thesis approach to take, keep in mind the complexity of the topic and the length of the paper. In a long paper on a complex topic, the reader may welcome the clarity of the closed thesis, but in a short essay on a simple topic the closed thesis is probably not necessary and may be too mechanical.

Keep in mind that a thesis is not necessarily restricted to one sentence as in the examples above. In fact, it's not unusual for a closed thesis to require a paragraph. And remember too, that a well-thought-out and clearly expressed thesis will guide writer and reader, keeping both focused on the question at issue and the writer's position.

EXERCISE 4B

Identifying the Issue, Question at Issue, and Thesis

Complete the following sets by supplying the missing element.

1. *Issue:*
   Question at Issue: Should eighteen-year-old women be required to register for the draft?
   Thesis: In order to promote equality between the sexes, eighteen-year-old women should be required to register for the draft.
2. *Issue:* U.S. intervention in the Middle East
   Question at Issue: Should the United States have gone to war against Iraq?
   Thesis:
3. *Issue:* Health care
   Question at Issue:
   Thesis: The government should institute a National Health Program to provide free medical care to all its citizens.

SHAPING A WRITTEN ARGUMENT— RHETORICAL STRATEGIES

What do we mean by *rhetorical*? The term **rhetoric** has various shades of meaning, but the following definition adapted from Aristotle provides the most useful approach for our purposes: "The art of using language to good effect, to prove, to convince, to persuade."

And thus to argue. The structure of written argument as we know it today dates back to the orations of Greece and Rome. The following features of classical argument, modified by contemporary rhetoric, can serve us well as long as we recognize that they are options, not requisite components. We write to communicate, not to fit a formula or fulfill a set of narrow expectations.

The Introduction

How you begin your argument will depend on the issue, the audience, and your own style. The key question is: how much can you expect your readers to know about your question at issue? If your subject has received a great deal of recent media attention, you will probably not need to supply very much background. If, on the other hand, your subject is rather obscure or quite technical, then you will most likely have to supply your readers with the necessary background information—the history of the case or the specific circumstances which gave rise to the present problem—so that they can understand the argument to follow.

If not much background is required, you may want to begin your essay with a relevant narrative, either actual or fictional, which illustrates your question at issue. For example, if your subject is euthanasia, you may want to describe a day in the life of a terminally ill patient. Such a scene will capture the reader's interest—not a necessity but sometimes a valuable rhetorical strategy. Or you may choose to open with an opposing view and build your argument on a refutation of what is often the prevailing wisdom on an issue.

No matter what approach you choose, you have considerable flexibility. Your introduction may be a single paragraph or run to three or four paragraphs depending on the strategies you choose and the amount of background required. Usually, although not always, you will state your position (your thesis, the conclusion of your argument) somewhere in the introductory paragraphs so that your reader is clear about the purpose of the essay.

For a variety of introductory strategies, examine the three sample essays in Exercise 4E. In "Capital Punishment," you will find an introduction composed of two paragraphs, the first making a concession, the second moving toward the writer's thesis at the end. The author of "The Colorization of Black-and-White Films" opens with a literary quotation, briefly explores its relevance to his topic, and quickly reaches his thesis, which is stated indirectly but clearly. Randy Shilts, in a professional newspaper essay on a politically complex topic, provides considerable background information before arriving at his thesis.

The Development of Your Argument

Once again, the possibilities, while not infinite, are numerous. You will need to present as many strong premises in support of your position as necessary. These in turn will have to be elaborated, explained, and defended with as much specific detail, example, and illustration as you can provide. You may draw on personal experience, research, and respected authorities to support your position. Called, in classical rhetoric, the *confirmation* of your position, this support should be connected explicitly to your thesis unless the logical ties are self-evident. As Plato said in the *Phaedras*, "What is stated outright will be clearer than what is not."

Sometimes one premise will require a whole paragraph or more. Others may need only a few sentences and can be effectively grouped with additional premises. Here are two examples of paragraphs lifted from the middle of student essays, one which develops a single premise in some detail, another which groups a series of premises together in one paragraph.

A single premise paragraph:

Since the NCAA policy of random drug testing was begun one year ago, public debate on this issue has increased and the idea of drug testing for college athletes is being challenged for a variety of reasons. The strongest argument against drug testing of college athletes is that it is unconstitutional. An athlete should be entitled to the same constitutional rights as other citizens, and drug testing violates both the Fourth Amendment's provisions against unreasonable search and seizure, and the Fifth Amendment's provision of the right to refuse to furnish potentially incriminating evidence about one's self°. As various forms of drug testing have been subjected to legal challenges, the court rulings have generally been that drug testing is, indeed, unconstitutional. In 1986, Time magazine reported that ". . . a number of judges have already ruled that mass testing violates workers' constitutional rights to privacy and protection from self-incrimination," and quoted Federal Judge Robert Collins, who called a U.S. Customs Service drug testing program "unreasonable and wholly unconstitutional" (December 15, p. 35). In 1986 the Appellate Division of the New York State Supreme Court ruled that probationary teachers in a Long Island school district could not be compelled to submit to urinalysis because the tests would be an unconstitutional invasion of privacy (Kaufman, 19). In the case of Simone Le-Vant, the Stanford diver who has so far been the only athlete to challenge the NCAA drug tests in court, *The New York Times* reported that Judge Peter G. Stone of the Santa Clara county Superior Court agreed with the athlete and her attorney that mandatory urine tests were an obtrusive, unreasonable, and unconstitutional invasion of privacy (March 12, 1987).

A multipremise paragraph:

Although it is a controversial proposition, legalizing drugs has many advantages. First of all, it will free the now overburdened legal system to do its job dispensing justice. Cases will be processed with greater speed since the system won't be overwhelmed with drug cases. And with the legalization of drugs, violent drug related crimes will decrease. Prisons will be less crowded, which in turn will allow serious offenders to serve longer terms. Law enforcement officials will be freed to combat other serious crimes more effectively. With the money saved from law enforcement and legal procedures, a more effective campaign of educating the public on the maladies of drugs can be mounted, and more money will be available for rehabilitation of drug addicts. Finally, by legalizing drugs, we can slow down the spread of AIDS among IV drug users, who will be able to get clean needles and not have to share with other drug addicts, many of whom are infected with AIDS. The positive results of legalizing drugs definitely outweigh the negative consequences.

How many premises should an argument have?

It would seem that the greater the number of premises, the stronger the argument, but this quest for quantity should not be at the expense of quality; in other words, weak or questionable premises should not be included just to increase the number of premises. It's possible to have a very strong argument with only one or two premises if those premises are extremely convincing and are developed in convincing detail.

The Conclusion

We have no simple rule of thumb here other than to suggest you conclude your essay rather than simply stop. If your paper is long and complex, you

---

°Given the length of this paragraph, some writers might choose to divide it in two, starting a new paragraph here where the examples begin. Paragraphing, while certainly not arbitrary, can be flexible and should serve the needs of the reader as well as the logic of the argument.

need to help your reader by briefly summarizing where you have been and what you propose. If you present only a tentative or partial thesis in the introduction, then you need to be sure that your final position is clear in the conclusion. If you think that further investigation is still needed before you can arrive at a responsible "conclusion" on the issue, then recommend what direction you think such investigation should take. If, as a result of your argument, you have definite recommendations for action, your conclusion can carry such recommendations.

You and your readers should feel satisfied at the close of your paper. This does not mean that every paper needs a long and redundant formulaic conclusion. Once again we refer you to the sample essays in Exercise 4E for models.

And so your argument assumes its shape. Commenting on effective rhetoric, Plato, quoting Socrates, summed it up this way in *Phaedrus*:

> Every discourse, like a living creature, should be so put together that it has its own body and lacks neither head nor feet, middle nor extremities, all composed in such a way that they suit both each other and the whole.

A DIALECTICAL APPROACH TO ARGUMENT

Effective argument is more than the straightforward presentation of a thesis, premises, and their support. Most issues worth arguing today are complex, with evidence sometimes contradictory or ambiguous. Arguments on such issues should reflect a flexible mind, one capable of thinking *dialectically*. From this term's various meanings, we can extract a definition of **dialectic** appropriate for written argument:

> a method of argument that systematically weighs contradictory ideas with a view to resolution of their contradictions; the act of disclosing the contradictions in an opponent's argument and overcoming them

It is this interplay of conflict among seeming opposites that can help us arrive at some form of "truth" or resolution. Through logical disputation we test and explore our ideas as we search for a viable position. As German philosopher Georg Hegel saw it, the dialectic is a *process* of change whereby an idea, a *thesis*, is transformed into its opposite, *antithesis*. The combination of the two is then resolved in a form of truth, *synthesis*. Aristotle described this final common ground as *stasis*.

English philosopher John Stuart Mill was trained by his father to argue both sides of every question and was taught that you had no right to a belief unless you understood the arguments for its opposite. And cognitive psychologist Piaget maintained that one mark of a maturing mind is the ability to take another's point of view and thus be capable of holding two conflicting views on the same issue.

Dialectical thinking moves us to a richer form of argument in which the process of interweaving premises and counterarguments leads us to a new, stronger position on the issue.

Addressing Counterarguments

To take this dialectical approach to argument, you as a writer must pay careful attention to opposing views, acknowledging within your paper important **counterarguments** and thus those members of your audience who might hold them.

But, one might ask, why aid and abet the opposition by calling attention to their arguments? For a number of good reasons such strategies can actually strengthen your own position.

By *anticipating* your opponent's reasoning, you can often disarm the opposition. The "I recognize that. . . ." approach can be very effective, showing the writer's knowledge of the opposition's viewpoint.

You can make your own position stronger when you state and then *refute* opposing premises by demonstrating their weakness or falseness. You must handle refutation tactfully, however, if you hope to convince those opposed to your position. If you treat them with contempt, as though they are shortsighted and thickheaded for holding the position they do, you will only alienate them and defeat your own purpose, which is to have your views heard.

By addressing counterarguments to your position, you also appear more reasonable, more fair. You are seen not as narrow-minded, dogmatic, or unheedful of others' views, but as broad-minded and aware of complexity and so ultimately as more intelligent, reliable, and thus credible.

And when you *acknowledge* the possibility of merit in some of your opponents' reasoning, you have taken the ultimate step in establishing yourself as a "generous" thinker. Arguments are rarely truly one-sided, no matter how strong your convictions. When you can *concede* a point, you move closer to a middle ground, opening a line of communication and thus increasing your chances of winning your final point.

You may even discover weaknesses and contradictions in your own thinking as you sort through the reasoning of your opponents. It is not easy to abandon cherished beliefs, but clear thinkers often must.

How much counterargument?

How much counterargument should writers include in their papers? There is no precise answer to this question. If the writer has strong refutations for every one of the opposition's premises, then she may want to include all these premises. If, on the other hand, a writer thinks the premises she has to support her conclusion are stronger than her refutation, she may want to include only a minimum of counterargument. In any case, a writer cannot ignore the most compelling opposing premises even if they provide the greatest challenge to the writer's own view. For example, in a paper in favor of euthanasia, the writer would have to deal with the widely held belief that euthanasia is a form of murder or suicide.

Refutation and concession

As you can see from this discussion, there is more than one way to address counterarguments. But address them you must, since to present a contradictory position and then leave it alone would confuse your reader. Here are two possible responses:

1. **Refutation:** Present a counterargument and then explain why this position is false, misleading, irrelevant, or weak; discredit it in some well-reasoned way.

From a student essay in support of a law sanctioning active euthanasia:

Some say death and suffering are in keeping with God's universal plan for humanity. Functioning to educate, to prepare people for the painless eternity of heaven, the dying process, no matter how long or how agonizing, has both spiritual and moral purpose. **To believe this argument though, one must believe there is life after death and many do not. So why can't people live and die in accordance with their own value system? Let both the religious and secular have some control of their own destiny; give those who choose to die that alternative, while honoring the belief of those who do not.** [emphasis added]

2. **Concession:** Recognize the merit of a counterargument and so concede that point or (as in our example below) a feature of it. If, for example, you are arguing in favor of euthanasia and want to refute the counterargument that euthanasia is a form of murder, you might begin this way:

Although I also believe that life is sacred and murder is wrong, I don't think that ending the life of a brain-dead patient is equivalent to murder since in the true sense of the word "life," this patient is not living.

Rogerian strategy

For a deeper appreciation of concession we turn to the psychology of communication, particularly the work of Carl R. Rogers, a psychotherapist and communication theorist.

Carl Rogers recognized that people tend to establish barriers, grow more rigid in their beliefs when threatened, and are thus less open to alternatives. Therefore, if we view argument, whether spoken or written, as a dialogue, as an open exchange of ideas directed toward mutual understanding rather than as a hostile contest between adversaries, we may find a more responsive audience and thus have greater success with changing people's opinions. If we are genuinely concerned with communicating our ideas to others, we must cultivate the audience to whom we direct these ideas. To achieve this end, we must develop *empathy*—the ability, in Roger's words, "to see the expressed idea and attitude from the other person's point of view, to sense how it feels to him, to achieve his frame of reference in regard to the thing he is talking about." ("Communication: Its Blocking and Its Facilitation," *Et cetera*, vol IX, no. 2.) It is through empathy that we can most successfully understand another's position and so concede appropriate points, often gaining rather than losing ground in the process.

Take, for example, the issue of the death penalty. If a writer can understand why someone believes the death penalty serves as a deterrent and can acknowledge that understanding, a reader who favors the death penalty will be more inclined to consider the writer's arguments opposing the death penalty. The reader will feel less threatened as the writer reduces the gap between them and replaces hostile judgment with "mutual communication," helping a defensive opponent to see alternatives to her beliefs. Such a commitment can, as Rogers points out, carry risks. As a writer begins to "really understand" another person's point of view, she runs "the risk of being changed" herself. This spirit of conciliation and cooperation can sometimes be painful. But the gain in understanding can pay off handsomely as rigidity and defensiveness evolve into problem solving.

These ideas are not entirely new. Well over two thousand years ago, Aristotle spoke of an essential triad in argument, *logos*, *ethos*, and *pathos*:

logos   the argument itself (derived from the Greek, meaning both "word" and "reason")

ethos   the disposition of the writer (speaker) to present herself well

pathos   empathy for the audience

MACHLIS

Carl Rogers and Aristotle both suggest that effective argument depends not only on a well-informed writer but also on a writer who is acutely aware of her audience and well disposed toward them.

The alternatives for organizing Rogerian concessions within an essay are the same as those discussed above under refutation and concession and as illustrated in the sample essays in Exercise 4E.

Can you identify the Rogerian strategy in this cartoon?

"He says his ballads sing of the brotherhood of man, with due regard for the stabilizing influence of the nobility."

When There Is No Other Side

What makes an issue worth arguing? While there are no fast rules, issues inappropriate for argument fall into three general categories. Some positions are simply too offensive to the majority of writers or readers. Arguments advocating racial bigotry, for example, fall into this category. Others are so personal or so self-evident that they don't lend themselves to intelligent debate. Take for example the following claims:

Chocolate ice cream is far superior to strawberry.

or

Free, quality education should be provided for all children in America.

Neither proposition lends itself to the kind of exploration we have been discussing in this chapter, in the first instance because it concerns a personal and insignificant preference, and in the second because no one could in all seriousness argue against it.

For an effective argument

> support your own position as thoroughly as possible
>
> present relevant opposing views
>
> provide appropriate concessions and refutations
>
> develop empathy for your audience

APPLICATION TO WRITING

Logical Joining of Contrasting and Concessive Ideas

To express contrast and concession, so necessary for effective written argument, you need to manipulate your sentences to convey logical relationships. We introduced principles of logical joining with indicator words in Chapter 3 and continue that discussion here.

EXERCISE 4C

Expressing Contrast and Concession

Below are three different attitudes on smoking in the workplace. Read the passages carefully, examine the logical relationship between ideas, then state the position of each writer and explain how you reached your decision.

1. The battle rages on. Whereas some contend that smoking, as a direct threat to health, should be banned in the workplace, others maintain that forbidding smoking is too extreme a measure. Recent medical evidence does suggest that cigarette smoke may be harmful to non-smoking bystanders as well as smokers, but smokers argue their emotional health is at stake. They point out that such discrimination threatens

their constitutional civil rights, while executives and non-smoking employees claim that medical costs from health problems and time lost from work justify such restrictions of personal choice.

2. Although most people recognize that smoking is a direct threat to health, making nonsmoking a condition of employment constitutes a new form of discrimination.

3. While banning smoking on the job can create serious personnel problems for a company, current medical evidence strongly supports those who argue for a completely smoke-free work environment.

As you have no doubt noticed, it is through the different choices of joining words that these writers established their slant on the issue here. Let's review these distinctions:

COORDINATING CONJUNCTIONS	SUBORDINATING CONJUNCTIONS	MAJOR TRANSITIONS
contrast:	contrast & concession:	contrast & concession:
but	while	however
yet	whereas	on the other hand
	although	
	though	

The Concessive Sentence

The degree to which subordinating conjunctions express concession can vary according to the content of the sentence. In sentence 3 above, the writer recognizes the merit of a counterargument. But in some cases you may simply acknowledge your opponent's position without really conceding it, as in the following example:

Although smokers defend their constitutional rights, the health of a non-smoker should come first.

EXERCISE 4D

Making Rhetorical Choices

Try joining the following pair of sentences in three different ways: from the perspective of a film buff, a responsible financial planner, and someone genuinely uncommitted.

1. I desperately want to see the new Spike Lee movie.

2. I know I need to save money for books, not to mention groceries.

EXERCISE 4E

Identifying Rhetorical Features of Argument

Three well-developed arguments follow, two written by students and one by Randy Shilts (Pulitzer Prize winner for *And the Band Played On*, an examination of the AIDS crisis). They all use the rhetoric of argument effectively. In the first student essay, we identify the elements presented in this chapter:

thesis

premises

counterarguments

concessions and refutations used to address opposing views

Rogerian strategy

We ask you to identify these same features in the second student essay and the Shilts piece (or one of these if your class has time constraints).

Capital Punishment:
Help or Hindrance to American Society

The newspaper headlines are appalling: a young man is brutally murdered by a gang of thugs when he attempts to defend his parents from attack; a woman jogger is abducted, raped, and killed, her mutilated body dumped like garbage in a ditch by the side of the road; a small child dies from the multiple broken bones and internal injuries received at the hands of his abusive parents. How is it possible to remain calm and rational when confronted with such senseless violence and cruelty directed by human beings against one another, especially when the result is disability or death for the victim? Perhaps it is not surprising to see members of our society, angry and afraid, attempting to deal with increasing criminal violence by supporting the use of capital punishment.

More and more, our society relies on capital punishment to protect citizens by preventing and deterring violent crime: to avenge through retributive justice the pain and suffering inflicted by criminals on victims and their families, and to provide a kind of "collective relief" to its members by disposing of people who are aberrant, offensive, and unmanageable. However, I believe capital punishment should be abolished within the United States because I am convinced that imposition of the death penalty is not the only effective way to decrease the incidence of violent crimes; the execution of criminals does not necessarily bring about justice; and the "sigh of relief" afforded society through the use of capital punishment actually results in the dehumanization of our society as a whole.

Obviously, the execution of convicted criminals can be viewed as a means of protecting society, since a dead person is unable to commit further crimes, violent or otherwise. However, because there is no way to predict accurately whether or not a criminal would break the law again, two problems arise. First, it is impossible to know exactly how well capital punishment succeeds in preventing crimes of violence because the number of crimes prevented by execution cannot be accurately known. Second, in order to provide society with maximum protection, *every* criminal convicted of violent crime must be executed to ensure he will not repeat his crime. Given these problems, the continued use of capital punishment as a crime prevention measure seems unjustifiable and brutal, especially when long-term imprisonment can provide virtually the same amount of protection to society without taking human life.

Similarly, the deterrent effects commonly attributed by society to use of the death penalty cannot be demonstrated because they cannot be measured. Social scientists have no way of computing the number of violent crimes *not* committed, nor can they know the motivation of each violent criminal when he makes the decision whether or not to break the law. However, if capital punishment works to deter violent criminals, as its use increases the incidence of crimes of violence in our nation should show a correspondent decrease, which is unfortunately not the case. In this instance as well, the use of long-term imprisonment appears to have the same deterrent effect as imposition of the death penalty, without unnecessary loss of life. In light of these facts, clearly the use of capital punishment is not the best way of either preventing or deterring violent crime in our society.

When a murder has been committed, it is easy to view imposition of the death penalty as a good way to "even the score." Recently, I read a magazine article documenting an interview with a man whose only son had been murdered. The father kept repeating his wish to attend the execution of his son's convicted killer so he would know the boy's death has been avenged and "justice" done. Although I sympathize with the father's grief, several questions keep running through my mind: Is it really possible to "get even"? Will executing the murderer bring the son back to life? Will it obliterate the pain and terror the boy felt at the time of his death? How is "justice" served by trying to erase the death of one person by killing another? Perhaps my math is faulty, but I do not understand how one dead body added to another dead body can equal

(margin annotations)
Concession   Thesis

Counter-argument   Refutation

Counterargument   Refutation

Refutation

3

4

5   Rogerian Strategy

Refutation

anything but two dead bodies. And I have another question: What happens if the wrong person is arrested, tried, convicted, and executed? To make an all-too-possible mistake and execute the wrong person in the name of justice would be the ultimate *injustice*. In order for the use of the death penalty to be viable, its application must be foolproof. Since the possibility of error exists, the use of capital punishment can never guarantee that justice will be carried out.

Premise

Last of all—and most of all—I am concerned about what happens to a society whose members condone capital punishment. I believe few of us would be willing to witness an execution, much less participate by shooting the gun, throwing the electrical switch, or dropping the cyanide pellet to kill another person, even someone convicted of a heinous crime. Yet we seem to be perfectly willing to tell the government to do our dirty work for us, somehow believing personal responsibility can be eluded if the killing is delegated to an invisible civil servant paid to do the job. However, whether we like it or not, each member of our society becomes individually responsible when group approval is given for the taking of human life. Capital punishment involves the killing of a human being in the attempt to justify one murder by the commission of another, and human life is devalued when we succeed in distancing ourselves from that knowledge. Instead of strengthening our society, the use of capital punishment weakens it by allowing us to ignore the inherent humanity of *every* person.

6

Dependence on the execution of criminals is one way of attempting to deal with the increase of violent crime plaguing American society; yet it is not the only way of handling the problem, nor is it the best way. The use of capital punishment does not stop crimes or violence and it does not assure justice will be done. It does, however, damage our society by causing it to resort to violence in an attempt to control violence. Therefore, because use of the death penalty does not help society but actually hinders it, I suggest capital punishment no longer be allowed within the United States.

7

Mickey Lee Christensen

The Colorization of Black-and-White Films

I have heard of your paintings too, well enough; God has given you one face, and you make yourselves another.

—Hamlet, III, i

Perhaps Prince Hamlet himself could fashion an argument eloquent and strong enough to deter those intent upon performing an injustice which, although relatively unimportant when measured against greater tribulations in our time (or Hamlet's), constitutes nothing less than a crime against art: the colorization of black-and-white films.

1

Behind this effort to "colorize" black-and-white films of the '30s, '40s, and '50s is Ted Turner, whose corporation Turner Broadcasting acquired the rights to Metro-Goldwyn-Mayer's (MGM) film library. He retained the services of a professional "colorizing" company to color, with the assistance of computer technology, black-and-white films.

2

Colorization alters, indeed perverts, a completed, collaborative work. My first argument against colorization is theoretical, even moral, rather than practical: The worst thing about colorization of classic black-and-white films is that some person or technology utterly uninvolved with the process of actually making the film changes it without the consultation or control of the original creators. Any film director will tell you that he or she designs a set, lights a scene, and costumes actors in certain ways in order to bring out the best effects of color or black-and-white film. When shooting color, for example, a director will use particular colors in a set to evoke particular subconscious reactions in a viewer; when not using color, however, a director will disregard color as such, and focus on the gradations of black, white, and gray in order to achieve her or his effect. But in colorization, a person or staff who had nothing to do with the original collaborative process makes these after-the-fact creative decisions.

3

Let's take as an example a scene from William Wyler's *Wuthering Heights*, released in 1939, and starring Laurence Olivier and Merle Oberon. There's a scene on Peniston Crag where Heathcliff reaffirms his love for Cathy: the heather waves in the brisk wind as the two raven-haired, fair-skinned lovers look out over the expanse of the moors. In black-and-white, Wyler had to make such decisions as what type of lighting would best suit the curves of Oberon's face, and the angles of Olivier's; whether the heather would be a deeper or lighter hue than the crag; how to light the lovers in the foreground in order to convey a sense of depth of the moors in the background. In colorization, some staff person, maybe even a well-intentioned budding craftsperson, would make such decisions as: Should the blush in Oberon's cheek match the color of the heather or should it complement it? Is Olivier's hair brown-black or blue-black? Are the moors blue-green or Kelly green? Perhaps a skillful colorizer could create a pleasing balance of color, invent an artful one (although in practice such is not the case, as I will discuss later); the question is not whether a colorization technician is capable of producing a pleasing colorized image, the question is whether it is right to allow such post facto decisions to be made. Because those doing the colorization are totally outside of the creative process, their single-handed alteration of a completed work seriously undermines the original intentions of the creators.

4

In defense of colorization, Turner says that it will allow "young people to see films they would not otherwise want to watch." Allowing for the moment that Turner has his finger firmly on the pulse of young America, one has to wonder why we should stop at colorizing films in an

5

effort to pander to our perceptions of what youth wants. Why not update other classics in other media? We could start with Gershwin songs, most of which I'm sure are embarrassingly hackneyed or simply inscrutable to Turner's youth: "'S Wonderful" would become "'S Gnarly" or "'S Rad"; "I've Got A Crush on You" could be youthfully updated to "I Like the Cut of Your Spandex." Experience shows that when someone wants to change something wonderful into something pedestrian or offensive, he or she ostensibly has America's youth in mind; however, young people are no more or less likely to like or dislike a movie because it's in color or black-and-white than anyone else—one has simply to note the plethora of black-and-white rock videos to see that color has nothing to do with what can appeal to youth.

So why is Turner doing it? Clearly, Turner has embarked on this mission to color in order to make money. Fine. Some argue in his defense that the original black-and-white films were made for the same reason, and that they really don't constitute "art" the way, say, a Beethoven string quartet or novel by Flaubert does. There is an element **6** of truth in this: most old black-and-white films, like most current films, were made to make money, and as such are merely disposable entertainment, created to make a quick commercial kill and then mercifully forgotten. Turner, however, wants to color, not these hundreds of marginal forgotten films, but the classics of black-and-white cinema in which interest has never waned: "Casablanca," "The Maltese Falcon," "Miracle on 34th Street," even "Citizen Kane." These films are nothing if not works of high craftsmanship and even of art—their unwavering popularity certainly should secure their special place in cinema history in their original form.

All of my arguments up to now have been based on the theoretical right of an artist or group of artists not to have their work tampered with after the fact, regardless of the quality of the alteration. Practically **7** speaking, however, the effect of colorization in its present form is anything but realistic and artistic. The colors in a colorized film are weak and inconsistent, and remind one of the photographs from the 20's and 30's which had been "colorized." In these colorized films, the edges of the color move outside of the area in which they belong—the blue sky spills over to give brown mountains unnatural sky-blue tops, copper hair drips its redness onto a blue skirt, which leaves an unbecoming blue smudge on the once alabaster neckline of our fair heroine. The overall effect is certainly less than credible, and is usually distracting.

It has been said that colorization is not unlike applying makeup to a cadaver. This is true, and not just because of how unreal the color looks in both instances; in both cases, an important decision has been made without the consent of the person or persons involved. And like the **8** cadaver, many of the directors and craftspeople who made the original films have since passed away, and therefore cannot speak out against colorization of their work. Even if we could think of no other reason to stop colorization, we should stop it out of the memory for those gone; we are obligated to leave their work as they left it.

One can imagine Turner and Co. applying the first computer-assisted colors to the beloved sled "Rosebud" in "Citizen Kane"; suddenly, there is a rumble in the lab, the furniture shakes, the building sways. Given the scientific bent of the staff, they would think they had sat *9* through a minor earthquake and continue diligently with their work— they would never imagine that Orson Wells was turning over in his grave.

Thomas Logan

Free Needles Would Be a Help in S.F.

If there is any city to which San Francisco can look for lessons concerning the controversy over providing free needles to drug addicts, it would *1* be far across the Atlantic beneath the brooding bluffs of Scotland's Edinburgh Castle.

The tragedy of AIDS in Edinburgh offers a chilling warning of what *2* San Francisco can expect if this city doesn't move decisively to make needles more freely available.

The Edinburgh experience grew largely out of a shortage of marijuana in 1982, a scarcity that quickly made heroin a fashionable drug. In *3* early 1984, police realized that heroin use was out of control, so they launched a crackdown on drug paraphernalia, confiscating the needles that addicts used to inject the narcotic.

In Scotland's other major metropolis, Glasgow, heroin also spread *4* rapidly among local drug users, but police there took no comparable measures against the possession of syringes.

The lack of clean needles in Edinburgh meant that addicts were forced to share needles. Dr. Roy Robertson, Edinburgh's leading *5* authority on AIDS among drug addicts, estimates that within 18 months of the arrival of AIDS in Scotland, more than half of the city's addicts were infected with the human immunodeficiency virus.

Just 30 miles away in Glasgow, where needles were available, stud- *6* ies have found that only 4 percent to 7 percent of addicts are infected.

Today, Scotland is facing the disastrous consequences of the Edinburgh needle shortage. About 60 percent of the 1,200 known HIV- infected people in Scotland are intravenous drug users, most of them in *7* Edinburgh. Problems with heterosexual transmission of the virus from addicts to their girlfriends—and then to the women's babies—have followed.

"Making needles available to addicts is not the only answer to the problem of AIDS among drug users," concludes Robertson, "but cer- *8* tainly, it has to be part of the solution."

Just about every health expert who has considered the problem agrees.   9

To be sure, a society that offered nothing more to its addicts than free needles would be both cruel and cynical. The long-term answer to the connection between AIDS and the drug culture lies in expanded drug treatment centers that can help the addict stop using altogether.   10

This solution, however, is expensive. President Ronald Reagan's AIDS commission put a $3 billion price tag on its proposal for expanded drug treatment, and neither the Reagan nor Bush administrations have moved to give anything resembling this level of support.   11

Even if the money were available, neither the facilities nor the personnel to staff them are now in place. Training the number of drug counselors needed would take another year or two, federal officials say.   12

Moreover, some addicts have shown no willingness to make use of recovery facilities even when they are available. The very nature of drug addiction means that not all those who are sick will want to be cured.   13

Until these addicts want treatment and until the necessary staff and facilities exist to help them, it only makes sense that needles be made more easily available.   14

The issue has an unparalleled urgency on the West Coast, particularly in San Francisco. On the East Coast, among the AIDS-ravaged addicts of New York and New Jersey, attempt to prevent AIDS among needle users have come far too late. Between 50 percent and 75 percent of addicts in some of these Eastern cities are HIV-infected.   15

In San Francisco, HIV infection rates among addicts are substantially lower, generally estimated at between 13 percent and 20 percent. We still have the time and opportunity to stop AIDS from spreading like a prairie wildfire among the addict population.   16

The viral incursion, however, is growing. And the stories of Edinburgh and New York tell us what will happen here if officials don't move fast. The virus will continue to move, even if government officials don't.   17

Most opposition to free needles has tended to come from black community leaders. They worry that easier access to needles condones drug use and encourages youths to shoot up.   18

San Francisco Health Commissioner Naomi Gray, the only black on the commission, went so far as to equate free-needle programs with the "genocide" against poor people. The revulsion black leaders feel toward narcotics is understandable; after all, they've seen their communities ravaged by addiction and its related crimes.   19

But there's no evidence whatsoever that easier access to needles in any way encourages drug use. And rhetorical concerns about hypothetical genocide should not overshadow the stark truth that a real genocide of minorities looms ahead if AIDS is not checked among addicts now.   20

The distribution of uncontaminated needles to those who already are using drugs is a first, albeit limited, step toward preventing this mass death.   21

In the past, the history of the AIDS epidemic has largely been written in stories of lost opportunities, unheeded warnings and unnecessary deaths that inevitably follow actions not taken.   22

The resolution to San Francisco's free-needle controversy in the weeks ahead will determine whether, in the future, we recall the lives we saved or the deaths we witnessed.   23

Randy Shilts

ARGUMENT AND EXPLANATION—DISTINCTIONS

When preparing Writing Assignments 7 and 8, you will need to argue for a position, not simply explain a position. As you elaborate support for premises in written argument, you will often rely on explanation—of terminology, of background, of your reasoning—but you must not lose sight of your purpose, which is to persuade your reader of the wisdom of your position.

An **argument** is an attempt to establish a basis for belief, for the acceptability of your conclusion. In argument, you present reasons for your conclusion in order to convince someone of your point of view.

In **explanation**, on the other hand, you are clarifying why something has happened or why you hold a given opinion.

Look at these examples:

I'm convinced he committed the crime because his fingerprints were on the murder weapon.

We are given a reason for believing that he committed the crime. We have an *argument*.

He committed the crime because he needed money.

We are given a reason why he committed the crime. We have an *explanation*.

What about these? Which illustrates argument, which explanation?

Don't go to that market because it's closed for renovation.

Don't go to that market because the prices are higher than anywhere else and the checkout lines are slow.

EXERCISE 4F

Distinguishing Arguments from Explanations

Read the following editorials carefully and identify arguments and explanations. How do they differ in purpose? Explain your answers with references to specific passages in the columns.

They're Getting Older on Campus

The average age of college students went up a couple of years after World War II when millions of servicemen used their GI Bill benefits to return to school. The age also climbed during the Vietnam war for an opposite reason: people could beat the draft by staying in school. Now, a state survey of the composition of the 1.68 million people enrolled for credit in California's public colleges and universities shows that the trend toward an aging student population is continuing—for a number of unrelated reasons.   *1*

The average age of all freshmen enrolled in the state's community colleges, for instance, is 21.9 years. And the average age of part-time community college freshmen is 30.8 years. The average age of state university full-time graduate students is 30.8 years but this average age stretches from 28.2 years at San Luis Obispo to 36.9 years at Cal State Bakersfield. The average age of women master's degree candidates is 33.7 years, almost two and a half years older than that of males. At one state university, Dominguez Hills, which has heavy minority enrollment, the average age of senior students was 28.9 years.   *2*

Dr. Horace Crandell of the staff of the California Postsecondary Education Commission compiled the study and terms the results "startling." He speculates that some delay occurs because many students study only part-time before amassing enough units to transfer to U.C. or a state university.   *3*

Financial pressures force people to take longer to attain degrees. Many of these students are also delayed, he believes, because they must first complete remedial courses. Many minority students are simply poorly prepared for the demands of higher education. Some of the older student population results, Crandell believes, because of decisions to change careers or life goals. And some of the increase in age may be because of unexpected unemployment and the need to prepare for a different occupation.   *4*

The students are also showing a marked interest in their pocketbooks. Huge increases have taken place since 1980-81 in mathematics and computer enrollments; environmental majors have declined by almost one-half.   *5*

It was not all that long ago that student activists warned their peers not to trust anyone over 30. Now an awful lot of people over 30 seem to be right there on campus hitting the books. The change is astonishing.   *6*

Ethnic Restriction at Lowell High

A patently unfair policy that needs adjustment has been applied to academically elite Lowell High School, ordered to deny admission to superbly qualified students because they just happen to fall within an ethnic quota.   *1*

Under a 1982 court-ordered desegregation plan, alternative schools such as Lowell must limit the enrollment of any one ethnic group to 40 percent of the student body and must admit members of at least four ethnic groups. Chinese students at Lowell have reached 44.1 percent of a student population of 2807. The percentage of Chinese students throughout the entire San Francisco public school district of 65,000 students is 22.3 percent.   *2*

Lowell High School features a disciplined, academic regimen, with emphasis on college-preparatory courses. Its admission standards are high, requiring an almost straight-A average and test scores above the 97th percentile.   *3*

Strict enforcement of the five-year-old integration decree, made at the behest of several groups that participated in the plan, means that half a hundred outstanding students of Chinese origin who have already qualified for Lowell will have to go elsewhere. Some observers believe this is a welcome development that tends to diffuse academic skills throughout the district, with bright students serving as lightning rods for their dull fellows.   *4*

Superintendent Ramon Cortines feels, too, that other public high schools offer equivalent educational opportunities.   *5*

A well-balanced school population is a desirable concept, but Lowell has long attracted a citywide selection of scholars that has made it one of the most prestigious secondary schools in the country. Its enrollment should not be confined to a strict ethnic percentage.   *6*

FOUR APPROACHES TO WRITING ARGUMENTS

The next four writing assignments all focus on argument. Writing Assignment 7 serves as preparation for Writing Assignment 8. Writing Assignment 9 presents a more complex and thus more challenging approach to an issue. Assignment 10 focuses on working collaboratively with classmates on complex issues chosen by the class.

WRITING ASSIGNMENT 7

Arguing Both Sides of an Issue

The topic   Below is a list of proposals advocating a position on a social issue. Choose *one* and write two arguments, one defending and one refuting the proposal.

For each argument, convey clearly the position you are taking by writing a short thesis (the conclusion of your argument) at the top of the page. For each position, provide relevant reasons (premises) which are, to the best of your knowledge, accurate. You will have two separate papers with a paragraph for each reason. While each paragraph should be written coherently with fluent sentences, you don't, at this stage, need to provide logical transitions between paragraphs for a coherent whole. And you need not provide an introduction, conclusion, or research. All this will come later in Writing Assignment 8.

Make your selection with care, for you will be spending considerable time on this one issue.

1. Both professional and college athletes should be tested for drugs.
2. An employer should have the right to require drug testing of employees.
3. Parental permission should be required for a minor to have an abortion.
4. High school students should have to maintain a C average in order to participate in competitive sports.
5. Doctors should be permitted to perform euthanasia upon patients who ask to die.
6. The practice of surrogate motherhood should not be legal.
7. School administrators should be allowed to censor student newspapers.
8. Colleges should practice affirmative action in their admission policies.
9. Congress should pass legislation making English the official language of the United States Government.
10. If another issue interests you more—for instance, a campus topic or a controversy in your neighborhood—you may write on it. Be sure the issue is one worth arguing from both sides and can be expressed as a proposal similar to those above. You may, of course, change any of the given topics to suit your own purpose.

Audience   A wide range of your peers, those who would agree with you, those who disagree, and those who have not, as yet, formed any opinion.

Purpose   To present both sides of a controversial issue so you and your readers are forced to consider alternatives to one position.

WRITING ASSIGNMENT 8

Taking a Stand

The topic   In this essay you will take a stand on the issue you debated in Writing Assignment 7, constructing as persuasive an argument as possible.

Your thesis may express a strong position either for or against the proposition you addressed in the previous assignment, or may be qualified as appropriate to reflect your view of the issue. (See the discussion of the thesis earlier in this chapter.)

To support your position fully, you will draw on the premises you presented in Writing Assignment 7, discarding reasoning that seems weak or irrelevant, adding reasons where you find gaps in your earlier paper. Strengthen your argument with as much available data as you think necessary to make your case. As you expand your argument, you will probably need to consult outside sources—newspapers, magazines, books, and individual authorities—for supporting information. Be sure to cite all references. For guidelines, consult Appendix II, Research and Documenting Sources.

To address opposing views, you will select the most important premises from your list of arguments on the other side of your position and briefly address them, acknowledging, conceding, and refuting in the manner best suited to your stand on the issue. Do not elaborate the opposing views in the same way you have your own premises.

For help in organizing your paper, refer once again to the sample essays in Exercise 4E.

To complete the assignment, include the following attachments:

Your issue, question at issue, and thesis

Your principal argument set out in standard form (see Chapter 3)

Peer editing You may find it useful to edit a first complete draft with classmates. Bring photocopies of your paper to class and exchange papers with one or more students, asking questions, noting strengths and weaknesses on each others' drafts.

Audience The same as for Writing Assignment 7.

Purpose To present a convincing, balanced, fair argument for your position on a controversial argument in order to persuade your readers to adopt your point view.

A checklist of essential components for this essay:

A clear thesis to guide you as a writer and prepare your reader

Support for this thesis—plenty of well-reasoned premises supported with examples, explanation, and analysis

Counterarguments with appropriate concessions and refutations

Sentences logically joined for contrast and concession, cause and effect

Transitions between paragraphs to keep ideas flowing

WRITING ASSIGNMENT 9

Exploring an Argument in Depth

Not all issues lend themselves to a pro or con, "yes" or "no" argument. In Writing Assignment 7 you argued two opposing positions on the same question at issue, and then in 8 took a position on that issue. For this paper, you will address an issue in more of its complexity, considering arguments from as many sides as possible and coming to a conclusion that seems reasonable in light of your in-depth exploration. Such topics often present paradoxes in which two contradictory claims may both merit approval.

In such a conclusion, you may incline to one position or another, or may settle for explaining and clarifying the issues without going so far as to make a definitive decision. For an example of this kind of argument, look ahead to the editorial from *The New Republic* near the end of this chapter or to the essay, "The Invasion of the Niña, the Pinta and the Santa María," in Chapter 5.

The topic   A current controversial issue of interest to you, one that suggests more than a simple pro and con approach.

A checklist for this essay:

An introduction that presents the question at issue with appropriate background and acknowledges its complexity.

A detailed discussion of arguments for as many positions as possible.

Refutations and concessions as appropriate for a thoughtful examination of alternatives.

Your personal recommendation on the issue, based on an evaluation in which you weigh the strengths and weaknesses of the positions you have presented. Your recommendation may be in favor of one of the positions you've presented, a synthesis of them, a call for further investigation, or a summary of possible alternatives.

Because you will be presenting a number of viewpoints, you must make sure your readers know which point of view you are expressing at any given point in the paper. Clear and logical transitions between points will help you accomplish this (note discussion of indicator words in Chapter 3 and contrast and concession earlier in this chapter), as will smooth attributions of quotations and references to the ideas of others (see Appendix II).

Be prepared to face a degree of chaos as you sort out the different perspectives. Don't be afraid of the inevitable confusion that a more complex issue often produces. It is through such a thinking and writing process that critical thinking takes place.

Once again, you may want to edit a draft with classmates.

Audience The same as for Assignments 7 and 8.

Purpose To clarify your audience's understanding of a complex controversial issue.

 ## WRITING ASSIGNMENT 10

Collaborating on a Complex Issue

Here we offer an alternative approach to writing the kind of argument presented in Assignment 9. Rather than preparing your paper on your own, you will be working with a group of classmates.

Once out in the world, writing for business, politics, for many jobs, you will find that much of the writing you do is collaborative.

The topic Each member of the class will submit two or three controversial issues. From this list, the class will select four or five topics around which research groups will form on the basis of preference. You should end up with groups of five or six students.

Here are the guidelines for working with classmates to construct a written argument.

1. The topic research groups will meet in class to narrow the issue to a specific question at issue.
2. Students will conduct research to find at least one relevant article addressing the question at issue and make copies for members of the group. Because these articles are to represent the various positions on the question at issue, members of the group must confer to ensure that the articles together do reflect the diverse points of view.
3. Students will reduce the central argument of their own articles to standard form (see Chapter 3).
4. Each group will meet as often as necessary, in class and out as time permits, to share and discuss these materials. Members of each group will also have an opportunity to discuss the organization and development of their papers.
5. The class will choose whether students complete these papers on their own, or whether they work together as a group to compose one final product as a fully collaborative effort.
6. Each group may want to select the best paper to read to the class, or in the case of collaborative papers, there may be time to hear them all.

Audience The same as for Writing Assignments 7, 8, and 9.

Purpose To present different perspectives on an issue and to engage or persuade an audience through collaborative effort.

Response to a complex issue The editor of *The New Republic* faced just the kind of complexity described above when he explored the legal issues surrounding so-called hate speech. Before explaining why he takes the position he does, he offers a number of different perspectives, sorting out who sides with whom and why. This essay may help you see possibilities for organizing Writing Assignments 9 and 10.

Breaking the Codes

One year ago Robert Viktora, white and 18 years old, was arrested for burning a cross on the lawn of the only black family in his St. Paul, Minnesota, neighborhood. Rather than booking him for trespassing or disturbing the peace, police charged him under a local ordinance prohibiting "bias-motivated disorderly conduct." The law makes it illegal to place "on public or private property a symbol, object, appellation, characterization, or graffiti, including but not limited to, a burning cross or Nazi swastika, which one knows or has reasonable grounds to know arouses anger, alarm, or resentment in others on the basis of race, color, creed, or religion or gender."   *1*

A Minnesota District Court judge struck down the ordinance as unconstitutional, citing the 1989 Supreme Court decision establishing that flag burning was a constitutionally protected form of expression. The court found that the ordinance was "content-based" (it depended on the message of a given action), failed to serve a "compelling state interest," and was overly broad. Six months later the Minnesota   *2* Supreme Court reversed the decision, saying that cross burning was "deplorable conduct the City of St. Paul may without question prohibit." Last week the Supreme Court agreed to hear the case, *R.A.V.* v. *St. Paul*.

The issues raised in the case have split those who usually find themselves in the same corner on First Amendment questions. The Anti-Defamation League has sided with the prosecution, claiming that the burning of a cross is not "expressive or symbolic conduct" protected by   *3* the First Amendment. The ADL supports the Minnesota Supreme Court in its application of the "fighting words" doctrine, which says that words "which by their very utterance inflict injury or tend to incite an immediate breach of the peace" are not protected by the First Amendment. On the other side is the American Civil Liberties Union, which argues that the St. Paul law is unconstitutional both because it is based on message, not action, and because it is "hopelessly vague," and thus subject to abuse and arbitrary enforcement.

The Court's decision will hinge on the question of whether hate speech is one of the few kinds of expression not protected by the Bill of Rights. The two relevant exceptions recognized by law are "fighting words" (*Chaplinsky* v. *New Hampshire*) and speech that provokes "imminent lawless action" (*Brandenburg* v. *Ohio*). Proponents of legislation banning hate speech use these exceptions to argue that hate speech is not a protected freedom under the First Amendment. *4*

This is a superficially appealing, but dangerously narrow, reading of the Bill of Rights. The Constitution does not protect speech likely to incite violence. However, there is a rational and discrete standard upon which the Court makes this exception. It is not legitimate to limit expression solely because it arouses "anger, alarm, or resentment in others," as the St. Paul ordinance does. This, after all, gives the "others" a kind of veto power over the act or speech. The Supreme Court prohibited this vague standard in 1978 when it left intact a lower court's verdict in *Village of Skokie* v. *National Socialist Party of America*. The decision held that a march by members of the American Nazi Party could not be forbidden merely because it would offend residents of the predominantly Jewish Chicago suburb. *5*

The ACLU's arguments for overturning the St. Paul law, and ones like it, are entirely persuasive. The organization acknowledges that there is a "fighting words" exception to the First Amendment, which it underscores by pointing to existing public nuisance laws that it deems constitutional. These ordinances are better than the ordinance in dispute because they are content-neutral, proscribing certain actions regardless of their meaning, while the St. Paul ordinance is content-based. The ACLU points out that the Court has typically found content-based laws to be unconstitutional (most recently in the flag burning decisions, *Texas* v. *Johnson* and *United States* v. *Eichman*) because they give way to subjective interpretations. *6*

Content-based laws carry two dangers. The first is that they can turn epithets into ideas. Shouting "nigger," "kike," or "fag" is not a contribution to the grand clash of ideas out of which the liberal faith holds that truth will emerge. Neither, we think, is the burning of a cross (or a flag). But when such words or acts are suppressed by the state not because of their thuggery but precisely because of their meager political or social "content," that "content" is invested with an undeserved retrospective dignity. Epithets do not enlarge the marketplace of ideas, but suppressing them diminishes it. *7*

The second, and more important, danger of content-based laws is that they will be used to punish legitimate statements that upset people. A debate over the merits of affirmative action could provoke such a reaction, as it did four years ago at the University of California, Los Angeles. A student columnist for a campus newspaper wrote an article criticizing the administration for suspending an editor of a paper in which a cartoon ridiculing affirmative action appeared. The student *8* columnist was in turn suspended from his editorial position by a member of the faculty, a move that was reversed only after the ACLU supported his case.

Restrictions on hate speech have also become popular as a way to respond to expressions of racism on college campuses. Almost 200 universities around the country have implemented speech codes. These regulations often mirror the St. Paul ordinance in blurring the line between offensive conduct and offensive ideas. Private institutions do not have the same legal obligation to the First Amendment as governments or state schools, but they have as high a moral obligation to it. In places devoted to free debate, limiting expression based on its content is more, not less, foolhardy. Laws and codes that prohibit the content of speech, no matter how offensive it may be, come nowhere near addressing the underlying causes of such bigotry; they merely stifle its effects. They are an unprincipled way out.   *9*

The error of those who support hate crime legislation is in trying to fight racism by squelching it, rather than answering it with their own better arguments. As Justice Louis Brandeis said in 1927, "The remedy to be applied is more speech, not enforced silence." In prohibiting notions of racial and ethnic superiority, in enforcing silence, the government makes bigots into First Amendment martyrs and elevates noxious prejudices to the status of political ideas.   *10*

Hate crimes need not go unpunished in the absence of hate crime legislation, since most are also real crimes. In the Viktora case, the ACLU and the defense do not contend that the defendant could not have been prosecuted under other existing laws against trespassing, vandalism, harassment, and disorderly conduct. Police simply chose the wrong law to enforce. It makes better sense, legally and morally, to prosecute someone for harassment, trespassing, or disturbing the peace without judging the content of their expression than it does to proscribe certain forms of expression.   *11*

Laura Jones, a member of the St. Paul family on whose lawn the cross was burned, recognizes this distinction: "He has a right to say anything he wants to," she said of Viktora. "But he doesn't have the right to come up on our property and threaten us . . . He had to come through the fence to do that."   *12*

SUMMARY

Successful writing depends on both a sequential and a recursive writing process which breaks down into three fluid stages—creating, shaping, and correcting.

Convincing arguments usually contain an introduction to the topic, a thesis stated or clearly implied, well-supported premises, acknowledgement of opposing views, and a conclusion.

Successful written argument depends on a dialectical approach in which writers address both their own position and opposing views.

Expressing relationships between ideas, particularly contrast and concession, requires joining sentences for logic and fluency.

Collaboration on the production of a written argument can be helpful and reflects the process often used in the working world.

KEY TERMS

Brainstorming a strategy for generating ideas in which you spontaneously jot down thoughts as they come to you—words and phrases.

Freewriting a strategy for generating ideas in which you write continuously in sentences without editing the ideas or sentence structure.

Issue any topic of concern and controversy.

Question at issue a particular aspect of the issue under consideration.

Thesis a statement of a writer's position; in argument, a response to the question at issue, the conclusion of the central argument in an essay.

Rhetoric the art of using language to good effect, to prove, to convince, to persuade.

Dialectic a method of argument that systematically weighs contradictory ideas with a view to resolution of their contradictions.

Counterargument an opposing view in an argument.

Refutation an explanation of why a position is false or weak.

Concession a statement that grants the opposing view.

Rogerian strategy an explicit effort to see ideas from an opponent's point of view; the cultivation of empathy for the opposition; a concept derived from the research of psychologist Carl Rogers.

Argument an attempt to establish a basis for belief; to present reasons for your conclusion in order to convince someone of your point of view.

Explanation an attempt to clarify why something has happened or why you hold a given opinion.

Chapter
5

Evaluating Arguments: Premises

What is true is what I can't help believing.

—Oliver Wendell Holmes

*L*ogicians have evolved a number of precise tools for assessing arguments, sometimes making distinctions between deduction and induction (see Chapters 6, 7, and 8). But before we turn to such classifications, let's begin with what we already know. As we discovered in Chapter 4, in order to decide exactly what we believe on a particular issue and to present a convincing case for our beliefs, we have to be thorough in exploring arguments both for and against our positions. And we must be confident that the supporting premises are as reliable as we can make them. This, however, is where the difficulty can arise. How can we be sure that the premises offered by others or those we use in our arguments are reliable, are **acceptable**?

ACCEPTABILITY OF PREMISES—DETERMINING WHAT IS REASONABLE TO BELIEVE

In order to decide whether or not to accept a particular conclusion, we must examine premises very closely. If we find them acceptable, then we must accept the conclusion—provided the reasoning is valid (see Chapter 7). If we cannot accept the premises, then we cannot accept the conclusion. But what makes a premise acceptable? We offer some guidance for evaluating the *acceptability of premises,** but keep in mind that even after careful analysis,

---

*We are indebted to Trudy Govier, Anthony Blair, and Ralph Johnson for their discussion of the term "acceptable."

the acceptability of some premises will remain debatable. In such cases we must rely on the relevance and acceptability of the other premises to determine the cogency of the argument, and thus the strength of the conclusion. In many cases additional justification must be offered before a premise becomes acceptable, but at some point reason demands we accept—or reject—a premise and stop our search for further support.

A systematic approach can be helpful in evaluating premises. Begin by determining, to the degree possible, which of the following categories best characterizes the premise under scrutiny. Once you have decided what kind of premise you are examining, you will be better equipped to decide whether it is credible, whether it requires further support and if so what kind of support, or whether it should be dismissed as unacceptable.

Claims Necessarily True by Virtue of Language

Is the premise *necessarily* true? Is it impossible for it to be false because of the language of the proposition?

> Men who marry become husbands.

> Either the Red Sox will win the American League pennant or they won't.

Claims of Fact

Is the premise a *factual* proposition that is common knowledge, known to virtually all or easily verifiable, with no widely known evidence against it?

> The earth is round.

> The Second Amendment addresses the right to bear arms.

> No U.S. president is currently allowed to serve a third term.

If one weren't already confident that all three of these assertions were true, minimal research would quickly verify them. But in this category we often encounter statements that, while undeniably "factual," can still be debatable in terms of accuracy.

> A fully grown, mature tree gives off as much carbon dioxide as it takes in, whereas a young, growing tree "scrubs" the atmosphere by taking in far more than it emits.

> A mature tree continues to grow and gives off more oxygen than it does carbon dioxide.

These two potentially contradictory statements with distinctly different connotations were claimed as "facts" by two seemingly knowledgeable authors of letters to a newspaper. Arguing on opposite sides of the controversy surrounding attempts to preserve virgin forests along the Pacific coast, these two advocates claimed as facts totally incompatible premises. Here are the two letters in their entirety.

Tree Facts

Editor—This is in response to the several recent letters regarding saving the redwoods.

Fact: There is already a working forest management plan in effect, which has led to an ever increasing number of trees.

Fact: There are already in excess of 250,000 acres of virgin timber preserved for eternity in state and national forests.

Fact: A fully-grown, mature tree gives off as much carbon dioxide as it takes in, whereas a young, growing tree scrubs the atmosphere by taking in far more than it emits.

Fact: Louisiana Pacific was asked by the federal government, as part of the "Hands Across America" program, to build a plant and drying facility in Mexico. As they are not shipping logs there, only raw timber, the sawmill at Somoa, Calif., will continue to operate.

Earth First and their ilk are doing a great job manipulating the media and misleading the public. The above facts have been distorted or suppressed by the eco-terrorists in an attempt to create controversy and garner an emotional response from the populace.

Do not be sucked in by their "everyman versus the evil corporation" rhetoric.

P. Sandberg
San Carlos
June 28, 1990

More 'Tree Facts'

Editor—The letter to the editor from P. Sandberg (Chronicle, June 28) under the headline "Tree Facts," is not factual at all.

Among the statements listed as facts, the most serious error is the assertion that there are already in excess of 250,000 acres of virgin timber preserved "for eternity" in state and national forests. With reference to the coast redwood, there are approximately 250,000 acres of lands within the native range of the coast redwood protected in state and national parks. Of this total, there are 60,000 acres of old-growth redwoods in the state park system and 20,000 acres in Redwood National Park. At the most, then, there are 80,000 acres of virgin redwoods, less than 5 percent of the original coast redwood forest, in protected status in parks.

Briefly as to the other "fact": A mature tree continues to grow and gives off more oxygen than it does carbon dioxide. The distinction between shipping logs and shipping raw timber is a fine one—merely taking the bark off a log and squaring it for shipment is a very minor part of the process of manufacturing finished lumber. Forest management plans, often poorly enforced, may allow a large number of new seedlings to become established, but the short logging cycles being implemented by the timber industry will never allow these young trees to live more than 80 to 100 years. Redwoods will live 1,500 to 2,000 years if not subjected to logging.

> John B. DeWitt
> Executive Director
> Save-the-Redwoods League
> San Francisco
> July 3, 1990

What is a reader to make of these contradictory "facts"?

Both letters share the assumption that preservation of some old growth trees is desirable, but their authors differ markedly on the appropriate means to such an end. Most people connected with the lumber industry, at all levels, would be inclined to accept Sandberg's argument, while the majority of environmentalists would consider Dewitt's reasoning acceptable. But before uninformed or skeptical readers could be satisfied, they would require further support for all of the claims made here. Had the writers supplied additional statistics, biological data, and interpretations of such evidence and clarified possible discrepancies in language (Is the "mature tree" of Dewitt the equivalent of Sandberg's "fully-grown, mature tree"?), the reader would be better able to make a judgment on what action would be necessary to preserve coast trees.

Claims of Authority

Is the premise supported by an appropriate *authority* on the subject?

The Surgeon General warns that smoking is injurious to health.

Vladimir Horowitz, the internationally acclaimed pianist, preferred the Steinway piano.

Studies conducted by *The New York Times*, *The Los Angeles Times*, and the ABC Network suggest that increasing numbers of viewers object to TV violence.

Given the respected authority of the sources above, we would be inclined to accept the premises.

But in the "Tree Facts" letters, it would be helpful to know more about P. Sandberg. Is he/she a forester, an employee of the lumber industry? We know that John B. Dewitt is an executive of a conservation organization directly involved in saving redwoods. Weighing the vested interests of each advocate would help in sorting out which "tree facts" are acceptable.

When the authority cited is a statistical study (as in the third example above), we need to remember that statistical surveys can be reliable, unreliable, or open to further interpretation. Statistics can "lie"; don't let the authority of numbers seduce you.

In constructing your own arguments be prepared to cite, explain, and if necessary defend your sources when relying on authority. (For a warning about arguments based on inappropriate authority, see Chapter 9, and for documentation of sources, see Appendix II.)

On some occasions, eyewitness reports and individual experiences, your own or those of others, can serve as valuable evidence from "authority." Here acceptability will rest on how your audience views you as a witness or on their evaluation of a witness you cite and the circumstances under which a report was made. The celebrated Japanese movie, "Rashomon," in which four witnesses give different reports of the same crime, and numerous other tales, such as Lawrence Durrell's *Alexandria Quartets* or Ford Maddox Ford's *The Good Soldier*, illustrate how perceptions of the same event can vary.

Claims of Judgment

Is the premise a *judgment*?

In this, the category found most frequently in argument, the distinctions between acceptable and unacceptable can quickly become blurred, and controversy arises.

Certain judgments are taken for granted, become a part of a culture's shared belief system, and are unlikely to be challenged under most circumstances.

Taking the property of others is wrong.

People who physically abuse children should be punished.

But many judgments will not be universally accepted without considerable well-reasoned support, or may be rejected regardless of additional premises and cogent reasoning. For instance, as the following judgments illustrate, convincing advocates on the opposite side of the gun control issue can seem impossible.

The Second Amendment guarantees every individual the right to bear arms.

The Second Amendment guarantees only a "militia," not every individual, the right to bear arms.

Frequently a judgment is complicated by potentially ambiguous language. Words and their meanings can be and often are more complex than a dictionary definition.

Art that is considered obscene can have no aesthetic value.

Note that in this premise, the acceptability will rest on both the judgment itself and the interpretation of two terms: obscene and aesthetic. But don't let quibbles over definition distract you from the heart of otherwise strong arguments. You'll find additional discussion of this issue under definition in Chapter 10.

A caution: When feelings run high, or when we find ourselves short on information about a particular issue, we may be tempted to attack the conclusion of an argument with which we disagree. The important point here is that to refute an argument successfully, we must begin by evaluating the premises, one by one, rather than moving in on the conclusion first. At the same time, we must avoid the risk of allowing a healthy skepticism to grow into incapacitating cynicism. What we must search for is a balance between probing questions and a generous tolerance as we evaluate the premises on which a conclusion rests. As Tom Bridges of Montclair State University puts it, "The goal of inquiry is not objective truth, but reasonable belief, *pistis*—the state of being persuaded."

EXERCISE 5A

Evaluating Premises in a Short Argument

Examine the following arguments and for each:

1. Write it in standard form.
2. Determine which of the categories discussed above most accurately describes each premise.
3. Evaluate the acceptability of the premises so as to establish the relative strength or weakness of each argument. Which premises will you accept as given? Why? Which premises are unacceptable? Why? What could the writer do to make a premise acceptable? Are there assumptions that need to be challenged?

* a. Executives of several timber companies operating in Northern California have testified that more than 250,000 acres of virgin timber are protected in state and national forests. Such preserves are adequate for saving the old-growth redwoods. Thus, they argue, further restrictions on logging are unnecessary.

   b. Government should not be in the business of funding the arts. Too many social needs go unmet to warrant spending money on artists, and many Americans resent having their tax dollars spent on work that often offends them. This view has been vigorously supported by Jesse Helms, a senior member of the U.S. Senate, who blew the whistle on what he saw as obscene and sacrilegious art paid for by the NEA (National Endowment for the Arts), a government-subsidized agency.

Niculae Asciu

c. Because of the complexity of our tax system, most American taxpayers are unable to complete their own income tax forms but must
hire accountants to do it for them. To simplify our tax system, we
should adopt a modified flat tax. According to Hoover Institution
economists Robert Hall and Alvin Rabushka, such a tax would also
eliminate most deductions and exemptions, closing the many loop-
holes the rich now take advantage of. In addition, it would eliminate
the double taxation of corporate profits, which are first taxed when
earned, and then taxed again when distributed to shareholders.
Such taxation discourages savings and investment, the opposite of
what the economy needs.

EXERCISE 5B

Evaluating Your Own Premises

Choose one of the arguments above and construct an argument of similar
length which presents the opposite conclusion. Then follow the steps outlined
above for evaluating the premises you have provided.

EXERCISE 5C

Evaluating Editorials

Turn back to Exercise 4E in Chapter 4 and reread the editorial by Randy Shilts; then read the following editorial by Abe Mellinkoff. After analyzing both pieces carefully, evaluate each one according to the following steps. This exercise can be done individually in writing or together in classroom groups.

1. Isolate the central argument and write it out in standard form.
2. Evaluate the central premises in support of the conclusion according to the categories discussed above.
3. On the basis of your premise evaluation, discuss the strengths and weaknesses of each argument.

New Way To Fight AIDS On Wrong Track

Unfortunately for patients, doctors are sometimes very slow in finding a cure for a new illness. That's when quacks rush in to fill the time gap. Better something than nothing is the excuse given for listening to these false practitioners. The AIDS epidemic seems to be plagued with false remedies.   **1**

The latest quickie system to put a halt to the spread of AIDS is the free exchange of hypodermic needles. The process is both simple and logical. The only wonder is why it took years to get popular.   **2**

Here's how it works: A drug abuser who has AIDS passes the needle he has just used to a friend. When used the second time, the AIDS virus is transmitted. But if the second user only had a brand new needle, the argument runs, he would get his drug high and no AIDS virus.   **3**

Varied Success

The system of exchanging a clean needle at no charge for each addict who brings in a dirty one has been set up with varied success. After several months in New York, somewhere between fifty and a hundred addicts have taken advantage of that city service. An unofficial system in San Francisco is run by dedicated volunteers.   **4**

Campaigns are underway here and in other cities to spread the exchange system. Why not? The shortest rebuttal has come from the offices of Drug Czar William Bennett. The official message would become: "Don't take drugs, but if you do take them, take them safely. That's not helpful, it's pernicious."   **5**

National Scourges

Certainly it would put a mark of legality on drug addition. If the government is to certify drugs free of the AIDS virus, the next step would be an official stamp of purity on the drugs themselves.   **6**

Both drugs and AIDS are national scourges. It's quite possible that making drugs even quasi-legal might boost their use. We can't afford to   **7** risk that even if this outwardly appealing AIDS program goes down a drain already used for other unsuccessful plans to fight AIDS.

APPLICATION TO WRITING

Summaries

One way to explore an argument and reveal the important premises leading to a conclusion is to write a summary. Once you have isolated the premises and connected them in a condensed but logically flowing summary, you are in a strong position to evaluate their acceptability and at the same time to show yourself and your readers that you fully understand a written argument. Close, critical reading requires concentration; writing, in a compressed, organized form, can serve your understanding of what you have read.

Strategies for Writing a Summary

Read the piece you want to summarize carefully, identify the question at issue, and mark off the conclusion and important premises. Some of these may be implicit rather than explicit. A short summary sentence written in the margin beside each important premise and the conclusion(s) can be helpful. Write out the conclusion in a single summary sentence and then expand this central idea with a short version of the premises that are offered in its support. To insure a smoothly written, coherent summary, provide appropriate indicator words (conjunctions and transitional phrases) to join sentences and connect ideas (see Chapter 4 for more on joining).

How Long Should a Summary Be?

Summaries come in many lengths, from one sentence to several pages, depending on the purpose of the summary and the length of the piece to be summarized. Note, for example, the brief summaries at the conclusion of each chapter in this text. A good summary will be both complete and concise. To meet these conflicting goals, you must convey the essence of the whole piece without copying whole passages verbatim or emphasizing inappropriate features of the argument. Background information, detailed premise support, and narrative illustrations are usually omitted from summaries, and paraphrases of ideas rather than direct quotations, except for a few words here and there, are preferred.

> SUMMARIES SHOULD BE CONCISE, COMPLETE, AND COHERENT AND WRITTEN IN YOUR OWN WORDS.

WRITING ASSIGNMENT 11

Constructing a Summary and Response

A. The following newspaper essay presents several points of view. Read it carefully, identify the question at issue, and sort out the various arguments offered.

You will discover that this piece is similar in structure to the arguments discussed in Writing Assignment 9 in Chapter 4. It is complex and weighs several positions rather than taking a stand on one side of the issue only.

B. Identify the conclusions to the arguments Alessandra Stanley discusses and supply the key premises in their support. Her premises for one position seem more numerous and compelling than those for the other and thus the author's bias is implicit, even if she has stated no explicit conclusion of her own.

C. Now write a summary of the article (approximately 150–200 words). You may want to compare summaries with classmates.

D. Having read the article critically and organized your interpretation in writing, evaluate the central premises according to the four premise categories discussed earlier in this chapter.

E. Write a letter to the editor of *The New York Times* in which you express your opinion of Stanley's article and your position on the issues she raises. Discuss the premises she presents, and, if you think of others not mentioned in the article, include them. Letters to newspapers, like summaries, are usually compressed, so you will need to be economical and selective with words here, limiting yourself to between 300 and 400 words.

Audience   Readers of *The New York Times* who will need the key points of the original argument before they move on to your response.

Purpose   To present an insightful analysis of a complex argument in order to illuminate the issue for your readers.

The Invasion of the Niña, The Pinta and The Santa María

Amid many passages complaining about the weather and the mood of his men, there are a few sentences in Christopher Columbus's diary that read as if penciled in later to meet contemporary rules of political correctness.

Take an entry from December 12, 1492, describing Columbus's discovery of a "very young and beautiful girl," a native Bahamian woman who was sent, presumably as a gift, to the Admiral's cabin. "I clothed her and gave her glass beads, hawks' bells and brass rings, and sent her back to the land very honorably, as I always do," he wrote.

Unfortunately for the explorer, he is not best remembered for his chivalry. Instead, as the quincentenary of his historic "encounter" (the notion of "discovery," among many other things, is hotly contested) approaches in 1992, he is sailing headlong into a revisionist squall as daunting as anything he encountered on the Atlantic.

The Italian explorer known to generations of schoolchildren as the first American hero is being counter-commemorated by American Indian groups and others as a founding father of colonial greed, slavery and genocide. (Those who claim that Leif Ericsson found the New World first, of course, dismissed Columbus long ago as a Gianni-come-lately.)

The Alliance for Cultural Democracy, with headquarters in Minneapolis, will not be celebrating Christopher Columbus next year. Its members publish a quarterly newsletter, "Huracán," devoted to tracking official quincentennial ceremonies and listing alternatives. The alliance has for its symbol a drawing of a galleon with a red slash through it.

"Our perspective is what Columbus did to initiate the age of modern colonialism," said Ricardo Levins Morales, a founding member of the alliance. "As long as that history remains untaught," Mr. Morales said, "it's like the abusive family dynamic — if the abuse is denied, the pattern of abuse is likely to continue."

The National Council of Churches is not far behind. Its members have voted to condemn Columbus's arrival as an "invasion" and plan to hold counterdemonstrations to the Catholic Church's plans for a celebration of 500 years of Christianity.

Christopher Columbus "symbolizes everything that is against basic American values," said Jack Weatherford, a professor of anthropology at Macalester College, in St. Paul, and a leading anti-Columbus scholar. Mr. Weatherford notes that Columbus never actually came to mainland North America (he landed in the Caribbean). He says that the navigator started the Atlantic slave trade and that his heroic status was a cynical invention of Washington Irving. Mr. Weatherford argues that after the war with the British in 1812, Americans were searching for a non-Anglo-Saxon national hero, and Irving served up Columbus.

In addition to the much ballyhooed novel "The Crown of Columbus," written by Louise Erdrich and her husband, Michael Dorris, two writers who tirelessly celebrate their American Indian ancestry, other revisionist works have appeared in anticipation of 1992. In "The Conquest of Paradise," Kirkpatrick Sale stresses the explorer's legacy of environmental destructiveness — and his lack of imagination. It seems that besides despoiling the New World, Columbus traveled like a trunk, failing to take any note of America's natural wonders. (His diary is peppered with such perfunctory descriptions as "big and little birds of all sorts.")

Anti-Columbus fervor on the left has, of course, unleashed a counterattack from the right. For conservatives, the heroine of the moment is Lynne Cheney, chairwoman of the National Endowment for the Humanities, who denied a grant for a documentary called "1492: Clash of Visions," which unfavorably depicted Columbus and the Spanish conquistadors. Ms. Cheney complained that the film was not balanced, and criticized it in particular for dwelling on Spanish human rights violations while whitewashing the less attractive features of Aztec civilization, such as cannibalism. "Besides, Columbus never even *met* the Aztecs," she said.

Columbus's defenders have not been helped by the fact that John Goudie, the chairman of the presidential commission in charge of coordinating the international quincentennial, was forced to resign last year after reports of financial improprieties. (The commission and Spain are currently bickering over who will pick up the bill for the main event of 1992, an Atlantic crossing by replicas of the Niña, the Pinta and the Santa María.)

But the politicization of Columbus has obscured the fact that Columbus-bashing is a proud American tradition. One of the few facts schoolchildren retain about the explorer, besides the date of his voyage and the color of the ocean (blue), is that his discovery was a colossally mistaken search for a new route to India. Columbus's historic error has delighted generation after generation of snickering third graders.

The Encyclopedia Americana fastidously credits the Italian navigator with leading "the first recorded European expedition to cross the Atlantic Ocean in warm or temperate climes," before quickly pointing out that he "was not the first European to land in the Americas."

There have always been those who think Columbus might have been Jewish, but the Encyclopedia Judaica does not seem eager to claim him. "He was himself mysterious about his background, which he wished to conceal," according to the entry on Columbus, "however, he boasted cryptically about his connection with King David." The encyclopedia lists some clues that have led scholars to believe Columbus was Jewish, then adds tartly, "The mystery regarding Columbus' origins is largely the outcome of his own mendacity."

Daniel J. Boorstin, librarian emeritus of the Library of Congress, does not appear to be all that impressed with Columbus, either. In his book, "The Discoverers," he repeatedly reminds his readers that Vasco da Gama was a much better sailor. He does grudgingly give Columbus points for "salesmanship." As Mr. Boorstin describes it, Columbus's wheedling around the court of Queen Isabella and King Ferdinand to peddle his pet project, "The Enterprise of the Indies," seems pathetic. The explorer comes off like some independent Hollywood producer desperately trying to pitch a movie deal to an all-powerful, indifferent studio.

The new Hollywood has bucked the revisionist fad and is unabashedly championing Columbus as a Renaissance Rambo. There are two competing big-budget Columbus productions. One features Timothy Dalton, the latest James Bond, as the explorer, and will be directed by George P. Cosmatos, who also directed "Rambo II." Mario Puzo wrote the screenplay. The film's producer, Ilya Salkind, produced the Superman movies.

The other movie, which will star the French actor Gerard Depardieu, is to be directed by Ridley Scott ("Alien"). Mr. Depardieu's Columbus is expected to have his wily moments, but like the Timothy Dalton version, he will be a heroic, larger-than-life figure. Patrick Wachsberger, president of Odyssey, the French company that is financing the Depardieu version, explained, "Nobody goes to the movies to see anything but a hero."

REASON, INTUITION, AND IMAGINATION

> The heart has its reasons which reason knows nothing of.
>
> —Blaise Pascal

Before moving on to analyzing patterns of logic in the next chapters, we need to pause for a moment to reflect on the broader issues of truth and acceptability. As writer Mary Midgley argues in *Can't We Make Moral Judgments?*

> There is no single infallible form of knowledge, forming a standard against which all others must be measured. . . . Instead, there are many different ways of knowing, each with their own standards and their own suitable kinds of evidence. . . . The pattern of our knowledge is much more like that of a forest of different interdependent plants, or a city of different interconnected buildings, than of a single enormous building piled on a single foundation-stone.

Intuition, imagination, and creativity as well as logic are ways of knowing. What roles do they play in constructing acceptable arguments? If we are to account for a full range of human experience, we need to listen to the poets as well as logicians. Novelist Thomas Mann, looking at the function of myth, found it "better to be warned by a haunting image than to be caught defenseless by the real thing." And poet John Ciardi found reason inadequate for explaining the natural world.

Who could believe an ant in theory?
A giraffe in blueprint?
Ten thousand doctors of what's possible
Could reason half the jungle out of being.

In his novel *The Lyre of Orpheus*, Robertson Davies—like most artists, a searcher after truth—expresses a distrust of logic. He describes it as "a means of straining out of every problem the whisperings of intuition, which is a way of seeing in the dark."

But we are not ready to dismiss logic. We do not, in fact, see logic and intuition as mutually exclusive, but rather value the poet's vision as part of the reasoning process and respect the boundaries of reason pushed to embrace imagination as a component in determining what is "true," what is *acceptable*. Sometimes a **metaphor** can carry, through images and associations, an understanding beyond what explicit reasoning can convey. The paradoxes and ambiguities found in literature often capture truths and realities too subtle for our intellects alone but understood intuitively. In the Taoist tradition of China, imagination and dreams are regarded as no less real than what is called, in the Western tradition, reality.

EXERCISE 5D

Truth and the Literary Imagination

Read the three passages below, choose one, and write a short analysis of what the author is suggesting about truth. What does it say about the author's view of the world?

1. It's not writ down in any map. True places never are.

—Herman Melville, *Moby Dick*

2.   Did Chuang Chou dream
      he was the butterfly,
        Or the butterfly
      that it was Chuang Chou?

      In one body's
   metamorphoses,
        All is present,
   infinite virtue!

      You surely know
   Fairyland's oceans
        Were made again
   a limpid brooklet,

      Down at Green Gate
   the melon Gardener
        Once used to be
   Marquis of Tung-ling?

      Wealth and honor
   were always like this:
        You strive and strive,
   but what do you seek?

         —Li Po, Old Poem

3. Tell all the Truth but tell it slant—
   Success in Circuit lies
   Too bright for our infirm Delight
   The Truth's superb surprise

The Lightning to the Children eased
With explanation kind
The Truth must dazzle gradually
Or every man be blind—

—Emily Dickinson, Poem #1129

ANALOGY

One creative way to mount an argument can be through **analogy**—a comparison of two things, alike in certain respects. The point is made by comparing something more familiar, sometimes more vivid, occasionally absurd, with an object or idea in need of clarification or logical support. For example, early in this century, it was known that the atmospheric conditions of the planet Mars are similar to those of Earth. From this similarity, it was argued by analogy that Mars must be inhabited by living beings similar to those on Earth. The comparison serves as a premise; to evaluate its acceptability, the reader must closely examine the essential characteristics of the people, places, or things being compared. Over time, scientific study has discredited this Earth/Mars analogy, and thus the premise (though some still believe that Mars is inhabited by living beings).

As we explain under fallacies in Chapter 9, analogies can prove treacherous in argumentation, but this risk is no reason not to flex your own creative powers in the art of analogous thinking and writing. Just remember to avoid the temptation to succumb to wild conjecture. Be sure your comparisons are strong and logical enough to carry your conclusion.

EXERCISE 5E

Evaluating an Analogy

Read the following excerpt from "In Defense of Abortion" by Judith Jarvis Thomson and evaluate the effectiveness of her analogy.

In Defense of Abortion

Most opposition to abortion relies on the premise that the fetus is a human being, a person from the moment of conception. The premise is argued for, but, as I think, not well. But I shall not discuss any of this. For it seems to me to be of great interest to ask what happens if, for the sake of argument, we allow the premise. How, precisely, are we supposed to get from there to the conclusion that abortion is morally impermissible? Opponents of abortion commonly spend most of their time establishing that the fetus is a person, and hardly any time explaining the step from there to the impermissibility of abortion. Perhaps they think the step too simple and obvious to require much comment. Or perhaps instead they are simply being economical in argument. Many of those who defend abortion rely on the premise that the fetus is not a person, but only a bit of tissue that will become a person at birth; and why pay out more arguments than you have to? Whatever the explanation, I suggest that the step they take is neither easy nor obvious, that it calls for closer examination than it is commonly given, and that when we do give it this closer examination we shall feel inclined to reject it.

I propose, then, that we grant that the fetus is a person from the moment of conception. How does the argument go from here? Something like this, I take it. Every person has a right to life. So the fetus has a right to life. No doubt the mother has a right to decide what shall happen in and to her body; everyone would grant that. But surely a person's right to life is stronger and more stringent than the mother's right to decide what happens in and to her body, and so outweighs it. So the fetus may not be killed; an abortion may not be performed.

It sounds plausible. But now let me ask you to imagine this. You wake up in the morning and find yourself back to back in bed with an unconscious violinist. A famous unconscious violinist. He has been found to have a fatal kidney ailment, and the Society of Music Lovers has canvassed all the available medical records and found that you alone have the right blood type to help. They have therefore kidnapped you, and last night the violinist's circulatory system was plugged into yours, so that your kidneys can be used to extract poisons from his blood as well as your own. The director of the hospital now tells you, "Look, we're sorry the Society of Music Lovers did this to you — we would never have permitted it if we had known. But still, they did it, and the violinist now is plugged into you. To unplug you would be to kill him. But never mind, it's only for nine months. By then he will have recovered from his ailment, and can safely be unplugged from you." Is it morally incumbent on you to accede to this situation? No doubt it would be very nice of you if you did, a great kindness. But do you have to accede to it? What if it were not nine months, but nine years? Or longer still? What if the director of the hospital says, "Tough luck, I agree, but you've now got to stay in bed, with the violinist plugged into you, for the rest of your life. Because remember this. All persons have a right to life, and violinists are persons. Granted you have a right to decide what happens in and to your body, but a peron's right to life outweighs your right to decide what happens in and to your body. So you cannot ever be unplugged from him." I imagine you would regard this as outrageous, which suggests that something really is wrong with that plausible-sounding argument I mentioned a moment ago.

WRITING ASSIGNMENT 12

Creating an Analogy

In a short paper (one to two pages), illustrate a point by analogy. Not every notation of similarity serves an argument. In both writing and speech, we use analogies to illustrate or amplify ideas. In this assignment you may choose to argue or simply to describe or explain with analogy. You may want to create an analogy that supports a counterargument to Thomson's position.

SUMMARY

In argument, it is important to evaluate both your own premises and those of others. To help you determine whether or not premises are acceptable, place them in descriptive categories before evaluating them. Is a given premise

1. necessarily true?
2. a fact?
3. of or from authority?
4. a judgment?

One way to clarify, emphasize, and evaluate key points in a written argument, or other piece of discourse, is to condense ideas in a summary.

Sometimes the poetic imagination can help us unravel and express meaning. In addition to the principles of logic and explicit reasoning, intuition and metaphor—including analogy—play an important role in clear and creative thinking and writing.

KEY TERMS

Acceptable reliable, what is reasonable to believe.
Metaphor a figure of speech which imaginatively compares one object with another in order to expand our understanding of the object being compared.
Analogy a comparison of two things for the purpose of illustrating a point.

Chapter
6
Deductive and Inductive Reasoning

There is a tradition of opposition between adherents of induction and deduction. In my view, it would be just as sensible for the two ends of a worm to quarrel.

—Alfred North Whitehead

*D*ifferent logicians tend to make different distinctions between deductive and inductive reasoning, with some going so far as to declare, as Whitehead did, that such a distinction is spurious. But classifications, if carefully made, help us to understand abstract concepts, and scientists and humanists alike often refer to patterns of reasoning as deductive or inductive.

KEY DISTINCTIONS

The key distinctions between deduction and induction are generally seen as falling into two categories.

Necessity versus Probability

In a *deductive argument*, the conclusion will follow by **necessity** from the premises if the method of reasoning is valid, as in this familiar bit of classical wisdom:

1. All men (updated—people) are mortal.
2. Socrates is a man (person).
   ∴ Socrates is mortal.

In an *inductive argument*, the conclusion can only follow with some degree of **probability** (from the unlikely to the highly probable). British philosopher Bertrand Russell made the point implicitly but emphatically in

The Problems of Philosophy: "The man who has fed the chicken every day throughout its life at last wrings its neck instead." The chicken reasons thus—

1. He has fed me today.
2. He has fed me this next day.
3. He has fed me this day too.
4. He has fed me yet another day.
    etc.
    ∴ He will feed me tomorrow.

The poor chicken has made a prediction, and a reasonable one, based on its past experience.

A related distinction here becomes clear. The premises of a deductive argument contain all the information needed for the conclusion, whereas the conclusion of an inductive argument goes beyond the premises. For this reason, some prefer the certainty of deduction to the probability of induction. Italian author Italo Calvino describes such a person in his novel, *Mr. Palomar*:

> To construct a model—as Mr. Palomar was aware—you have to start with something; that is, you have to have principles, from which, by deduction, you develop your own line of reasoning. The principles—also known as axioms or postulates—are not something you select; you have them already, because if you did not have them, you could not even begin thinking. So Mr. Palomar also had some, but since he was neither a mathematician nor a logician, he did not bother to define them. Deduction, in any case, was one of his favorite activities, because he could devote himself to it in silence and alone, without special equipment, at any place and moment, seated in his armchair or strolling. Induction, on the contrary, was something he did not really trust, perhaps because he thought his experiences vague and incomplete. The construction of a model, therefore, was for him a miracle of equilibrium between principles (left in shadow) and experience (elusive), but the result should be more substantial than either.

Ambrose Peré, an Italian Renaissance physician, revealed his distrust of induction when he defined inductive diagnosis as "the rapid means to the wrong conclusion." One assumes that he would have argued for the value of a few well-learned principles behind one's observations.

From General to Specific, Specific to General

In a *deductive* argument the inference usually moves from a generalization to a particular, specific instance or example that fits that generalization. Two examples:

1. All students who complete this course successfully will fulfill the critical thinking requirement.
2. Jane has completed this course successfully.
    ∴ Jane has fulfilled the critical thinking requirement.

1. Children born on a Saturday will "work hard for a living."

2. Nick was born on a Saturday.

∴ Nick will work hard for his living.

You may not believe this folk wisdom, especially if you were born on a Saturday, but the line of reasoning is still deductive.

In an *inductive* argument the inference usually moves from a series of specific instances to a generalization.

1. Temperatures in the western states have been above normal this year.

2. Temperatures in the Midwest have been above normal this year.

3. Temperatures in the East have been above normal this year.

4. Winter all over the nation was milder than usual.

5. Drought has been increasing across the country.

∴ The first stages of the dreaded "Greenhouse Effect" are upon us.

Sometimes in inductive reasoning, we begin with a hypothesis, an unproved theory or proposition, and gather the data to support it. For instance, when Jonas Salk thought his vaccine would cure polio, he first had to test it inductively by administering it to a broad sample before concluding that the vaccine prevented polio.

THE RELATIONSHIP BETWEEN INDUCTION AND DEDUCTION

In Exercise 6B we ask you to distinguish between inductive and deductive reasoning, but in reality the two are inextricable. Consider the source for the generalizations upon which deductions are based. In some cases they seem to be the laws of nature (or of God if one is religiously inclined), but more often than not we arrive at these generalizations by means of repeated observations. Throughout history, people have observed their own mortality, so we can now take that generalization—all people are mortal—as a given from which we can deduce conclusions about individual people. Induction has, in this case, led to a trusted generalization which in turn allows us a "necessary," or deductive, inference.

Humorists have sometimes turned these concepts on their heads. Here's Woody Allen reflecting on deduction: "All men are Socrates." And Lewis Carroll, in "The Hunting of the Snark," on induction: "What I tell you three times is true."

In a more serious approach, Robert Pirsig, in his philosophical novel *Zen and the Art of Motorcycle Maintenance,* and Thomas Huxley, the British scientist and writer of the nineteenth century, attempt to explain deduction, induction, and the relationships between them in language we can all understand. Their point is that these terms were never intended to be the exclusive domain of academics but, rather, descriptive of the ways in which we all think every day.

Note how the following two excerpts from their work—"The Method of Scientific Investigation" by Huxley and a chapter from Pirsig's novel—explain both the differences between induction and deduction and their dependence on one another.

The Method of Scientific Investigation

The method of scientific investigation is nothing but the expression of the necessary mode of working of the human mind. It is simply the mode at which all phenomena are reasoned about, rendered precise and exact. There is no more difference, but there is just the same kind of difference, between the mental operations of a man of science and those of an ordinary person, as there is between the operations and methods of a baker or of a butcher weighing out his goods in common scales, and the operations of a chemist in performing a difficult and complex analysis by means of his balance and finely graduated weights. It is not that the action of the scales in the one case, and the balance in the other, differ in the principles of their construction or manner of working; but the beam of one is set on an infinitely finer axis than the other, and of course turns by the addition of a much smaller weight.   *1*

You will understand this better, perhaps, if I give you some familiar example. You have all heard it repeated, I dare say, that men of science work by means of induction and deduction, and that by the help of these operations, they, in a sort of sense, wring from Nature certain other things, which are called natural laws, and causes, and that out of these, by some cunning skill of their own, they build up hypotheses and theo-   *2* ries. And it is imagined by many, that the operations of the common mind can be by no means compared with these processes, and that they have to be acquired by a sort of special apprenticeship to the craft. To hear all these large words, you would think that the mind of a man of science must be constituted differently from that of his fellow men; but if you will not be frightened by terms, you will discover that you are quite wrong, and that all these terrible apparatus are being used by yourselves every day and every hour of your lives.

There is a well-known incident in one of Molière's plays, where the author makes the hero express unbounded delight on being told that he had been talking prose during the whole of his life. In the same way, I trust, that you will take comfort, and be delighted with yourselves, on the discovery that you have been acting on the principles of inductive   *3* and deductive philosophy during the same period. Probably there is not one here who has not in the course of the day had occasion to set in motion a complex train of reasoning, of the very same kind, though differing of course in degree, as that which a scientific man goes through in tracing the causes of natural phenomena.

A very trivial circumstance will serve to exemplify this. Suppose you go into a fruiterer's shop, wanting an apple,—you take up one, and, on biting it, you find it is sour; you look at it, and see that it is hard and green. You take up another one, and that too is hard, green, and sour. *4* The shopman offers you a third; but, before biting it, you examine it and find that it is hard and green, and you immediately say that you will not have it, as it must be sour, like those that you have already tried.

Nothing can be more simple than that, you think; but if you will take the trouble to analyse and trace out into its logical elements what has been done by the mind, you will be greatly surprised. In the first place you have performed the operation of induction. You found that, in two experiences, hardness and greenness in apples went together with sourness. It was so in the first case, and it was confirmed by the second. True, it is a very small basis, but still it is enough to make an induction from; you generalise the facts, and you expect to find sourness in apples where you get hardness and greenness. You found upon that a general law that all hard and green apples are sour and that, so far as it goes, is a perfect induction. Well, having got your natural law in this way, when you are offered another apple which you find is hard and green, you say, "All hard and green apples are sour; this apple is hard and green, therefore this apple is sour." That train of reasoning is what logicians call a syllogism, and has all its various parts and terms,—its major premiss, its minor premiss and its conclusion. And, by the help of further reasoning, which, if drawn out, would have to be exhibited in two or three other syllogisms, you arrive at your final determination, "I will not have that apple." So that, you see, you have, in the first place, established a law by *5* induction, and upon that you have founded a deduction, and reasoned out the special particular case. Well now, suppose, having got your conclusion of the law, that at some time afterwards, you are discussing the qualities of apples with a friend: you will say to him, "It is a very curious thing,—but I find that all hard and green apples are sour!" Your friend says to you, "But how do you know that?" You at once reply, "Oh, because I have tried them over and over again, and have always found them to be so." Well, if we were talking science instead of common sense, we should call that an experimental verification. And, if still opposed, you go further, and say, "I have heard from the people in Somersetshire and Devonshire, where a large number of apples are grown, that they have observed the same thing. It is also found to be the case in Normandy, and in North America. In short, I find it to be the universal experience of mankind wherever attention has been directed to the subject." Whereupon, your friend, unless he is a very unreasonable man, agrees with you, and is convinced that you are quite right in the conclusion you have drawn. He believes, although perhaps he does not know he believes it, that the more extensive verifications are,—that the more frequently experiments have been made, and results of the same kind arrived at,—that the more varied the condititions under which the same results are attained, the more certain is the ultimate conclusion, and he disputes the question no further. He sees that the experiment has been tried under all sorts of conditions, as to time, place, and people, with the same result; and he says with you, therefore, that the law you have laid down must be a good one, and he must believe it.

In science we do the same thing;—the philosopher exercises precisely the same faculties, though in a much more delicate manner. In scientific inquiry it becomes a matter of duty to expose a supposed law to every possible kind of verification, and to take care, moreover, that this is done intentionally, and not left to a mere accident, as in the case *6* of the apples. And in science, as in common life, our confidence in a law is in exact proportion to the absence of variation in the result of our experimental verifications. For instance, if you let go your grasp on an article you may have in your hand, it will immediately fall to the ground. That is a very common verification of one of the best established laws of nature—that of gravitation. The method by which men of science establish the existence of that law is exactly the same as that by which we have established the trivial proposition about the sourness of hard and green apples. But we believe it in such an extensive, thorough, and unhesitating manner because the universal experience of mankind verifies it, and we can verify it ourselves at any time; and that is the strongest possible foundation on which any natural law can rest.

Mechanics' Logic

Two kinds of logic are used (in motorcycle maintenance), inductive and deductive. Inductive inferences start with observations of the machine and arrive at general conclusions. For example, if the cycle goes over a *1* bump and the engine misfires, and then goes over another bump and the engine misfires, and then goes over another bump and the engine misfires, and then goes over a long smooth stretch of road and there is no misfiring, and then goes over a fourth bump and the engine misfires again, one can logically conclude that the misfiring is caused by the bumps. That is induction: reasoning from particular experiences to general truths.

Deductive inferences do the reverse. They start with general knowledge and predict a specific observation. For example, if, from reading the hierarchy of facts about the machine, the mechanic knows the horn *2* of the cycle is powered exclusively by electricity from the battery, then he can logically infer that if the battery is dead the horn will not work. That is deduction.

Solution of problems too complicated for common sense to solve is achieved by long strings of mixed inductive and deductive inferences that weave back and forth between the observed machine and the mental hierarchy of the machine found in the manuals. The correct program for this interweaving is formalized as scientific method.

3

Actually I've never seen a cycle-maintenance problem complex enough really to require full-scale formal scientific method. Repair problems are not that hard. When I think of formal scientific method an image sometimes comes to mind of an enormous juggernaut, a huge bulldozer—slow, tedious, lumbering, laborious, but invincible. It takes twice as long, five times as long, maybe a dozen times as long as informal mechanic's techniques, but you know in the end you're going to *get* it. There's no fault isolation problem in motorcycle maintenance that can stand up to it. When you've hit a really tough one, tried everything, racked your brain and nothing works, and you know that this time Nature has really decided to be difficult, you say, "Okay, Nature, that's the end of the *nice* guy," and you crank up the formal scientific method.

4

For this you keep a lab notebook. Everything gets written down, formally, so that you know at all times where you are, where you've been, where you're going and where you want to get. In scientific work and electronics technology this is necessary because otherwise the problems get so complex you get lost in them and confused and forget what you know and what you don't know and have to give up. In cycle maintenance things are not that involved, but when confusion starts it's a good idea to hold it down by making everything formal and exact. Sometimes just the act of writing down the problems straightens out your head as to what they really are.

5

The logical statements entered into the notebook are broken down into six categories: (1) statement of the problem, (2) hypotheses as to the cause of the problem, (3) experiments designed to test each hypothesis, (4) predicted results of the experiments, (5) observed results of the experiments and (6) conclusions from the results of the experiments. This is not different from the formal arrangement of many college and high-school lab notebooks but the purpose here is no longer just busy-work. The purpose now is precise guidance of thoughts that will fail if they are not accurate.

6

The real purpose of scientific method is to make sure Nature hasn't misled you into thinking you know something you don't actually know. There's not a mechanic or scientist or technican alive who hasn't suffered from that one so much that he's not instinctively on guard. That's the main reason why so much scientific and mechanical information sounds so dull and so cautious. If you get careless or go romanticizing scientific information, giving it a flourish here and there, Nature will soon make a complete fool out of you. It does it often enough anyway even when you don't give it opportunities. One must be extremely careful and rigidly logical when dealing with Nature: one logical slip and an entire scientific edifice comes tumbling down. One false deduction about the machine and you can get hung up indefinitely.

7

In Part One of formal scientific method, which is the statement of the problem, the main skill is in stating absolutely no more than you are positive you know. It is much better to enter a statement "Solve Problem: Why doesn't cycle work?" which sounds dumb but is correct, than it is to enter a statement "Solve Problem: What is wrong with the electrical system?" when you don't absolutely *know* the trouble is *in* the electrical system. What you should state is "Solve Problem: What is wrong with cycle?" and *then* state as the first entry of Part Two: "Hypothesis Number One: The trouble is in the electrical system." You think of as many hypotheses as you can, then you design experiments to test them to see which are true and which are false. *8*

This careful approach to the beginning questions keeps you from taking a major wrong turn which might cause you weeks of extra work or can even hang you up completely. Scientific questions often have a surface appearance of dumbness for this reason. They are asked in order to prevent dumb mistakes later on. *9*

Part Three, that part of formal scientific method called experimentation, is sometimes thought of by romantics as all of science itself because that's the only part with much visual surface. They see lots of test tubes and bizarre equipment and people running around making discoveries. They do not see the experiment as part of a larger intellectual process and so they often confuse experiments with demonstrations, which look the same. A man conducting a gee-whiz science show with fifty thousand dollars' worth of Frankenstein equipment is not doing anything scientific if he knows beforehand what the results of his efforts are going to be. A motorcycle mechanic, on the other hand, who honks the horn to see if the battery works is informally conducting a true scientific experiment. He is testing a hypothesis by putting the question to Nature. The TV scientist who mutters sadly, "The experiment is a failure; we have failed to achieve what we had hoped for," is suffering mainly from a bad scriptwriter. An experiment is never a failure solely because it fails to achieve predicted results. An experiment is a failure only when it also fails adequately to test the hypothesis in question, when the data it produces don't prove anything one way or another. *10*

Skill at this point consists of using experiments that test only the hypothesis in question, nothing less, nothing more. If the horn honks, and the mechanic concludes that the whole electrical system is working, he is in deep trouble. He has reached an illogical conclusion. The honking horn only tells him that the battery and horn are working. To design an experiment properly he has to think very rigidly in terms of what directly causes what. This you know from the hierarchy. The horn doesn't make the cycle go. Neither does the battery, except in a very indirect way. The point at which the electrical system *directly* causes the engine to fire is at the spark plugs, and if you don't test here, at the output of the electrical system, you will never really know whether the failure is electrical or not. *11*

To test properly the mechanic removes the plug and lays it against the engine so that the base around the plug is electrically grounded, kicks the starter lever and watches the spark-plug gap for a blue spark. If *12* there isn't any he can conclude one of two things: (a) there is an electrical failure or (b) his experiment is sloppy. If he is experienced he will try it a few more times, checking connections, trying every way he can think of to get that plug to fire. Then, if he can't get it to fire, he finally concludes that *a* is correct, there's an electrical failure, and the experiment is over. He has proved that his hypothesis is correct.

In the final category, conclusions, skill comes in stating no more than the experiment has proved. It hasn't proved that when he fixes the electrical system the motorcycle will start. There may be other things *13* wrong. But he does know that the motorcycle isn't going to run until the electrical system is working and he sets up the next formal question: "Solve problem: what is wrong with the electrical system?"

He then sets up hypotheses for these and tests them. By asking the right questions and choosing the right tests and drawing the right conclusions the mechanic works his way down the echelons of the motorcy- *14* cle hierarchy until he has found the exact specific cause or causes of the engine failure, and then he changes them so that they no longer cause the failure.

An untrained observer will see only physical labor and often get the idea that physical labor is mainly what the mechanic does. Actually the physical labor is the smallest and easiest part of what the mechanic does. By far the greatest part of his work is careful observation and precise *15* thinking. That is why mechanics sometimes seem so taciturn and withdrawn when performing tests. They don't like it when you talk to them because they are concentrating on mental images, hierarchies, and not really looking at you or the physical motorcycle at all. They are using the experiment as part of the program to expand their hierarchy of knowledge of the faulty motorcycle and compare it to the correct hierarchy in their mind. They are looking at underlying form.

EXERCISE 6A

Analyzing Pirsig and Huxley

1. In your own words, state Huxley's thesis.
2. According to Pirsig, what is the most important part of the mechanic's work?
3. How does Pirsig define induction and deduction?
4. Which method of reasoning—induction or deduction—does the scientific method rely on?

EXERCISE 6B

Distinguishing Inductive from Deductive Reasoning

Read the following passages carefully and determine which are based on deductive reasoning and which on inductive. Briefly explain your answers.

* **1.** Marie must be out of town. She hasn't answered her phone in a week, nor has she returned the messages that I have left on her answering machine. When I drove past her house last night, I noted that the lights inside and out were off.

  2. Cat lovers do not care for dogs, and since Colette had numerous cats all of her life, I assume she did not care for dogs.

  3. According to polls taken prior to the Republican convention, the Democratic candidate held a substantial lead in the presidential race. We are now confident that he will win in November.

* **4.** Every Frenchman is devoted to his glass of *vin rouge*. Philippe is a Frenchman so he too must be devoted to that glass of red wine.

  5. For Iranians, life remains a struggle. Personal freedoms are severely curtailed. Through systematic segregation at work and in public places, women remain the second-class citizens that they became during Ayatolla Khomeini's years. And with an average income of $100 a month, the Iranian middle class is straining in the face of 40 percent inflation rates. (from "Iran Gingerly Tries a Bit of Pragmatism" by Youssef M. Ibrahim)

  6. As an expert testified on the MacNeil/Lehrer News Hour following the *Challenger* disaster in 1986, the solid rocket booster had proved safe in over 200 successful launchings of both space shuttles and Titan missiles. It was reasonable to conclude that the same rocket booster would function properly on the *Challenger* mission.

  7. Students educated in the past two decades are not as well informed as were students attending universities prior to the mid-1960s. Because our rising generation of leaders has been educated in the past two decades, they are not as well informed as those leaders who preceded them. [This line of reasoning is suggested in two popular books on contemporary values and education: *The Closing of the American Mind* and *Cultural Literacy*.]

  8. When people are confident and cheerful they are generally inclined to spend more freely. With this in mind, we have designed these ads to project a feeling of cheerful confidence that should encourage viewers to spend more freely on your product. [ad agency pitch to a potential client]

EXERCISE 6C

Identifying Your Own Reasoning Processes

Think about your own reasoning processes for a minute. Calvino (see above) maintains that we can't begin thinking without deductive "principles." But would you get very far in your day without resorting to an inductive thinking process as well?

Jot down two personal examples of your reasoning processes: one illustrating deductive reasoning, the other, inductive.

APPLICATION TO WRITING

Deduction, Induction, and Organizational Patterns

Textbooks about writing frequently describe organizational patterns for essays as being strictly deductive or inductive. It is true that a written argument may start with a broad generalization offered as a given upon which applications to more specific circumstances may be built. Such a shape does resemble one definition of deduction—a generalization applied to a particular instance or example. A paper that assumes the majority of mothers are working outside the home today could then go on to argue for a particular course of action to address problems surrounding the trend of both parents working outside the home.

Often a collection of specific data—empirical observations, examples from research, and statistics—can add up to a generalization in the conclusion and thus appear to reflect the inductive process. A survey of urban households, for example, could, with careful analysis, lead to a conclusion about trends in family eating habits.

But, as Pirsig and Huxley emphasize, it takes an interplay of the two thinking methods to reflect accurately how we arrive at our conclusions. The writer of the paper on family eating habits would be likely to start speculating on why trends in family meals have changed and possibly on what impact such changes would have on society. Such an approach would not be described as inductive, but, in fact, represents a combination of inductive and deductive reasoning.

So it would seem that while an essay may proceed from the particular to the general, mirroring the pattern of inductive reasoning, or from the general to the particular, mirroring deduction, any piece of writing as complex as an essay will involve both inductive and deductive reasoning even if the organization of the essay resembles one pattern more closely than another.

WRITING ASSIGNMENT 13

An Argument Following Two Patterns of Organization

While, as we have just explained, it is difficult to isolate deductive and inductive thinking in our writing process, for developing effective rhetorical skills, practice in different organizational patterns can be useful.

Select one controversial issue (you may want to look back at Writing Assignment 7 in Chapter 4 for ideas) and prepare two short position papers, one following a deductive pattern of reasoning, the other, an inductive. About two pages for each should be sufficient.

1. In the deductive version, you will state your thesis (see discussion in Chapter 4) clearly in the opening paragraph and provide evidence to support it—obviously not fully developed, given the relative brevity of the paper.
2. In the inductive version, you will present your supporting data first and let this evidence lead you, and your reader, to the conclusion(s) you draw, which you will state at the end.

Audience   The same wide range of your peers you addressed in the writing assignments in Chapter 4—those who would agree with you, those who disagree, and those who have not, as yet, formed any opinion.

Purpose   To determine, possibly from your classmates, which format is more effective.

SUMMARY

Inductive and deductive reasoning are distinct from one another in two ways.

1. In a deductive argument, the conclusion will follow by necessity from the premises if the method of reasoning is valid. But in an inductive argument, the conclusion can only follow with some degree of probability.
2. In a deductive argument, the inference moves from a generalization to a particular instance or example that fits that generalization. In an inductive argument, the inference usually moves from a series of specific instances to a generalization.

Induction and deduction are interdependent; it takes an interplay of the two thinking methods to reflect accurately how we arrive at our conclusions.

Chapter
7

Evaluating Deductive Arguments

"Contrariwise," continued Tweedledee, "if it was so, it might be; and if it were so, it would be; and if it isn't, it ain't. That's logic."

—Lewis Carroll

All good reasoning depends on seeing relationships between classes. A **class** in logic is all of the individual things—persons, objects, events, ideas—which share a determinate property, a common feature. What is that determinate property? Anything under the sun. A class may consist of any quality or combination of qualities which the classifier assigns to it. A class may be vast, such as a class containing everything in the universe, or it may be quite small, containing only one member, such as Uncle Fred's last girlfriend.

CLASS LOGIC

Making classes and assigning members to those classes is an essential part of everyday reasoning—it's how we order our experience. Indeed, each word in the language serves as a class by which we categorize and communicate experience. We can then take these words in any combination to create the categories or classes which serve our purpose.

A recent article in the *Journal of the American Medical Association*, for example, features a piece titled "Risk of Sexually Transmitted Diseases Among Black Adolescent Crack Users in Oakland and San Francisco." This title, which identifies one class (and the subject of the article), was created by combining eight classes: the class of things involving risk, the class of things which are sexually transmitted, the class of disease, the class of African Americans, the class of adolescents, the class of crack users, the class of persons living in Oakland, and the class of persons living in San Francisco.

Relationships Between Classes

There are three possible relationships between classes: **inclusion, exclusion,** and **overlap.**

Inclusion: One class is included in another if every member of one class is a member of the other class. Using letters, we can symbolize this relationship as all A's are B's. Using circle diagrams, also called Euler diagrams after Leonhard Euler, an eighteenth-century mathematician, we can illustrate a relationship of inclusion this way:

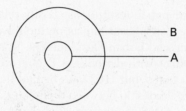

For example, the class of professional basketball players is included in the class of professional athletes since all professional basketball players are also professional athletes. The following diagram illustrates this relationship.

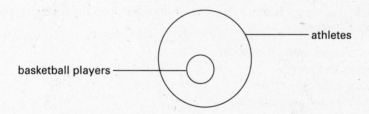

Exclusion: One class excludes another if they share no members, if no A's are B's. Such a relationship exists between handguns and rifles.

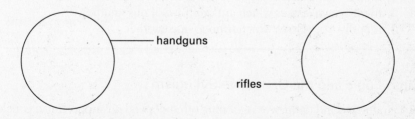

Overlap: One class overlaps with another if they have at least one member in common—if at least one A is also a B—for example, students at this university and students who like rap music.

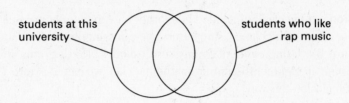

students at this university

students who like rap music

The way our public institutions classify relationships between groups of people can have a significant impact on their lives. HUD, the federal department of Housing and Urban Development, is authorized to allocate housing funds to individuals with disabilities. People with AIDS argue that they are entitled to such funds, but HUD has denied them any such subsidy. Clearly, HUD sees the relationship between disabilities and AIDS as one of exclusion while those with AIDS see their relationship to those with disabilities as one of inclusion.

EXERCISE 7A

Identifying Relationships Between Classes

Using circle diagrams, illustrate the relationships between the following pairs of classes.

   *1. cantaloupes and watermelons
   2. judges and lawyers
   3. Saabs and convertibles
   4. mollusks and amphibians
   5. cosmetics and hairspray
   6. the homeless and the mentally ill
   7. euthanasia and suicide

Now create your own classes.

   1. Identify two classes, one of which is inclusive of the other.
   2. Identify two classes which are exclusive of one another.
   3. Identify two classes which overlap one another.

Class Logic and the Deductive Syllogism

Both inductive and deductive reasoning often depend on supporting a conclusion on the basis of relationships between classes. Let's look first at deduction.

Deductive arguments usually involve more than two classes; in fact, the simplest form of deductive argument involves three classes. Remember this famous (modified) argument from Chapter 6?

> All people are mortal.
> Socrates is a person.
> ∴ Socrates is mortal.

The three classes are "people," "mortality," and "Socrates." We can use circle diagrams to illustrate the relationship between these three classes. The first premise asserts that the class of people is included in the class of mortality. The second premise asserts that the class of Socrates is included in the class of people; and thus the conclusion can claim that Socrates is included in the class of mortality.

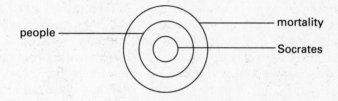

This type of argument is called a **categorical syllogism**—a deductive argument composed of three classes; such an argument has two premises and one conclusion derived from the two premises.

The subject and the predicate   To help identify the three classes of a categorical syllogism, you may want to identify the subject and predicate of each premise. Categorical propositions, and indeed all English sentences, can be broken down into two parts—the **subject** and **predicate.** These terms are shared by both grammar and logic and mean the same thing in both disciplines. The subject is that part of the sentence about which something is being asserted, and the predicate includes everything being asserted about the subject. In the first premise above, "all people" is the subject and "are mortal" is the predicate; in the second premise, "Socrates" is the subject and "is a person" is the predicate. The subject identifies one class, the predicate the other.

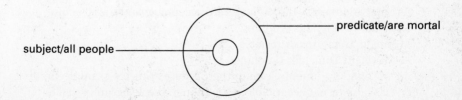

Note: If the premise stated "people are mortal" rather than "all people are mortal" the meaning would be the same since, if a class is not quantified in some way—some, many, few, one—it is assumed that the assertion refers to the entire class.

Truth, validity, and soundness   If the conclusion follows of necessity, inescapably, from the premises, as it does in the syllogism about Socrates, then it is a **valid** argument.

We frequently use the term "valid" in everyday language. For example, we say, "That's a valid point." But in logic **validity** has this very precise meaning: the conclusion follows of necessity from the premises, the form of the argument is correct, the line of reasoning conforms to the rules of logic. When we learn to evaluate the validity of a deductive argument, we can see what it means for a conclusion to follow inescapably from the premises.

Validity, however, is not the only requirement for a successful deductive argument; the premises must also be "true" or "acceptable" (see Chapter 5). Logicians use the term "true," a useful term when a proposition can be evaluated by absolute or mathematical standards. But in most of our arguments, we must settle for what is reasonable to believe, what has been adequately supported and explained. Such proof sometimes falls short of what can be claimed as "true," an absolute term too imposing, even intimidating, for many assertions which we would nonetheless be inclined to accept. Thus, we, like a number of others in the critical thinking field, prefer the term "acceptable" to "true."

To summarize, two requirements must be met for us to accept the conclusion of a deductive argument.

1. the structure of the argument must be *valid*—that is, the conclusion must follow of necessity from the premises
2. the premises must be *acceptable* (true)

A deductive argument whose premises are acceptable and whose structure is valid is a **sound** argument—a successful deductive argument. Put another way, if the argument is valid and the premises are acceptable, then the conclusion cannot be false.

Keep in mind that the terms validity and soundness can refer only to the argument as a whole. In contrast, individual statements can only be described as acceptable or unacceptable (true or false). We can't describe an argument as being true or a premise as valid.

Some examples of sound and unsound arguments:

1. A sound argument—the premises are acceptable and the structure valid.
   Drift-net fishing kills dolphins.
   Mermaid Tuna uses drift nets.
   ∴ Mermaid Tuna kills dolphins.
2. An unsound argument—one of the premises (in this example the first one) is false or not acceptable, even though the structure is valid.

All Latins are volatile.
Jesse is a Latin.
∴ Jesse is volatile.

3. An unsound argument—the premises are true but the structure is invalid.
All athletes are people.
All football players are people.
∴ All football players are athletes.

Note that in example 3, all the statements are true, both the premises and the conclusion, but since the structure of the argument is invalid—the premises do not lead inescapably to the conclusion—the argument is unsound.

Guilt by association   Let's look at another example of an invalid argument with true premises.

Drug dealers wear electronic pagers.
Doctors wear electronic pagers.
∴ Doctors are drug dealers.

All of us would reject this ridiculous argument, but this pattern of reasoning, erroneous as it is, is fairly common. One famous example took place in 1950 when communism was referred to as the "red menace," and Sen. Joe McCarthy and the House Un-American Activities Committee were beginning their witch-hunt against anyone who had ever had an association, no matter how slight or distant, with communism. It was in this climate of national paranoia that Republican Richard Nixon running against Democrat Helen Gahagen Douglas for a California senate seat presented the following argument, allowing the voters to draw their own conclusion.

Communists favor measures x, y, and z.
My opponent, Helen Gahagen Douglas, favors these same measures.
∴ Helen Gahagen Douglas is a Communist.

This kind of reasoning, based on guilt by association, is faulty (but often effective—Douglas lost the election) because it assumes that if two classes share one quality, they share all qualities. This reasoning is a source of much racism and sexism; it assumes that if two people are of the same sex or race they share not only that characteristic but an entire set of characteristics as well. But a simple diagram can illustrate where the logic fails.

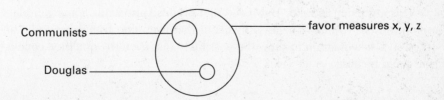

More on syllogisms   Before you examine some syllogisms on your own, we need to look once again at exclusion, overlap, and inclusion.

Examine the following example and use circle diagrams to illustrate the relationship between each of the classes to determine the validity of the reasoning.

> All Alice's friends are Libertarians.
> Deborah is not a Libertarian.
> ∴ Deborah is not a friend of Alice.

Were you able to illustrate by exclusion that this is a valid argument? Can you do the same for this one?

> None of Alice's friends are Libertarians.
> Deborah is not a friend of Alice.
> ∴ Deborah is not a Libertarian.

Can you illustrate why this reasoning is not reliable, why the argument is invalid?

So far we have been dealing with what we call a **universal proposition,** an assertion that refers to all members of a designated class. What happens when we qualify a premise with "some," and then have what logicians call a **particular proposition**? Let's look at an example.

> All gamblers are optimists.
> Some of my friends are gamblers.
> ∴ Some of my friends are optimists.

A diagram will illustrate that since the conclusion is qualified, it can follow from one qualified, or "particular," premise. Although it's possible for some friends to fall outside the class of gamblers and thus, perhaps, outside the class of optimists, the second premise guarantees that some (at least two) of my friends are included in the class of gamblers.

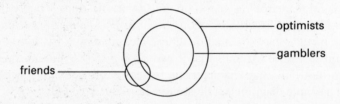

This argument is valid. But if the first premise also says "*Some* gamblers are optimists," you can't necessarily claim that even one friend has to be an optimist. Use a diagram to show the possibility that even the qualified conclusion could be false.

EXERCISE 7B

Determining the Validity of Categorical Syllogisms

Use Euler diagrams to determine the validity of the following categorical syllogisms.

Example   **1.** Stealing is a criminal act.
    2. Shoplifting is stealing.
        ∴ Shoplifting is a criminal act.

    VALID Inclusion

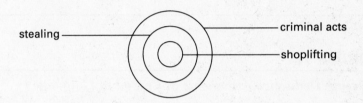

*1. Liberals want to ban offshore drilling.
    Conservationists want to ban offshore drilling.
    ∴ Conservationists are liberals.
*2. A cautious pilot wouldn't drink before a flight.
    Maxine is a cautious pilot.
    ∴ Maxine wouldn't drink before a flight.
3. All Jose's parrots understand Spanish.
    Pepe is his favorite parrot.
    ∴ Pepe understands Spanish.
4. Gauguin's paintings of Tahiti have brilliant and unrealistic colors.
    "Starry Night" has brilliant and unrealistic colors.
    ∴ "Starry Night" is a Gauguin painting of Tahiti.
5. Young men with shaven heads and swastikas tattooed on their arms are racists.
    John is a young man who doesn't shave his head or have a swastika tattooed on his arm.
    ∴ John is not a racist.
6. A democracy does not punish its citizens unfairly.
    The government of Kuwait sentenced a young man to 15 years in prison for wearing a Saddam Hussein T-shirt.
    ∴ The government of Kuwait is not a democracy.
7. Every pediatrician knows that each child develops at his own rate.
    Dr. Haskell knows that each child develops at his own rate.
    ∴ Dr. Haskell is a pediatrician.

*8. Some artists are completely self-absorbed.
Frida Kahlo was an artist.
∴ Frida Kahlo was completely self-absorbed.

9. Communists in Central America support the liberation movement.
Priests in Central America support the liberation movement.
∴ Priests in Central America are Communists.

*10. Killing the innocent is morally wrong.
Modern warfare always involves killing the innocent.
∴ Modern warfare is always morally wrong.

Create three categorical syllogisms of your own—one valid but unsound, one invalid, and one sound.

EXERCISE 7C

Evaluating Deductive Arguments in Everyday Language

Determine whether the following arguments are sound or unsound. First, reduce each one to a categorical syllogism (supplying any unstated premises or conclusions); then use circle diagrams to determine validity; and finally, evaluate each premise according to the categories of acceptability [see Chapter 5].

*1. Plagiarism is wrong, and paraphrasing the words of others without proper acknowledgment is the same as plagiarism, so paraphrasing the words of others without proper acknowledgment is wrong.

2. The time has come for the government to ban cigarette smoking on all international flights now that the National Academy of Sciences, in its comprehensive study of air quality in aircraft cabins, has declared that smoke in jetliners is harmful to health and safety. (Hint: The first premise of this argument is not stated.)

3. Mafia member Joe Bonano is guilty of criminal activities because he claimed the Fifth Amendment in the course of his trial. The Fifth Amendment, you will recall, is the privilege of a witness not to testify on the grounds that the evidence called for might be incriminating. One may choose not to testify against oneself, but there is a risk attached to this privilege. For we cannot avoid the fact that people who take the Fifth Amendment have something to hide—their guilt. In the case of Joe Bonano, that something to hide is his criminal activities.

WRITING ASSIGNMENT 14

Questioning Generalizations

The following generalizations could all be the first premise of a categorical syllogism. Choose one and write a paper in support of, or in opposition to, the claim.

1. Women are better dancers than men.
2. Men are better athletes than women.
3. Everyone is capable of being creative.
4. Nice guys finish last.
5. Appearances can be deceiving.
6. The purpose of a college degree is to prepare an individual for a career.
7. A college graduate will get a higher paying job than a high school graduate.
8. A woman will never be elected president of the United States.
9. All people are created equal.
10. War is a necessary evil.

This assignment could be postponed until you have covered Chapter 8 and completed Exercise 8D—Collecting Generalizations. With this option, you will submit the generalizations you collect after reading James Thurber's "What a Lovely Generalization!" and add these to the generalizations above, choosing one to support or refute.

Audience   A reader who is not strongly invested in the proposition one way or another but who is interested in hearing your point of view.

Purpose   To cast a critical eye on a generalization which people tend to accept without question.

HYPOTHETICAL ARGUMENTS

Another common type of deductive argument is the hypothetical or conditional argument which, unlike the categorical syllogism, is concerned not with classes but with conditions. For example:

If Maria drops that glass, it will break.

A condition is established which if met will lead to a specified consequence. The condition is called the **antecedent;** the consequence is called, appropriately enough, the **consequent.** The second premise, or minor premise, establishes whether or not that condition has been met.

Maria dropped the glass.

In this case, the antecedent has been affirmed. The conclusion then follows of necessity: The glass broke. The argument pattern looks like this:

If A, then B.
A.
∴ B.

The Valid Hypothetical Argument

This argument pattern *affirms the antecedent,*° and any argument which conforms to this pattern is valid; though of course whether or not the argument is sound, whether or not we accept the conclusion, depends on the acceptability of the premises as well as the validity of the argument.

Another valid argument pattern is one in which the minor premise *denies the consequent†*.

If Maria drops that glass, it will break.
It did not break.
∴ Maria did not drop it.

It follows that if the glass didn't break, Maria didn't drop it. Here's the form of this argument.

If A, then B.
Not B.
∴ Not A.

The rule governing the validity of a hypothetical argument is really quite simple: *The minor premise must either affirm the antecedent or deny the consequent.*

The Invalid Hypothetical Argument

Conversely, to deny the antecedent or affirm the consequent leads to invalidity. For example:

If Maria drops the glass, it will break.   [If A, then B.
Maria did not drop the glass.   Not A.
∴ The glass did not break.   ∴ Not B.]

°Logicians refer to this argument pattern as modus ponens.

†Logicians refer to this argument pattern as modus tollens.

It does not follow that if Maria does not drop it, it won't break since there are many other ways for the glass to break: Jack may drop it or someone may pour very hot liquid into it, just to name two possibilities.

To affirm the consequent will also produce an invalid argument.

If Maria drops the glass, it will break.	[If A, then B.
It broke.	B.
∴ Maria dropped it.	∴ A.]

If the glass did break it doesn't necessarily follow that Maria was the cause since, once again, there are many ways for a glass to meet such a fate.

To summarize: These two hypothetical argument patterns are valid.

If A, then B.	If A, then B.
A.	Not B.
∴ B.	∴ Not A.

These two hypothetical argument patterns are invalid.

If A, then B.	If A, then B.
Not A.	B.
∴ Not B.	∴ A.

Determining the validity of hypothetical reasoning reminds us that many conditions or causes can lead to the same result; we can't assume only one specific condition for a particular consequence unless we are told that this is the case.

Necessary and Sufficient Conditions

When there is a condition essential for a particular consequence, that condition is called a **necessary condition**—a condition without which the consequence cannot occur. Fire, for example, cannot occur without oxygen; oxygen then is a necessary condition of fire. But oxygen alone cannot start a fire—there must be matter to burn as well as something to ignite it—so it is not, by itself, a **sufficient condition.** A sufficient condition is one possible cause of a result but not the only one. The death of someone you love can serve as a sufficient condition for grief, but it is not a necessary condition; other events can also cause grief.

During the Senate Judiciary Committee hearings on the nomination of Clarence Thomas to the Supreme Court, a dispute ensued when Senator Alan Simpson maintained that Thomas's acknowledged good character should render him qualified for the Supreme Court. A law professor agreed that good character was an important ingredient for successful service on the Court, but explained that it was not the only desirable characteristic. Good character was indeed *necessary* but it was not *sufficient* to justify approval of Thomas, who many thought lacked judicial experience.

Logicians sometimes express a necessary cause as "if and only if." If, and only if, oxygen is present can fire start. Or, as writer Tobias Wolff (in *This Boy's Life*) remembers his mother warning him: "She said I could have the rifle if, and only if, I promised never to take it out or even touch it"—a necessary condition he failed to honor, unfortunately.

Hypothetical Chains

Hypothetical arguments may also consist of entire chains of conditions, as in the following example.

> If gun control advocates mount a very strong, well-funded campaign in the fall, then Congress will pass a law banning handguns.
> If Congress passes a law banning handguns, then fewer people will be able to purchase them.
> If fewer people are able to purchase them, then there will be fewer guns.
> If there are fewer guns, then there will be less violence in our society.
> ∴ If gun control advocates mount a very strong, well-funded campaign in the fall, then there will be less violence in our society.

The pattern is apparent:

> If A, then B.
> If B, then C.
> If C, then D.
> If D, then E.
> ∴ If A, then E.

If, in such a chain, the first condition is affirmed, the other conditional claims, like falling dominoes, lead us inescapably to the conclusion—providing, of course, that we accept the truth of the claims. In fact, the domino theory, which warned of a Communist threat to the United States and guided foreign policy in Central America for much of the twentieth century, is based on this kind of reasoning.

> If Nicaragua falls (to communism), then El Salvador will fall.
> If El Salvador falls, then all of Central America will follow.
> If Central America falls, then Mexico will fall.
> If Mexico falls, communism will be at our border.
> ∴ If Nicaragua falls, communism will be at our border.

Is this a sound argument? If not, why not?

Hypothetical Claims and Everyday Reasoning

As you prepare to do the following exercise on hypothetical arguments, keep in mind that such reasoning is not limited to logic texts but is a common feature of the thinking we do every day. For example:

If I miss that review session, I won't be prepared for the midterm.

If I don't stop at the grocery store on my way home, I won't have anything to eat for dinner.

As these examples indicate, we continually make conditional claims and decisions based on these claims and the outcome we desire. In the examples above, if the "I" of the sentences fails to affirm the antecedent, he must be prepared to accept the less than desirable consequences.

EXERCISE 7D

Determining the Validity of Hypothetical Arguments

Use argument patterns to determine the validity of the following hypothetical arguments.

*1. If most countries are opposed to South Africa's policy of apartheid, then it must be a bad policy. Indeed, most countries are opposed to apartheid. So it must be a bad policy.

  2. Doctors claim that if you drink large amounts of diet cola with saccharin, you'll get cancer. Fortunately, Calvin does not drink large amounts of saccharin-sweetened cola. He will not get cancer.

*3. If the burglar came in through the window, it would be unlocked. We found the window unlocked. We all agreed that the burglar must have come in through the window.

  4. If the burglar came in through the window, it would be unlocked. We found the window locked, leading us to believe that the burglar couldn't have come in through the window.

*5. If you respected my opinion, you would seek my advice. You don't seek my advice, so I can only conclude that you don't respect my opinion.

  6. If the government doesn't balance the budget, the deficit will increase. The facts speak for themselves: the deficit is increasing. Clearly, the government is not balancing the budget.

  7. If the governor makes a strong speech on the necessity of conserving water, he will be able to convince people to do so. Fortunately he has scheduled a press conference for that purpose, so people will conserve water.

  8. All the sportswriters agreed that if the 49ers didn't play well against the Redskins, the 49ers were destined to lose the all-important game. As we all remember, they lost in the closing minutes, leaving me with the unhappy knowledge that they didn't play well that day.

  9. If the paint is oil-based, the paintbrush cannot be cleaned with water, but the brush is being cleaned with water, so the paint must not be oil-based.

 10. If oil supplies from the Persian Gulf are reduced, the price of oil will rise in the United States. If the price of oil in the United States rises,

manufacturing costs will rise, and if this happens, an economic recession could develop. So if an economic recession does develop, we can certainly attribute it to reduced oil supplies from the Persian Gulf.

EXERCISE 7E

Analyzing a Timeless Argument

Reduce the following poem to a hypothetical argument containing two premises and a conclusion, and determine its validity. Hint: The first two stanzas contain the first and second premises respectively, and the last, the conclusion.

TO HIS COY MISTRESS

by Andrew Marvell (1621-1678)

Had we but world enough, and time,
This coyness, Lady, were no crime.
We would sit down, and think which way
To walk, and pass our long love's day.
Thou by the Indian Ganges' side
Shouldst rubies find; I by the tide
Of Humber would complain. I would
Love you ten years before the Flood,
And you should, if you please, refuse
Till the Conversion of the Jews.
My vegetable love should grow
Vaster than empires and more slow;
An hundred years should go to praise
Thine eyes, and on thy forehead gaze;
An age at least to every part,
And the last age should show your heart.
For, Lady, you deserve this *state*,   (dignity)
Nor would I love at lower rate.

But at my back I always hear
Time's winged chariot hurrying near;
And yonder all before us lie
Deserts of vast eternity.
Thy beauty shall no more be found,
Nor, in thy marble vault, shall sound
My echoing song; then worms shall try
That long-preserved virginity,
And your *quaint* honor turn to dust,   (proud)
And into ashes all my lust:

The grave's a fine and private place,
But none, I think, do there embrace.

Now therefore, while the youthful hue
Sits on thy skin like morning dew,
And while thy willing soul *transpires*   (breathes out)
At every pore with instant fires,
Now let us sport us while we may
And now, like amorous birds of prey,
Rather at once our time devour
Than languish in his slow-*chapped* power.   (jawed)
Let us roll all our strength and all
Our sweetness up into one ball,
And tear our pleasures with rough strife
Thorough the iron gates of life;
Thus, though we cannot make our sun
Stand still, yet we will make him run.

EXERCISE 7F

Paraphrasing a Twentieth-Century Response to Marvell's Poem

Paraphrase the argument in this reply to Marvell.

THE COY MISTRESS REPLIES

Lysander Kemp

If time, whose gentle Trot was right,
Hast learnt to gallop over-night;
If this *capacious* World so soon   (able to contain much)
Is shrunk, and shrivell'd like a prune;
If heav'nly Virtue's now a crime,
Concupiscence instead sublime: (strong sexual desire)
Then these are Marvell's marvels, known
To his gross wit, and his alone;
Such fables cannot frighten mee
Out of my precious Chastity.

Yet, if hee'll quit his prattling talk
Of flesh to dust, of bones to chalk,
Of wintry Toombes, and am'rous worms,
And seek my love with fairer terms;
I'll melt, I'll be no longer coy,
Welcoming honourable Joy:
Then we'll turn pale, and lose our breath,

And find a livelier kind of Death:
For, if today he'll wed me right,
Why then, I'll die with him tonight.
If not, then Fie to his rough strife,
He wants a *bawd,* and not a Wife.   (prostitute)

EXERCISE 7G

Evaluating an Argument for Peace

Using your own words, reduce this poem to a hypothetical argument and
determine its validity. Hint: The first premise is stated in the last stanza, but
the minor premise and the conclusion are implicit.

DULCE ET DECORUM EST

by Wilfred Owen (1893-1918)

Bent double, like old beggars under sacks,
Knock-kneed, coughing like hags, we cursed through sludge,
Till on the haunting flares we turned our backs
And towards our distant rest began to trudge.
Men marched asleep. Many had lost their boots
But limped on, blood-shod. All went lame; all blind;
Drunk with fatigue; deaf even to the hoots
Of tired, outstripped Five Nines that dropped behind.

Gas! Gas! Quick, boys!—An ecstasy of fumbling,
Fitting the clumsy helmets just in time;
But someone still was yelling out and stumbling
And flound'ring like a man in fire or lime . . .
Dim, through the misty panes and thick green light,
As under a green sea, I saw him drowning.

In all my dreams, before my helpless sight,
He plunges at me, guttering, choking, drowning.

If in some smothering dreams you too could pace
Behind the wagon that we flung him in,
And watch the white eyes writhing in his face,
His hanging face, like a devil's sick of sin;
If you could hear, at every jolt, the blood
Come gargling from the froth-corrupted lungs,
Obscene as cancer, bitter as the cud
Of vile, incurable sores on innocent tongues,—

My friend, you would not tell with such high zest
The old Lie: *Dulce et decorum est*
*Pro patria mori.**

Biographical note: This poem is especially poignant because its author, Wilfred Owen, died on the battlefield in the last week of the First World War at the age of 25.

APPLICATION TO WRITING

Parallel Structure and Class Logic

Our earlier discussion of classes applies not only to logic, syllogisms, and politics but also to sentence structure, specifically to parallel structure.

Parallel structure is simply a repetition of like grammatical units—a list of items if you will—often joined by conjunctions. The items in the list, however, must not only be grammatically similar but also relate logically to one another. Here's where class logic comes into play.

To understand what we mean, look at the following sentence.

The language used in the text will have to be looked at for sexism, racism, and bias.

The list in this sentence is "sexism, racism, and bias." The list is *grammatically* parallel because all three words in the list are nouns, but not *logically* parallel since sexism, racism, and bias are presented as three separate classes when in fact sexism and racism are particular forms of bias; they are included in the class of bias, not separate from it. One way to correct this faulty logic would be to replace "bias" with "other forms of bias" thus illustrating the logical and actual relationship—exclusion—which exists between the three classes.

EXERCISE 7H

Editing the Illogical Series

Revise the following sentences for logical classification.

* *1. In their attempt to excel, these people will often work extra hours and work through many lunch hours.
  2. I have seen city ordinances which do not allow smoking in restaurants popping up all over the place: in offices, in buildings.
  3. I asked Linda if she had any materialistic aspirations such as living in a mansion, having a nice car, or being extremely wealthy.

---

* "It is sweet and fitting to die for one's country." From the Latin poet Horace.

4. The customers at the bank where I work are wealthy depositors, checking account holders, cooperative individuals, and those who are thoughtlessly rude to me.

5. For the most part, he is handsome, active, and well-dressed, usually in expensive clothes or a suit and tie.

A Review of Parallel Structure

Look at the following two sentences:

> I came, I saw, I conquered.

> They plan to visit Rio, Madrid, and Bangkok.

Though quite different in content they are similar in form: they both illustrate parallel structure. As stated above, parallel structure is simply repetition, usually of the same grammatical structures used in the same way, sometimes of the same word or phrase, often joined by the conjunctions *and, but, or, yet.*

Parallelism is a useful rhetorical device, providing a powerful means of emphasizing relationships by organizing ideas into predictable patterns. We hear a repetition and expect the pattern to continue. Read the two sentences above. Listen to the "ring" of the first sentence and the aid to attention and memory such a rhetorical device provides. And then note the logical organization and its contribution to meaning in the second sentence; the grammatical grouping underscores the implicit relationships between these cities: historical cities of diverse beauty, international centers representing distinct cultures and interesting travel destinations.

When our expectations are thwarted, we may falter briefly in our reading or even lose the thread of the writer's thought. In most cases, our ear tells us when a series is wandering off the track, but sometimes it can be helpful to check the grammatical structure. Here is a strategy for examining your own sentences.

Think of parallel structures as lists, in the case above a list of cities to visit. We can illustrate this list and the need for it to conform to the principles of parallelism by placing parallel lines at its beginning:

> They plan to visit // Rio, Madrid, and Bangkok.

The conjunction "and" joins three proper nouns acting as direct objects of the verb "plan to visit."

We can do the same thing to more complicated sentences taken from Joan Didion's essay on Alcatraz, "Rock of Ages."

> It is not an unpleasant place to be, out there on Alcatraz with only // the *flowers* and the *wind* and a bell *buoy* moaning and the *tide* surging through the Golden Gate.... [a list of nouns as direct objects of the preposition "with"]

> Once a week the Harts take their boat to San Francisco to // *pick up* their mail and *shop* at the big Safeway in the Marina.... [a list of two infinitive phrases]

Mr. Scott, whose interest in penology dates from the day his office acquired Alcatraz as a potential property, // *talked about* // *escapes* and *security routines* and *pointed out* the beach where Ma Barker's son Doc was killed trying to escape. [This sentence contains two lists, one within the other—two verbs for the subject "Mr. Scott"; and two nouns acting as direct objects of "talked about."]

Now read the next sentence (aloud if possible) and hear how the loss of expected balance or harmony offends the ear.

When I should be studying, I will, instead, waste time by watching television or daydream.

The two verbs are not in the same form and are therefore not parallel. They can be made parallel by simply changing "daydream" to "daydreaming."

Sometimes faulty parallelism offends not only our ear but also our reason.

People who have "book smarts" usually work in places like // *libraries* or *assistants* to attorneys.

Though the writer has joined two nouns (grammatically compatible elements), an assistant of any kind cannot be a "place." He has lost control of the sentence because he has forgotten where the list begins. There is more than one way to fix this sentence, to make it logical and balanced. How would you correct it?

English, however, can be somewhat flexible when it comes to parallelism. For example, few readers would object to this sentence:

The bus system is economical, but it is crowded, uncomfortable, and may not be depended on.

Here the third element does not conform to the grammatical structure of the first two, yet it is neither confusing nor harsh in its rhythm. We could easily revise the ending to read "undependable," but some writers might prefer the original. Careful writers, however, make such decisions judiciously, generally preferring to maintain the grammatical and rhetorical integrity of a parallel series.

Before doing Exercise 7I, note the rhetorical effects of parallel structure on the following passage taken from *The Road to Coorain*, an autobiography by Jill Ker Conway, the first woman president of Smith College. Use our system of notation to mark off the different series or lists.

Those night train journeys had their own mystery because of the clicking of the rails, the shafts of light pouring through the shutters of the sleeping compartment as we passed stations, and the slamming of doors when the train stopped to take on passengers. In the morning there was the odd sight of green landscape, trees, grass, banks of streams—an entirely different palette of colors, as though during the night we had journeyed to another country. Usually I slept soundly, registering the unaccustomed sounds and images only faintly. This time I lay awake and listened, opened the shutters and scanned unknown platforms, and wondered about the future.

This passage has several parallel lists. Did you find them all?

EXERCISE 7I

Supplying Parallel Elements

Complete these sentences with a parallel element.

1. Writing a good paper is a task that demands // hard work, patience, and...
*2. She // rushed home, threw her assorted debris into a closet, and...
3. Fewer and fewer Americans are buying houses these days // not because they don't want to own their own home but...
4. The first lady is a woman who // has an open mind but...
5. The first lady is a woman who has // an open mind and...

In the following sentences, identify the misfit—the element of the sentence which is not parallel—and revise the sentence so that all the elements of the list are parallel.

*6. Many influences shape a child's development: family, church, peer groups, economic, social, and school.
7. Do you live in an area where knife wounds, killings, and people are raped are as common as the sun rising in the morning?
8. He helped to wash the car and with cleaning out the garage.
9. Free inquiry in the search for truth sometimes necessitates the abandonment of law and order but which always demands freedom of expression.
10. Pineapple juice is my favorite because it is a good source of energy, it isn't artificially sweetened, and because of its low cost.
11. The president launched a campaign against drunk driving and promoting the use of seat belts.

As a final exercise in parallel structure, write three of your own sentences—one with two or more verbs sharing the same subject, one with two or more adjectives, and one with two or more nouns. Use as your subject a topic you are currently writing on for this or another class.

Parallelism—The Open and Closed Series

A series can be open or closed. For example:

The state must balance its budget by eliminating free school lunches, afterschool childcare, and driver education classes.

The list is complete. The writer is recommending that three government benefits be terminated. But what if the writer only wants to suggest the kinds of cuts the legislature should make? He might write,

The state must balance its budget by eliminating free school lunches, afterschool childcare, driver education classes, etc.

This version indicates an open series, one that is not complete but is, instead, representative. A writer of a memo can use "etc." to indicate the representative nature of his list, but "etc." is not appropriate in a more formal piece of writing such as an editorial, an essay, or even a letter to the editor. So how can we write an open series without resorting to the vague and lazy "etc."? Simply remove the "and" from the list. Joan Didion uses this strategy in describing Alcatraz:

> Alcatraz Island is covered with flowers now: orange and yellow nasturtiums, geraniums, sweet grass, blue iris, black-eyed Susans.

The absence of the "and" before the final element implies that the list is not exhaustive, that there may be other flowers on the island in addition to those she names.

Emphasizing Ideas with Parallelism

As we mentioned above, parallelism can be a powerful rhetorical device. Beyond the sentence, parallelism can provide emphasis and organize major ideas in paragraphs, particularly in argument. Note how *New York Times* columnist Anthony Lewis drives home his point in the following excerpt (italics added) from one of his editorials.

> A sigh of relief: That is the first reaction to the result in Louisiana. David Duke lost, and we can put aside our worst fears. America is not so susceptible to the virus of racism.

> But it is not really an occasion for relief when a man who as recently as two years ago openly peddled Nazi propaganda wins nearly 40 percent of the vote in an American state.

> It is not an occasion for relief when a former leader of the Ku Klux Klan can master the techniques of modern politics so well that for hundreds of thousands of voters he is a hero, the voice of their frustration.

> And it is not an occasion for relief when it takes weeks of effort, local and national, focused on a single election, to defeat such a man....

Note how the repetition of the phrase "it is not an occasion for relief when" provides not only emphasis but also coherence.

SUMMARY

There are three possible relationships between classes: inclusion, exclusion, and overlap.

Both inductive and deductive reasoning often depend on supporting a conclusion on the basis of relationships between classes.

For a categorical argument to be sound, the structure of the argument must be valid and the premises acceptable.

For a hypothetical argument to be valid the second, or minor premise, must either affirm or deny the consequent.

Parallelism is a useful rhetorical device, providing a powerful means of emphasizing relationships by organizing ideas into predictable patterns.

KEY TERMS

Class   a class in logic is all of the individual things—persons, objects, events, ideas—which share a determinate property.

Inclusion   a relationship between classes in which every member of one class is a member of another class.

Exclusion   a relationship between classes in which classes share no members.

Overlap   a relationship between classes in which classes share at least one member.

Categorical syllogism   a deductive argument composed of three classes; the argument has two premises and one conclusion derived from the two premises.

Subject   that part of the sentence about which something is being asserted.

Predicate   includes everything being asserted about the subject.

Validity   the conclusion follows of necessity from the premises; the form of the argument is correct.

Soundness   describes a deductive argument whose premises are acceptable and whose structure is valid.

Universal proposition   refers to all members of a designated class.

Particular proposition   refers to some members of a designated class.

Antecedent   the part of a hypothetical argument which establishes a condition.

Consequent   the part of a hypothetical argument which results from the antecedent.

Necessary condition   a condition without which the consequence cannot occur; for example, fire cannot occur without oxygen.

Sufficient condition   one condition among others which leads to a particular consequence; for example, a match is one way to start a fire but not the only way.

Parallel structure   a repetition of like grammatical units, often joined by the conjunctions and, but, or, yet.

Chapter
8

Evaluating Inductive Arguments

He uses statistics as a drunken man uses lamp-posts—for support rather than illumination.

—Andrew Lang

*T*he fundamental distinction between deductive and inductive reasoning lies in the relative certainty with which we can accept a conclusion (see Chapter 6). The certainty guaranteed when a deductive argument is validly reasoned from acceptable premises cannot be assumed in an inductive argument, no matter how carefully one supports the inference. The terms most appropriate for inductive arguments then are strong and weak, reliable or unreliable rather than valid and invalid.

Some logicians prefer the categories deductive and nondeductive to deductive and inductive, given the varied forms arguments can take when they don't conform to the rigorous rules of inference required for deduction.

GENERALIZATION

Determining cause and effect, formulating hypotheses, drawing analogies, arriving at statistical generalizations are all examples of nondeductive reasoning, or as we have chosen to call it, inductive reasoning. But in this chapter we concentrate on the **statistical generalization**. Such generalizations are best characterized as predictions, as claims about the distribution of a **projected property** in a given group or population, the **target population**. From the distribution of such a property in *part* of the target population, the **sample**, we infer a proposition, a conclusion which is either strong or weak depending on how carefully we conduct our survey. We make a prediction, an inference, about the unknown on the basis of the known; on the basis of our observations of the sample, we make a generalization about all of the population, including that part we have not observed closely.

Suppose we want to determine whether New York taxpayers will support a tax designated specifically for building shelters for the homeless. Here the projected property would be the willingness to support this particular tax (what we want to find out). The target population would be New York taxpayers. The sample would be that portion of New York taxpayers polled. From their answers, we would draw a conclusion, make a generalization about New York taxpayers in general: unanimous support, strong support, marginal support, little support, no support—whatever their answers warrant. But no matter how precise the numbers from the sample, we cannot predict with absolute certainty what the entire population of New York taxpayers will actually do. When we make an inference from some to all, the conclusion will always remain logically doubtful to some degree.

Let's look at another example.

For several years now, scientists and health officials have been alerting the public to the increased risk of skin cancer as the thinning of the ozone layer allows more of the harmful ultraviolet rays to penetrate the atmosphere. Imagine that the student health center at your school wanted to find out if students were aware of this danger and protecting themselves from it. In this case, the projected property would be taking preventative measures to protect oneself from the sun. The target population would be all the students attending your school, and the sample would be the number of students polled. Once again, any conclusions reached by the health center on the basis of its survey would be tentative rather than certain, with the certainty increasing in proportion to the size of the sample—the greater the number of students polled, the more reliable the conclusion, assuming the sample is representative as well.

The Direction of Inductive Reasoning

The direction of inductive reasoning can vary. We may start by noting specific instances and from them make general inferences, or we may begin with a general idea and seek specific examples or data to support it. The following example moves from specific cases to a generalization.

Observing a sudden increase in the number of measles cases in several communities, public health officials in 1990 inferred that too many infants were going unvaccinated.

Even here you may notice that our ability to think both deductively and inductively has a way of intertwining the two modes of thought, but the structure of this argument is still inductive, the conclusion being probable rather than guaranteed.

But often we start with a tentative generalization, a possible conclusion called a **hypothesis**, an assertion we are interested in proving.

Rousel Uclaf, the French manufacturers of a revolutionary new pill to prevent pregnancy and avoid abortion, hoped to prove that it was both effective and safe. In order to do so they had to conduct elaborate studies with varied groups of women over time. Until they had gathered such statistical support in a sample population, their claim that it was effective and safe was only a hypothesis, not a reliable conclusion. But once they had tested their product, RU 486, on 40,000 women in several European countries and found only two "incidents" of pregnancies and no apparent harm, they were ready to claim that RU 486 is reasonably safe and statistically effective.

Even here, the conclusion remains inductive—it is a highly probable conclusion but not a necessary one as it would be in deduction. Unfortunately, there are examples of such inductive reasoning leading to false (and disastrous) conclusions. Approved for use in Europe though not in the United States, the drug Thalidomide, given to pregnant women for nausea in the 1960s, caused many children to be born with grave deformities. And the Dalkon Shield, an intrauterine birth control device of the 1970s, although tested before being made available, caused sterility in many of its users.

Testing Inductive Generalizations

With inductive arguments, we accept a conclusion with varying degrees of probability and must be willing to live with at least a fraction of uncertainty. But the question will always remain, how much uncertainty is acceptable?

Criteria for evaluating statistical generalizations   *How* we infer our conclusions, the way in which we conduct our surveys, is crucial to determining the strength of an inductive argument. Whether we are constructing our own arguments or evaluating those of others, we need to be discriminating. Many of our decisions on political, economic, sociological, even personal issues depend on inductive reasoning. Scarcely a day goes by without an inductive study or poll reaching the news sections of daily papers or the evening news on TV—surveys show the president's popularity is rising or falling, Americans favor socialized medicine, one in five nongovernment workers is employed at firms with drug testing programs. A few principles for evaluating such generalizations can help us all examine the conclusions with the critical perspective necessary for our self-defense.

In order to accept a conclusion as warranted or reliable, we need to control or interpret the conditions of the supporting survey.

Two features of the sample are essential:

1. The *size* must be adequate. The proportion of those in the sample must be sufficient to reflect the total size of the target population. Statisticians have developed complex formulas for determining adequate size proportionate to a given population, but for our general purposes common sense and a little well-reasoned practice will serve. (Note, however, that the Gallup Organization polls 2,500 to 3,000 to determine how 80 million will vote in a presidential election and allows for only a 3 percent margin of error.)

2. The sample must be *representative*. It must represent the target population in at least two different ways.

  a. The sample must be selected *randomly* from the target population.

  b. It must also be *spread* across the population so that all significant differences within the population are represented. Such a contrived approach might seem contradictory to a random sample, but some conscious manipulation is often necessary to assure a sample that is genuinely typical of the target population.

Examine the following diagram to see these principles illustrated.

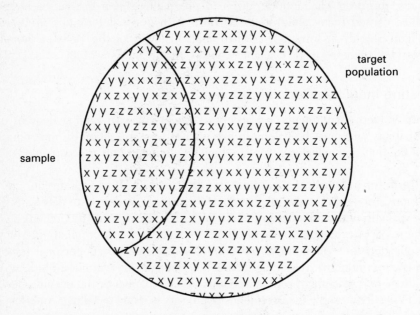

As you can see, we are back to classes (Chapter 7). The sample is a subclass included in the larger class of the target population. As we make inferences, we move from a conclusion about the smaller class, the sample, to a conclusion about the larger class, the target population.

Let's evaluate the reasoning in the following argument:

A visitor of modest means from a midwestern city comes to San Francisco for five days and is instructed by her friends to assess the prices of San Francisco restaurants; some of them are considering a trip there in the near future. Our tourist, let's call her Martha, picks up a guidebook and takes the first five restaurants listed in the book: Masas, Campton Place, Postrio, Trader Vic's, and Ernie's, all of which are located downtown. Verging on bankruptcy, poor Martha returns home with the report that restaurants in San Francisco are staggeringly expensive. For a resident of San Francisco, the error in her conclusion and the flaw in the reasoning that led to her false conclusion are easy to spot—she has inadvertently chosen five of the most expensive restaurants in the city. Before selecting her restaurants, she should have examined her guidebook carefully to be sure that her survey of restaurants was, to some degree, representative. The book clearly began with a list of the major splurges, and that was as far as Martha went.

With only five days, she was necessarily limited when it came to the *size* of her sample, and thus she would have to place a strong qualifier on any conclusion she drew. But with a little care, she could have aimed for a more *random* sample by investigating different sections of her guidebook, referring to more than one guide, and visiting various geographical areas of San Francisco. Such a sampling would also have helped her arrive at examples spread more effectively over different types of cuisine. A visitor intent on savoring the best fare regardless of cost would have done well following Martha's approach, but one interested in the prices was doomed to a distorted picture.

Can you identify the projected property, the target population, the sample, and the conclusion for this inductive argument?

Hasty generalizations

When, like Martha, we leap to an unwarranted conclusion, we commit the common logical fallacy of hasty generalization. If, for example, after one semester at a university as a student having had two professors who failed to return work, often missed class, or arrived late, you concluded that the university had a rotten faculty, you would be guilty of hasty generalization. The sample is clearly too small to warrant such a conclusion. For further discussion of this familiar weakness in reasoning, look ahead to Chapter 9.

COUNTEREXAMPLES

With any generalization supported by specific examples, one counterexample can discredit, or "embarrass," the conclusion. Warranted conclusions must be consistent with the data used in their support, and where necessary, qualified appropriately—"most," "some," "usually," "occasionally," "in most cases."

Thinking Critically about Statistics

Relying on numbers without thinking about alternative explanations can quickly lead to false conclusions. Statistics should contribute to reasoning, not serve as a substitute for it. Examine this example:

General Foods learned the danger of placing blind faith in statistical marketing research when they tested Great Shakes, a new drink mix. Surveys of customers in several cities indicated they were enthusiastically buying all the flavors, and General Foods immediately began marketing the product nationally. They were surprised by the disappointing sales. What they had failed to consider was the possibility that customers were simply sampling all the flavors, hoping to find one they liked, and once they had rejected all flavors they lost interest in Great Shakes.

Note also subtle slants in the emphasis given to statistics. In the same issue of a major daily newspaper, the summary caption on page one stated that, "A new poll finds that 1 in 5 Californians still resent Japan for the attack on Pearl Harbor," while the inside story was headed, "50 years after attack on Pearl Harbor, only 1 in 5 is still resentful, poll shows." What are the different implications of these two captions?

The following exchange of letters in *The Nation* illustrates just how tricky numbers can be and reminds us that we should not judge without reflection.

Sexism Rampant

Hunter, N.Y.
Your poetry competition and its result were remarkable ["Prizewinning Poets—1990," May 14]. Competitiveness is one of those traits of our present system I'd think you'd eschew. But what really irks me is your result: Four female poets win a competition cosponsored by a publication with a female poetry editor [Grace Schulman]. Yes, there were males on the judging panel just as the queens of old had eunuchs to attend them. Does *The Nation* mean to tell us there were no entries by male poets that remotely approached the quality (however that's judged) of the winners? I can imagine the screams from the gallery if the results were as one-sided in the other direction—four male winners of a prize offered by a publication with a male poetry editor.

If progressive principles include freedom from gender bias, you're as regressive as anyone, only you've exchanged Neanderthal attitudes for Amazonian. You're as helplessly carried about by the raging beast of gender prejudice as anyone you've ever criticized.

Dominick Amarante

Schulman Replies

New York City
The Discovery—*Nation* contest is nearly unique in that it is judged anonymously. Neither the judges nor I know the gender or the names of the poets who enter the competition. However, this information might enlighten Dominick Amarante: According to the laws of probability, if an equal number of male and female poets submit entries, one out of sixteen times all the winners will be female, or male.

Grace Schulman

EXERCISE 8A

Evaluating a Map

What do you make of the generalization drawn from this map? What evidence is offered for this conclusion? How strong is the argument?

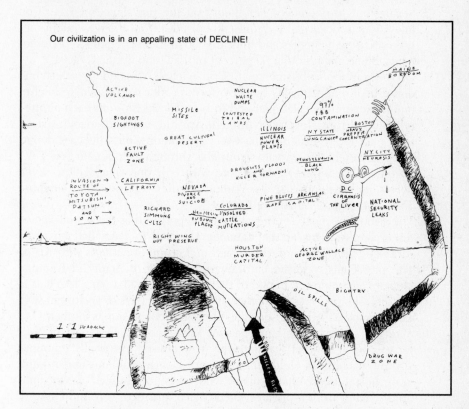

Our civilization is in an appalling state of DECLINE!

EXERCISE 8B

Evaluating Inductive Arguments

In the following inductive arguments, identify the conclusion, the projected property, the target population, and the sample. Then, drawing on the principles of reliable inductive generalizations, evaluate the argument.

* 1. The quality control inspector at Sweet and Sour Yogurt removes and tests one container out of approximately every thousand (about one every 15 minutes) and finds it safe for consumption. She then guarantees as safe all the containers filled that day.

2. In her book *Women and Love*, Shere Hite claims that a large percentage of American women are unhappy in their marriages and feel that men don't listen to them. She felt confident in her conclusions after mailing out 100,000 questionnaires to women's political, professional, and religious organizations and having 4 percent of the questionnaires returned.

3. Setting out to document her theory on the prevalence of racism on television, a sociologist examines 40 episodes from the new fall prime-time situation comedies and finds that 36 of them contain racist stereotypes. She concludes that 90 percent of television drama is racist.

* 4. On November 1, businessman Eric Nichols decided to select one domestic airline from his two favorites in order to consolidate his frequent flier mileage. He planned to base his decision on each airline's reliability. From November through April he made 20 evenly spaced trips on United, experiencing two cancellations, nine delayed departures, and eight late arrivals. From May through October, he flew TWA 22 times, but improved his record with only one cancellation, seven delays, and five late arrivals. Without further consideration, he chose TWA as the more reliable of the two.

5. The French Ministry of Social Affairs reported that three well-known research physicians at the Laennec Hospital in Paris had observed "dramatic biological improvements" in a group of patients with AIDS. The physicians reported a "dramatic" slowing of Acquired Immune Deficiency Syndrome in one of the six patients and a complete halt in the disease's progress in another after only five days of treatment with a compound called cyclosporine. (Hint: The conclusion is implicit.)

6. A recent study by the University of Medicine and Dentistry of New Jersey concluded that "women who were abused [physically, emotionally, or sexually] as children have more health problems and require more hospital care than women who were not abused." Seven hundred women from a private gynecological practice were interviewed. Mostly white, middle class with college degrees, they ranged in age from 16 to 76.

EXERCISE 8C

Finding Weaknesses in Inductive Arguments

In the following article, a critic points out weaknesses in an inductive argument. Analyze the original inductive study, then the critic's response, and summarize your findings according to these steps:

1. Identify the projected property, the target population, the sample, and the conclusion.

2. Explain the weaknesses as discussed by the critic and conclude with a discussion of your own opinion. Do you support the critic or the researchers who first presented the conclusions?

Dispute Over Claims of Ibuprofen Dangers

United Press International

Washington

Federal officials and makers of ibuprofen medicines yesterday disputed the conclusions of medical researchers who claim that a 12-patient study indicates that over-the-counter doses of the pain killer may cause kidney failure in high-risk people.

In a study published in the Annals of Internal Medicine, doctors from Johns Hopkins University medical school in Baltimore looked at the effects of ibuprofen and two other types of nonsteroidal, anti-inflammatory drugs in 12 women with chronic kidney problems but no obvious symptoms. Three of the patients developed complications.

But Food and Drug Administration spokeswoman Bonnie Aikman said yesterday that consumers have no cause for alarm about taking over-the-counter ibuprofen, as long as they read the label telling them to contact a doctor if they experience any unusual symptoms. That advice will be highlighted on ibuprofen labels starting in June, Aikman added.

The patients in the study were given the prescription-level does of ibuprofen—2,400 milligrams a day—two times the maximum daily dose recommended for over-the-counter versions of the drug.

Eight days into an 11-day course of treatment, three of the patients were judged to have severe enough kidney impairment that researchers stopped giving them the drug. When researchers later tried giving them lower doses of ibuprofen, 1,200 milligrams per day—or the top over-the-counter dose, two of the three patients again developed evidence of acute kidney failure.

Ibuprofen was recommended to patients by doctors nearly 50 million times in 1987, according to the National Disease and Therapeutic Index. An estimated 100 million people have used the nonprescription drug since it was introduced in 1984.

T. R. Reid, a spokesman for the Upjohn Co. of Kalamazoo, Mich., maker of Motrin, a prescription ibuprofen medication, and Motrin IB, the over-the-counter version, called the conclusions of the Johns Hopkins study "warped."

Reid noted the study only looked at 12 patients, and all patients were predisposed to kidney failure. But his major objection was that its authors extended the findings about prescription ibuprofen to over-the-counter ibuprofen.

Other common over-the-counter products containing ibuprofen are Nuprin, made by Bristol-Myers Squibb Co. of New York, and Advil, made by Whitehall Laboratories Inc. of New York.

"We do not believe the findings of this study apply to the safety of nonprescription ibuprofen in the general population," Whitehall said in a statement.

Reid said labels on prescription Motrin already inform doctors there is a slim risk—1 percent or less—of kidney complications from prolonged use of the drug.

In addition, the Upjohn Company said labels on nonprescription ibuprofen tell people with serious medical conditions, such as poor kidney function, to consult with their doctors before starting any new over-the-counter medication.

EXERCISE 8D

Collecting Generalizations

Humorist James Thurber had fun exploiting our tendency to overgeneralize. Read his essay and then collect two "Lovely Generalizations" from the world around you. From his absurd examples it is easy to see the dangerous thinking that can spring from similar patterns of thinking, particularly racial and ethnic stereotyping and its painful, sometimes tragic, consequences. Indeed, some of Thurber's examples are sexist. Can you identify them? (Note the suggestion for a writing assignment combining your generalizations with those given in Writing Assignment 14 in Chapter 7.)

What a Lovely Generalization!

I have collected, in my time, derringers, snowstorm paperweights, and china and porcelain dogs, and perhaps I should explain what happened to these old collections before I go on to my newest hobby, which is the true subject of this monograph. My derringer collection may be regarded as having been discontinued, since I collected only two, the second and last item as long ago as 1935. There were originally seventeen snowstorm paperweights, but only four or five are left. This kind of collection is known to the expert as a "diminished collection," and it is not considered cricket to list it in your *Who's Who* biography. The snowstorm paperweight suffers from its easy appeal to the eye and the hand. House guests like to play with paperweights and to slip them into their luggage while packing up to leave. As for my china and porcelain dogs, I disposed of that collection some two years ago. I had decided that the collection of actual objects, of any kind, was too much of a strain, and I determined to devote myself, instead, to the impalpable and the intangible.

Nothing in my new collection can be broken or stolen or juggled or thrown at cats. What I collect now is a certain kind of Broad Generalization, or Sweeping Statement. You will see what I mean when I bring out some of my rare and cherished pieces. All you need to start a collection of generalizations like mine is an attentive ear. Listen in particular to women, whose average generalization is from three to five times as broad as a man's. Generalizations, male or female, may be true ("Women don't sleep very well"), untrue ("There are no pianos in Japan"), half true ("People would rather drink than go to the theater"), debatable ("Architects have the wrong idea"), libellous ("Doctors don't know what they're doing"), ridiculous ("You never see foreigners fishing"), fascinating but un-demonstrable ("People who break into houses don't drink wine"), or idiosyncratic ("Peach ice cream is never as good as you think it's going to be").

"There are no pianos in Japan" was the first item in my collection. I picked it up at a reception while discussing an old movie called "The Battle," or "Thunder in the East," which starred Charles Boyer, Merle Oberon, and John Loder, some twenty years ago. In one scene, Boyer, as a Japanese naval captain, comes upon Miss Oberon, as his wife, Matsuko, playing an old Japanese air on the piano for the entertainment of Loder, a British naval officer with a dimple, who has forgotten more about fire control, range finding, marksmanship, and lovemaking than the Japanese commander is ever going to know. "Matsuko," says the latter, "why do you play that silly little song? It may be tedious for our fran." Their fran, John Loder, says "No, it is, as a matter of —" But I don't know why I have to go into the whole plot. The lady with whom I was discussing the movie, at the reception, said that the detail about Matsuko and the piano was absurd, since "there are no pianos in Japan." It seems that this lady was an authority on the musical setup in Japan because her great-uncle had married a singsong girl in Tokyo in 1912.

Now, I might have accepted the declarations that there are no saxophones in Bessarabia, no banjo-mandolins in Mozambique, no double basses in Zanzibar, no jew's-harps in Rhodesia, no zithers in Madagascar, and no dulcimers in Milwaukee, but I could not believe that Japan, made out in the movie as a great imitator of Western culture, would not have any pianos. Some months after the reception, I picked up an old copy of the *Saturday Evening Post* and, in an article on Japan, read that there were, before the war, some fifteen thousand pianos in Japan. It just happened to say that, right there in the article.

You may wonder where I heard some of the other Sweeping Statements I have mentioned above. Well, the one about peach ice cream was contributed to my collection by a fifteen-year-old girl. I am a chocolate man myself, but the few times I have eaten peach ice cream it tasted exactly the way I figured it was going to taste, which is why I classify this statement as idiosyncratic; that is, peculiar to one individual. The item about foreigners never fishing, or, at any rate, never fishing where you can see them, was given to me last summer by a lady who had just returned from a motor trip through New England. The charming generalization about people who break into houses popped out of a conversation I overheard between two women, one of whom said it was not safe to leave rye, Scotch, or bourbon in your summer house when you closed it for the winter, but it was perfectly all right to leave your wine, since intruders are notoriously men of insensitive palate, who cannot tell the difference between Nuits-St.-Georges and saddle polish. I would not repose too much confidence in this theory if I were you, however. It is one of those Comfortable Conclusions that can cost you a whole case of Château Lafite.

I haven't got space here to go through my entire collection, but there is room to examine a few more items. I'm not sure where I got hold of "Gamblers hate women"—possibly at Bleeck's—but, like "Sopranos drive men crazy," it has an authentic ring. This is not true, I'm afraid, of "You can't trust an electrician" or "Cops off duty always shoot somebody." There may be something in "Dogs know when you're despondent" and "Sick people hear everything," but I sharply question the validity of "Nobody taps his fingers if he's all right" and "People who like birds are queer."

Some twenty years ago, a Pittsburgh city editor came out with the generalization that "Rewrite men go crazy when the moon is full," but this is perhaps a little too special for the layman, who probably doesn't know what a rewrite man is. Besides, it is the abusive type of Sweeping Statement and should not be dignified by analysis or classification.

In conclusion, let us briefly explore "Generals are afraid of their daughters," vouchsafed by a lady after I had told her my General Wavell anecdote. It happens, for the sake of our present record, that the late General Wavell, of His Britannic Majesty's forces, discussed his three daughters during an interview a few years ago. He said that whereas he had millions of men under his command who leaped at his every order, he couldn't get his daughters down to breakfast on time when he was home on leave, in spite of stern directives issued the night before. As I have imagined it, his ordeal went something like this. It would get to be 7 A.M., and then 7:05, and General Wavell would shout up the stairs demanding to know where everybody was, and why the girls were not at table. Presently, one of them would call back sharply, as a girl has to when her father gets out of hand, "For heaven's sake, Daddy, will you be quiet! Do you want to wake the neighbors?" The General, his flanks rashly exposed, so to speak, would fall back in orderly retreat and eat his kippers by himself. Now, I submit that there is nothing in this to prove that the General was afraid of his daughters. The story merely establishes the fact that his daughters were not afraid of him.

If you are going to start collecting Sweeping Statements on your own, I must warn you that certain drawbacks are involved. You will be inclined to miss the meaning of conversations while lying in wait for generalizations. Your mouth will hang open slightly, your posture will grow rigid, and your eyes will take on the rapt expression of a person listening for the faint sound of distant sleigh bells. People will avoid your company and whisper that you are probably an old rewrite man yourself or, at best, a finger tapper who is a long way from being all right. But your collection will be a source of comfort in your declining years, when you can sit in the chimney corner cackling the evening away over some such gems, let us say, as my own two latest acquisitions: "Jewellers never go anywhere" and "Intellectual women dress funny."

Good hunting.

EXERCISE 8E

Putting Induction and Deduction Together

Read the following passage taken from Arthur Conan Doyle's story, *A Study in Scarlet*. Some critical thinkers have presented this passage as an example of deduction, others as induction. What do you think? Try to construct a deductive syllogism and then list the inductions that led to your premises. How sound is your syllogism?

A Study in Scarlet

"I wonder what that fellow is looking for?" I asked, pointing to a stalwart, plainly dressed individual who was walking slowly down the other side of the street, looking anxiously at the numbers. He had a large blue envelope in his hand, and was evidently the bearer of a message.

"You mean the retired sergeant of Marines," said Sherlock Holmes.

"Brag and bounce!" thought I to myself. "He knows that I cannot verify his guess."

The thought had hardly passed through my mind when the man whom we were watching caught sight of the number on our door, and ran rapidly across the roadway. We heard a loud knock, a deep voice below, and heavy steps ascending the stair.

"For Mr. Sherlock Holmes," he said, stepping into the room and handing my friend the letter.

Here was an opportunity of taking the conceit out of him. He little thought of this when he made that random shot. "May I ask, my lad," I said, in the blandest voice, "what your trade may be?"

"Commissionaire, sir," he said, gruffly. "Uniform away for repairs."

"And you were?" I asked, with a slightly malicious glance at my companion.

"A sergeant, sir, Royal Marine Light Infantry, sir. No answer? Right, sir."

He clicked his heels together, raised his hand in salute, and was gone.

I confess that I was considerably startled by this fresh proof of the practical nature of my companion's theories. My respect for his powers of analysis increased wondrously. There still remained some lurking suspicion in my mind, however, that the whole thing was a prearranged episode, intended to dazzle me, though what earthly object he could have in taking me in was past my comprehension. When I looked at him, he had finished reading the note, and his eyes had assumed the vacant, lack-lustre expression which showed mental abstraction.

"How in the world did you deduce that?" I asked.

"Deduce what?" said he, petulantly.

"Why, that he was a retired sergeant of Marines."

"I have no time for trifles," he answered, brusquely; then with a smile, "Excuse my rudeness. You broke the thread of my thoughts; but perhaps it is as well. So you actually were not able to see that that man was a sergeant of Marines?"

"No, indeed."

"It was easier to know it than to explain why I know it. If you were asked to prove that two and two made four, you might find some difficulty, and yet you are quite sure of the fact. Even across the street I could see a great blue anchor tattooed on the back of the fellow's hand. That smacked of the sea. He had a military carriage, however, and regulation side whiskers. There we have the marine. He was a man with some amount of self-importance and a certain air of command. You must have observed the way in which he held his head and swung his cane. A steady, respectable, middle-aged man, too, on the face of him— all facts which led me to believe that he had been a sergeant."

"Wonderful!" I ejaculated.

"Commonplace," said Holmes, though I thought from his expression that he was pleased at my evident surprise and admiration.

WRITING ASSIGNMENT 15

Constructing the Ideal Man and Woman

Choose five to ten ads featuring either men *or* women from a single magazine, and from this sample note similarities to arrive at a composite portrait of the ideal man or woman as represented in this magazine. Support your generalizations with specific details from the ads. Then comment on how this image may reflect the values, interests, and socioeconomic level of the targeted readers of this particular magazine.

Don't simply list and describe each ad and its message. Instead, organize your paper around the generalizations which you draw from your sample, generalizations about the appearance and behavior of men and women.

It might be interesting for women to look only at ads featuring men, and for men to look at ads featuring women.

If time allows, work with other students in groups, sharing ads and perceptions. This collaborative brainstorming will provide you with many ideas for your essay.

Audience The men and women in the class.

Purpose To make explicit the implicit gender-based expectations and demands which our culture places on us.

WRITING ASSIGNMENT 16

Conducting a Survey: A Collaborative Project

Conduct a survey at your school to determine something of significance about the student body, and then write a report in which you state either a question or a hypothesis, describe the survey, and speculate on the results. (Apologies to statisticians for the oversimplification of a very complex task.)

The class as a whole can brainstorm possible questions to ask the student body, the target population. What do students think about the current administration on campus or in Washington? Our nation's involvement in the Middle East? Or a host of other political issues? How many students take a full academic load and work part-time as well? There are many possibilities.

Choose five or six topics from these many possibilities and divide into groups around them. These groups will then create a survey—a questionnaire appropriate to the topic they are researching—and a strategy for distributing it to a representative sample.

The next step is to collect, tabulate, and discuss the data. Either each student can then write her own report or the group can write a single report, assigning a section to each member of the group.

The report will contain the following:

1. A description of the survey
   What questions did you ask?
   When and where did you ask them?
2. A description of the sample
   Who did you ask?
   How many did you ask?
3. Evaluation of the survey
   Was the sample large enough?
   Was it representative?

Were your questions unbiased?
What could you do to make it better?
4. Analysis of the results
How does it compare to what you expected the results to be before you began gathering the data?
What do you imagine are the causes which led to these results?
What are the implications of the results?

Audience Your campus community—students, faculty, and staff.

Purpose To inform your campus community about its student members.

SUMMARY

The statistical generalization, based as it is on an inductive leap from some to all, will never be as certain as a conclusion drawn from sound deductive reasoning.

The direction of inductive reasoning can vary. We may note specific instances and from them make general inferences, or we may begin with a general idea and seek specific examples or data to support it.

For a statistical generalization to be reliable, the sample must be adequate in size and representative of the target population.

With any generalization supported by specific examples, one counterexample can discredit the conclusion.

KEY TERMS

Statistical generalization a prediction about the distribution of a particular feature in a given group.
Projected property what is to be determined about the target population.
Target population the group about which the conclusion will be drawn.
Sample the surveyed members of the target population.
Hypothesis a tentative generalization, a possible conclusion, an assertion we are interested in proving.

Chapter
9

More on Evaluating Arguments—Fallacies

It would be a very good thing if every trick could receive some short and obviously appropriate name, so that when a man used this or that particular trick, he could at once be reproved for it.

— Schopenhauer

WHAT IS A FALLACIOUS ARGUMENT?

A fallacious argument is one that is persuasive but does not logically support its conclusion. All fallacious arguments are therefore unsound; in other words, the conclusion does not follow from the premises. But not all unsound arguments are fallacious. What's the difference? A fallacious argument will usually be persuasive while not all unsound arguments are.

We can demonstrate the relationship between fallacious arguments and unsound arguments with Euler diagrams (see Chapter 7).

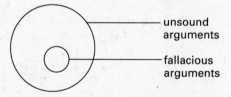

As this diagram indicates, all fallacious arguments are unsound, but not all unsound arguments are fallacious.

To further illustrate this distinction between an unsound and a fallacious argument, look at the following example.

Short people do not make good presidents.
The democratic candidate is short.
Therefore, the democratic candidate will not be a good president.

This argument is obviously unsound, but it is not persuasive and would convince no one. Technically, the line of reasoning is logical since the two premises lead inescapably to the conclusion. There is nothing fallacious in the *form* of this argument. The difficulty lies in the first premise. Because this is an absurd claim, and thus an unacceptable premise, we consider the argument unsound, but this is not the same as finding the reasoning fallacious.

Now let's look at a fallacious argument.

Senator X was expelled from college for cheating on an exam.
His wife divorced him because of his numerous affairs.
Therefore, he is a man without honor, a politician who cannot be trusted, and we should not support his National Health Bill.

This argument is also unsound but some may find it persuasive, believing that such a man could not propose worthwhile legislation. But since there is nothing in the premises which indicates flaws in the bill—only flaws in the man—the conclusion is not logically supported. The bill may be worthwhile despite the nature of the man who proposes it.

Fallacious reasoning may be intentional, as is sometimes the case with unscrupulous merchandisers and politicians, or it may be an innocent mistake resulting from fuzzy thinking or unexamined bias. In any case, if we are familiar with fallacies we can avoid them in our own thinking and writing. We can also spot them in the arguments of others, a skill which makes us wiser consumers and citizens.

There are many fallacies, a number of which tend to overlap. Our intention here is not to overwhelm you with an exhaustive list of fallacies and a complex classification scheme. Instead, we offer a list of the more common fallacies, presented in alphabetical order for easy reference.

Appeal to Authority

The opinion of an authority can support an argument only when it reflects his special area of expertise; the authority must be an expert on the subject being argued. If this is not the case, the appeal to authority is fallacious, as in the following example.

Abortion to save the life of a mother is an irrelevant issue because a former surgeon general, a well-known pediatric surgeon, claimed that in all his years of surgical practice he had never seen a case in which such a dilemma had arisen.

The problem here is that a pediatric surgeon is not an appropriate authority on an issue involving obstetrics.

Fallacious appeals to authority are bountiful in advertising which employs well-known actors and athletes to sell us everything from banking services to automobiles to coffee. Since many of these celebrities have no specialized knowledge—no authority—on the particular service or product they are promoting, they are not credible sources.

Appeals to authority also appear in the form of snob appeal or appeal to the authority of the select few. The following advertisement for a resort hotel illustrates this fallacy which appeals to people's desire for prestige and exclusivity.

Palmilla's not for everyone. The best never is.

Keep in mind that fallacious appeals to authority should not cause us to doubt all authorities, but rather encourage us to distinguish between reliable and unreliable sources.

Appeal to Fear

An appeal to fear attempts to convince by implicitly threatening the audience. Its efforts to persuade are based on emotion rather than reason. An ad for a business college uses this approach.

Will there be a *job* waiting when *you* leave college?

This ad attempts to frighten students by implying that unless they attend this business college, they will be unable to get a job after attending a four-year traditional college.

THE FAR SIDE By GARY LARSON

"Why, yes . . . we do have two children who won't
eat their vegetables."

Parents often rely on appeals to fear to persuade their children.

Appeal to Pity

An appeal to pity attempts to win our sympathy in order to convince us of the conclusion. Like an appeal to fear, it appeals to our emotions rather than our intellect. Some students use this approach when arguing for a particular grade.

> Professor Hall, I must get an A in your course. If you don't give me an A, I won't be able to go to law school.

As we know, a student's work in a course—papers, exams, participation—determines the final grade. The consequences of a grade, no matter how dire they may be, should have no effect in determining that grade.

Emotion, however, may play a part in argument, but its role must be minor, a backdrop to logical reasoning. In fact, effective arguments often begin with frightening statistics—"If nothing is done about the Greenhouse Effect, the earth's temperature will increase 10 degrees by the year 2000 with disastrous consequences for our environment." Or they may begin with an emotional illustration. For example, an argument for mandatory fencing around all private swimming pools may open with a description of a mother caring for a child who is brain damaged as a result of almost drowning in a private pool. Either of these introductions will capture the emotions and interest of the audience, but they should be followed by facts, appropriate appeals to authority, and logical reasoning.

Begging the Question

When a person begs the question, he offers no actual support for his conclusion while appearing to do so. Instead, he may argue in a circle, just restating, as a premise, his conclusion in different words.

> Students like rock music because it is the most enjoyable music around.

The writer is simply stating that students find rock music enjoyable because it is enjoyable. He begs the question. " They like it" means the same as "They find it enjoyable."

Or, take a couple of classics:

> Parallel lines will never meet because they are parallel.

> ...your noble son is mad.
> Mad call I it, for to define true madness,
> What is't but to be nothing else but mad?

> — Polonius to Queen Gertrude in *Hamlet*, II.ii

[We can discern something of Polonius' character from the manner of his argument.]

DENNIS the MENACE

"IT WAS SURE LUCKY YOU NAMED ME DENNIS...
'CAUSE THAT'S WHAT EVERBODY CALLS ME."

Dennis, like many children, follows a circular pattern of reasoning.

Some such fallacious arguments beg the question not by restating the conclusion, but by supporting the conclusion with assumptions (stated or hidden) that are as much in need of proof as the conclusion.

A familiar example is frequently offered by those opposed to rent control who argue that rent controls should be removed because such decontrol could result in a significant rise in housing construction and thus relieve the shortage of affordable rental units. A letter to the editor points out the weakness.

Editor: In your editorial concerning the housing crisis, you rely on one of the oldest rhetorical tricks of accepting as a given that which you could not possibly prove, that is, "There can be little question that removal of rent controls would result in a boom in apartment house construction . . ." If rent control is such an important factor, construction should have been booming in the '70s before rent control laws existed in our state. It wasn't . . .

Before we can accept the conclusion, the "truth" of the premise—that construction of new housing will increase if rent control laws are abolished—must be established.

We can also encounter question begging (avoiding the issue) in the form of an actual question, *a loaded question*. An example: Have you started paying your fair share of taxes yet? First, the questioner would have to establish what he means by "fair share," and then establish that the person to whom he addressed the question had not been paying it.

In some arguments, just a single word—reactionary, negligent, warmonger, deadbeat—can beg the question. Be on the alert for such prejudicial language.

Equivocation

Equivocation is the shifting of the meaning of a given term within a single argument. This fallacy stems from the often ambiguous nature of language. A term may be ambiguous because it has more than one meaning; for instance, the word "affair" may mean a party, a controversial incident, or an extramarital relationship. Look at this example:

> Antiabortion advocates stress that the unborn child has a right to life. But doesn't the woman hosting the child in her body have a right to her own life?

The fallacy of equivocation stems from the use of the term "right to life" in two different senses. In the first sentence, "right to life" refers to the child's biological existence independent of the mother. In the second sentence, the phrase does not refer to existence but to control over one's life. Such loose use of language does not effectively further the argument.

Let's look at another example.

> We are told by the government that to discriminate against a person in employment or housing is wrong and punishable by law. But we must discriminate when we hire an individual (Does he have the necessary experience?) or rent an apartment (Does he have sufficient income?). Discrimination is a necessary part of making such decisions.

In this example the word "discriminate" is the culprit. In the first sentence, "discriminate" refers to prejudice, to denying an individual employment or housing because of his or her race, sex, or religion. In the second sentence, "discriminate" refers to making careful distinctions between applicants on the basis of relevant issues.

Often equivocation is used to manipulate the language for rhetorical effect and positive associations, especially in advertising. A color film company refers to its product as "The Color of America," a slogan which is superimposed over images of Black and Asian American families. Hence, color refers to color film and to race, a clear case of equivocation.

In writing our own arguments, we can avoid equivocation by defining all ambiguous terms and being consistent in our use of them. (See Chapter 10 for definition strategies.)

**"Tonto, when I said put silver on the table,
I meant knives, forks, spoons."**

Tonto annoys the Lone Ranger when he equivocates, mistaking the horse
Silver for tableware.

False Analogy

An argument by analogy compares two or more things and suggests that since
they share certain characteristics, they probably share other characteristics as
well. In a false analogy, one compares two things in which the key features are
different.

Our involvement in the Middle East is justified or criticized on the basis
of reasoning by analogy. Those who favored the Gulf War argued that Saddam
Hussein is another Hitler and that his occupation of Kuwait, like Hitler's
occupation of Czechoslovakia, was a first step toward the goal of dominating
the entire region. If we had stopped Hitler there, World War II could have
been averted and millions of lives saved.

Those who were against the Gulf War argued that once again, as in Vietnam where 58,000 American lives were lost, the United States was involving
itself in the affairs of other countries with disastrous consequences for all.

Reasoning by analogy is appealing because it is vivid and accessible. But we must not accept analogies without careful examination. We must ask if the two things being compared are similar in ways that are significant to the point being made.

A mountain climber offers this analogy to minimize the danger of his sport.

> I don't want to die falling off a rock.... But you can kill yourself falling in the bathtub, too.

> — *John Bachar*

He is comparing two acts which are quite dissimilar, climbing a mountain and taking a bath, one a sport, the other a daily routine. And while it is possible to kill oneself slipping in the bathtub, if we were to compare the number of deaths in proportion to the number of bathers and the number of mountain climbers, we would surely find a higher incidence of deaths in mountain climbing than in bathing. In order to construct a more convincing analogy, the mountain climber should compare the risk in mountain climbing to another high-risk sport such as race car driving.

"For all his brilliance, we're going to have to replace Trewell. He never quite seems able to reduce his ideas to football analogies."

Many businessmen and politicians seem only too ready to reduce their ideas to sports analogies.

A "Dear Abby" reader writes in response to Abby's recommendation that young people use contraceptives for premarital sex, "We know that premarital sex is wrong, just as we know shoplifting is wrong." Dear Abby's reply points out the fallaciousness of this comparison.

> One of the most powerful urges inborn in the human animal is the sex drive. Nature intended it to ensure perpetuation of our species. It is not comparable with the temptation to swipe a candy bar or a T-shirt.

In debating whether or not it is appropriate for Miss America beauty contestants to have plastic surgery, those in favor of allowing such surgery compare it to other practices women use to improve their appearance such as makeup and hair color. *Boston Globe* columnist Ellen Goodman points out that this analogy is false since cosmetics are superficial while cosmetic surgery such as breast implants is physically invasive. She then offers a more accurate analogy—cosmetic surgery for beauty contestants is like steroids for athletes—each gives an unfair advantage to contestants involved in a competition.

False Cause

The fallacy of false cause is also called post hoc reasoning, from the Latin *post hoc, ergo propter hoc* which means "after this, therefore because of this." As this translation indicates, the fallacy of false cause assumes a cause-effect relationship between two events because one precedes another. It claims a causal relationship solely on the basis of a chronological relationship. Mark Twain uses this relationship for humorous effect.

> I joined the Confederacy for two weeks. Then I deserted. The Confederacy fell.

We know, as Twain did, that his desertion did nothing to end the Civil War, but this fallacy is not always so obvious. Look at the following example:

> Governor Robinson took office in 1990.
> In 1991, the state suffered a severe recession.
> Therefore, Governor Robinson should not be re-elected.
> (Hidden assumption: The governor caused the recession.)

Elected officials are often credited with the success or blamed for the failure of the economy. But in fact, anything as complex as the economy is affected by numerous factors such as inflation, environmental changes, the laws of supply and demand, just to name a few. Elected officials may indeed affect the economy but are unlikely to be the sole cause of its success or failure.

Determining the cause of all but the simplest events is extremely difficult. Post hoc reasoning is appealing because it offers simple explanations for complex events.

False Dilemma

A false dilemma presents two and only two alternatives for consideration when other possibilities exist. For this reason, a false dilemma is often referred to as either/or reasoning.

> Either you are in favor of recalling the mayor, or you are a supporter of his political platform.

We are presented with only two positions when in fact we may hold neither. We may want the mayor to continue in office because we believe him to be a strong administrator, but we may object to his proposal to encourage big business by lowering the business tax.

In his essay, "Love One, Hate the Other," movie critic Mick LaSalle rails against what he calls "false polarities." He offers the following examples: Lennon or McCartney, Monroe or Bardot, Hemingway or Fitzgerald, Freud or Jung. He calls them false "because, in each case, two elements are arbitrarily set apart as opposites when they are not opposite at all, and the idea is that we must choose between the two when there's no legitimate need to do that."

Narrowing to two choices is a strategy designed to forestall clear thinking and force a quick decision. This kind of reasoning can be seductive because it reduces the often difficult decisions and judgments we must make by narrowing complex problems and issues to two simple options.

"Damn it, Eddie! If you don't believe in nuclear war and you don't believe in conventional war, what the hell kind of war do you believe in?"

What alternative has the speaker completely overlooked?

Hasty Generalization

A hasty generalization is a conclusion based on a sample that is too small or in some other way unrepresentative of the larger population.

> Students in Professor Hall's eight o'clock freshman composition class are often late. There's no doubt that people are right when they claim today's college students are irresponsible and unreliable.

In this case the sample is both unrepresentative and too small; unrepresentative because we would expect an eight o'clock class to have more late students than classes offered later in the day, and too small because one section can't represent an entire freshman class.

It is impossible to avoid making generalizations, nor should we try to. But we must examine the basis for our generalizations to determine their reliability (see Chapter 8).

One way to avoid this fallacy is to qualify our generalizations with words such as "many" or "some." Most of us would accept the claim that "some women are bad drivers," but would reject and even be offended by the claim that "women are bad drivers."

Personal Attack

Often called by its Latin name, *ad hominem* ("against the man"), this fallacy substitutes for a reasoned evaluation of an argument an attack against the person presenting the argument. By discrediting the source, often in an abusive or irrelevant way, a person can disguise the absence of a substantive position.

> Because she is extremely wealthy and owns two luxurious homes, our mayor, Carolyn Quinn, cannot properly represent the people of this city.

But does a person's economic status necessarily rule out understanding of those in different circumstances?

A few years ago, conservative John H. Bunzel wrote a controversial book, *Challenge to American Schools*. In it he attacked the National Education Association for criticizing some reform ideas he admired—merit pay and standardized tests. He focused on their "leftist" politics rather than examining the reasons for their opposition.

Those given to Latin names like to label a particular kind of personal attack as *tu quoque*—"you also." In this instance, a person and thus his arguments are discredited because his own behavior does not strictly conform to the position he holds. We've all heard about the parent who drinks too much but admonishes his child about the dangers of drinking.

Anti-gun control groups were delighted when Carl Rowan, a prominent Washington columnist and a staunch advocate of gun control, wounded with an unregistered pistol a young man who broke into his backyard. But Rowan's failure to follow his own beliefs does not necessarily make his argument for gun control a weak one.

Poisoning the Well

A person poisons the well when he makes an assertion which precludes or discourages an open discussion of the issue. This assertion will intimidate the listener, who fears that any resistance on his part will lead to a personal disagreement rather than a critical discussion.

> Every patriotic American supports the war in the Gulf.

The listener must now prove his patriotism rather than express his doubts about the Gulf War, and the speaker avoids having to defend his conclusion with relevant premises.

Slippery Slope

We know this one by other names too: the domino theory, the ripple effect. One thing leads to another. People often claim that an action should be avoided because it will inevitably lead to a series of extremely undesirable consequences. Sometimes such a chain reaction is probable, but often it can be exaggerated for effect.

Look, if you give them a nuclear freeze, the next thing you know they'll want to outlaw war altogether.

If only all slippery slopes led to such a desirable outcome.

In a letter to the editor of a daily newspaper, a reader writes:

> The Handgun Initiative would create a huge bureaucracy equal to that in Russia, where handgun ownership is a serious crime. And we all know that bureaucracy in Russia kills people by locking them up in gulags. Are you ready for gulags in the U.S.?

Frances Fitzgerald, writing about the gay community in *The New Yorker*, cited the argument of one advocate who maintained that

> if San Francisco forced the closing of the bathhouses it would move quickly from there to concentration camps for gay men.

In both cases the writer described the downward slope as more precipitous than the evidence warranted, leading to erroneous conclusions.

Senator Jesse Helms, defending his anti-Communist stands, recognized the dangers of the slippery slope while heading in that direction himself in this masterpiece of mixed metaphor.

> We can't continue down the slippery slope of kicking our friends in the teeth.
>
> — Quoted in the *Durham Morning Herald*

Special Pleading

When an argument contains the fallacy of special pleading, it judges and labels the same act differently depending on the person or group who performs the act. It is the application of a double standard.

> The supplying of weapons to Central America by the Russians was an act of aggression. Our military aid to the region, however, helped the Freedom Fighters in their quest for peace.

In the 1980s, both the United States and Russia supplied military aid to Central America. But the language used to describe this act makes it appear as if what the United States did was admirable while what the Soviets did was reprehensible.

Straw Man

In a straw man argument, a person creates and then attacks a distorted version of the opposition's argument.

> The democratic candidate wants the federal government to house everyone, feed everyone, care for everyone's children, and provide medical care for everyone. And he's going to take 50 percent of every dime you make to do it.

This argument overlooks the candidate's proposal to reduce defense spending in order to meet his goals. Hence, this is an unfair presentation of the opposing view, but one that could be very effective in discouraging votes for the democratic candidate.

> **A caution:** Fallacies, as this chapter's epigraph points out, provide us with "short and obviously appropriate name[s]" for errors in reasoning, but we must not assume that all such errors can be labeled. Whenever we find fault with a particular line of reasoning we should not hesitate to articulate that fault, whether or not we have a label for it. On the other hand, we must be careful not to see fallacies everywhere, perhaps even where they don't exist. We must read critically, informed by our knowledge of fallacies; at the same time we should avoid tedious witch-hunts on the charitable assumption that most arguments are offered in good faith.

EXERCISE 9A

Identifying Fallacies

Identify by name the fallacies in each of the following arguments and justify your responses. You may want to turn to the end of the chapter for a chart of the fallacies.

> **Competition and collaboration:** An interesting approach to this exercise combines competition and cooperation. The class is divided into two teams who compete in identifying the fallacies, with team members cooperating on responses.

1. "I think if you look at the problems that are before us, on the whole they are problems that they have created. And so a willingness to be less creative is what is called for here." (Secretary of State George Shultz emphasizing, in 1982, that it would be up to the Soviet Union to initiate improved relations.)

°2. "Students should not be allowed any grace whatsoever on late assignments. Before you know it, they will no longer complete their work at all. If they don't do their assignments, they will be ignorant. If the students who are being educated are ignorant, then all of America will become more ignorant." (Thanks to a former student.)

3. America: Love it or leave it.

4. You can't expect insight and credibility from the recent book *The Feminist Challenge* because its author David Bouchier is, obviously, a man.

5. Politicians can't be trusted because they lack integrity.

6. Closing the gay baths to prevent the spread of AIDS is like closing bars to prevent the spread of alcoholism.

7. How long must we allow our courts to go on coddling criminals?

8. "I'm firm. You are stubborn. He's pig-headed." (Bertrand Russell)

*9. Anyone who truly cares about preserving the American way of life will vote Republican this fall.

10. "Why is it okay for people to choose the best house, the best schools, the best surgeon, the best car, but not try to have the best baby possible?" (A father's defense of the Nobel Prize winners' sperm bank.)

11. Socrates, during his trial in 399 B.C.: "My friend, I am a man, and like other men, a creature of flesh and blood, and not of wood or stone, as Homer says; and I have a family, yes, and sons, O Athenians, three in number, one almost a man, and two others who are still young; and yet I will not bring any of them hither in order to petition you for an acquittal." (Plato, the "Apology")

12. "All Latins are volatile people." (Senator Jesse Helms, on Mexican protests against Senate Foreign Affairs subcommittee hearings on corruption south of the border.)

13. Mark R. Hughes, owner of Herbalife International, was questioned by a Senate subcommittee about the safety of the controversial diet products marketed by his company. Referring to a panel of three nutrition and weight-control authorities, Hughes asked: "If they're such experts, then why are they fat?"

14. During these same hearings, Senator William Roth, R-Delaware, the Senate subcommittee chairman, reminded Hughes of criticism by some physicians that Herbalife fails to recommend that consumers seek guidance from doctors about their diets. "Do you believe it's safe to use your products without consulting a doctor?" Roth asked. "Sure," replied Hughes, 29. "Everybody needs good, sound, basic nutrition. We all know that."

15. When the Supreme Court ruled that school officials need not obtain search warrants or find "probable cause" while conducting reasonable searches of students, they violated freedoms guaranteed under the Bill of Rights. If you allow a teacher to look for a knife or drugs you'll soon have strip searches and next, torture.

*16. Since I walked under that ladder yesterday, I've lost my wallet and received a speeding ticket.

17. Sometimes, the *best* is not for everyone. (an ad for a "parisian boutique")

18. "I intensely believe that service is the highest form of being." (Susan Ford Vance, daughter of former President Jerry Ford, in an ad for a luxury hotel.)

19. We are going to have to ease up on environmental protection legislation or see the costs overwhelm us.

20. Any rational person will accept that a fetus is a human being.

21. "Editor—Is anyone really surprised that students' grades haven't improved when all they do is listen to rock 'n' roll? Rock lyrics don't ever develop into anything cohesive and the music never expands itself like real music does. All it does is just sit there and make a lot of very loud noise that goes boom, boom, boom, boom, boom that blots off the mind completely. How can a mind ever expand when that's all it ever takes in? It all started about 35 years ago with bubble-gum rock and then went into heavy metal and grades have been going down steadily ever since." (Bob Grimes in a Letter to the Editor, *San Francisco Chronicle*, May 5, 1989)

22. Heat Wave Blamed For Record Temperatures Across U.S. (a *Grass Valley Union* headline, August 16, 1988)

23. The erosion of traditional male leadership has led to an increase in divorce because men no longer possess leadership roles.

24. "Here they want to pay compensation to these Iranian people (whose families died when a U.S. cruiser in the Persian Gulf shot down an Iran Air flight) and they don't want to pay our attorney." (Ralph Dawson, conductor of the Concord Naval Weapons train that ran over protester Brian Wilson.)

25. Now, all young men, a warning take,
    And shun the poisoned bowl;   (alcohol)
    'Twill lead you down to hell's dark gate,
    And ruin your own soul.
    (Anonymous, from Carl Sandburg, ed., *The American Songbag*)

26. Editor: The Democratic controlled House, by jubilantly denying aid to Nicaragua's Contras, has strengthened the hand of communism in Central America. By suppressing a small war through their denial, they have guaranteed a full-scale war throughout all of Central America in the future, as country after country falls.

°27. I recently read about a homeless man with a burst appendix who was turned away from a hospital emergency room to die in the street. It's obvious that hospitals don't care about people, only money.

28. "You didn't have to come from Mars to direct *E.T.*, did you?" (Quincy Jones, producer of the film, *The Color Purple*, to Steven Spielberg, who was chosen to direct the film over the objections of the black community.)

29. I wouldn't consider reading William Safire's weekly language columns. How can you possibly respect him when you know that he wrote speeches for Nixon?

30. Do the vastly inflated salaries paid to professional athletes lead them into drug abuse?

31. The Nuclear Freeze movement was misguided and dangerous from the beginning, dependent as it was on "unilateral" disarmament. (A common argument of the movement's opponents. Those supporting the Nuclear Freeze movement actually proposed "bilateral" disarmament.)

32. Haemon: So, father, pause, and put aside your anger.
    I think, for what my young opinion's worth,
    That, good as it is to have infallible wisdom,
    Since this is rarely found, the next best thing
    Is to be willing to listen to wise advice.

   Creon: Indeed! Am I to take lessons at my time of life
    From a fellow of his age?
                             (Sophocles, *Antigone*)

°**33.** S & W vegetables are the best because they use only premium quality.

34. "We would not tolerate a proposal that states that because teenage drug use is a given we should make drugs more easily available." (Archbishop John R. Quinn in response to a National Research Council's recommendation that contraceptives and abortion be made readily available to teenagers.)

35. Reading test scores in public schools have declined dramatically. This decline was caused by the radical changes in teaching strategies introduced in the l960s.

36. The "window of vulnerability" developing in American defense makes it mandatory that we fund and develop more smart bombs.

37. "Just as instructors could prune sentences for poor grammar, so the principal was entitled to find certain articles inappropriate for publication—in this situation because they might reveal the identity of pregnant students and because references to sexual activity were deemed improper for young students to see." (From an editorial on the U.S. Supreme Court's decision to give public school officials broad powers to censor school-sponsored student publications.)

EXERCISE 9B

Analyzing an Editorial for Fallacious Reasoning

Read the following editorial by Abe Mellinkoff carefully and identify any examples of fallacious reasoning you find.

How to Change Your Drinking Habits

A lot of nice people who have given up on the Soviet Union and Red China, have lowered their sights. What they want to do now is improve **1** personal manners in public places. This may turn out to be even more difficult than improving our foreign affairs.

Their current goals are to settle the hash of those who throw empty beer cans out of car windows along the highway and those who leave their **2** empty Coke bottles at picnic grounds. Of course such practices are already illegal. But the reformers have a scheme to make them costly as well.

That's the essence of Proposition 11 on the November ballot. If it **3** passes, there will be a tortuous new history for each can or bottle.

The customer will pay a deposit of 30 cents per six-pack of beer or soft drink. Some weeks later, hopefully the customer will return his empties and get his money back. The grocer in turn must sort the cans **4** and bottles by type and brand and either take them to a recycling center, or wait until his wholesaler picks them up. For these time-consuming chores, he will get one cent a container.

If the plan works, there will be less litter out of town and more of it in the back of stores as grocers wait to get rid of their empties. But this is OK with the pushers of this initiative. They are operating on a policy that can best be summarized as *Damn-the-money. Full-speed-ahead*.   5

Other states—notably Oregon in the West—have already been suckered in by this anti-litter ploy. Everywhere prices on store shelves have gone up. A check of Safeway supermarkets in San Francisco and Portland on September 24 showed: Large-sized Pepsi's up 30 cents a six pack, large Cokes, up 28 cents; and Canada Dry club soda, 20 cents a quart.   6

In the words of Tom Kemp, top officer at the Coca Cola Bottling Co. of Los Angeles, "It's going to cost (the beverage industries) hundreds of millions of dollars. These (new) costs of distributing will become increased costs for the consumer. Any company that does not pass on its cost does not stay in business very long."   7

Of course the consumer can easily evade the new deposit law if it passes by merely changing his drinking habits. Wine—in fifths or jugs— is not covered and neither is the hard stuff. As a veteran picnicker, I can vouch that martinis ahead of time and chilled white wine during are every bit as satisfying as beer or the non-alcoholic bubbly stuff.   8

Once tried, many a picnicker will never go back to beer or 7-Up— deposit or no deposit.   9

WRITING ASSIGNMENT 17

Analyzing an Extended Argument

From the following collection of editorials, choose one on which to write an essay evaluating the argument. We suggest the following process for approaching this paper. Analyze each paragraph of your chosen editorial in order. Compose a list of the fallacies you find in each paragraph—give names of fallacies or identify weaknesses in reason (not all weaknesses can be precisely named) and illustrate with specific examples from the editorial. Avoid the trap of being too picky; you won't necessarily find significant fallacies in every paragraph. During this paragraph by paragraph analysis, keep the argument's conclusion in mind and ask yourself if the author provides adequate support for it.

Next, review your paragraph by paragraph analysis to determine the two or three major problems in the argument. Then group and condense your list of faults or fallacies, and in a coherently written essay organized around these two or three principal categories of weakness, present your evaluation of the argument. For example, if you find more than one instance of personal attack, you will devote one of your paragraphs to this fallacy and cite all the examples you find to support your claim. Follow the same procedure for other weaknesses. Identify each specific example you cite either by paraphrase or direct quotation, imagining as you write that the reader is not familiar with the editorial you are critiquing.

Audience College age readers who have not read the editorial and who are not familiar with all of the fallacies listed in the text.

Purpose To illustrate to a less critical reader that published arguments written by established professionals are not necessarily free of fallacious reasoning.

On Date Rape:

Dating is a very recent phenomenon in world history. Throughout history, women have been chaperoned. As late as 1964, when I arrived in college, we had strict rules. We had to be in the dorm under lock and key by 11 o'clock. My generation was the one that broke these rules. We said, "We want freedom—no more double standard!" When I went to stay at a male friend's apartment in New York, my aunts flew into a frenzy; "You can't do that, it's dangerous!" But I said, "No, we're not going to be like that anymore." Still, we understood in the '60s that we were taking a risk.

Today these young women want the freedoms that we won, but they don't want to acknowledge the risk. That's the problem. The minute you go out with a man, the minute you go to a bar to have a drink, there is a risk. You have to accept the fact that part of the sizzle of sex comes from the danger of sex. You can be overpowered.

So it is women's personal responsibility to be aware of the dangers of the world. But these young feminists today are deluded. They come from a protected, white, middle-class world, and they expect everything to be safe. Notice it's not black or Hispanic women who are making a fuss about this—they come from cultures that are fully sexual and they are fully realistic about sex. But these other women are sexually repressed girls, coming out of pampered homes, and when they arrive at these colleges and suddenly hit male lust, they go, "Oh, no!"

These girls say, "Well, I should be able to get drunk at a fraternity party and go upstairs to a guy's room without anything happening." And I say, "Oh, really? And when you drive your car to New York City, do you leave your keys on the hood?" My point is that if your car is stolen after you do something like that, yes, the police should pursue the thief and he should be punished. But at the same time, the police—and I— have the right to say to you, "You stupid idiot, what the hell were you thinking?"

I mean, wake up to reality. This is male sex. Guess what, it's hot. Male sex is hot. There's an attraction between the sexes that we're not totally in control of. The idea that we can regulate it by passing campus grievance committee rules is madness. My kind of feminism stresses personal responsibility. I've never been raped, but I've been very vigilant—

I'm constantly reading the signals. If I ever got into a dating situation where I was overpowered and raped, I would say, "Oh well, I misread the signals." But I don't think I would ever press charges.

The girl in the Kennedy rape case is an idiot. You go back to the Kennedy compound late at night and you're surprised at what happens? She's the one who should be charged—with ignorance. Because everyone knows that Kennedy is spelled S-E-X. Give me a break, this is not rape. And it's going to erode the real outrage that we should feel about actual rape. This is just over-privileged people saying they want the world to be a bowl of cherries. Guess what? It's not and it never will be.

Camille Paglia
San Francisco Examiner
July 7, 1991

Boxing, Doctors—Round Two

Before I went on vacation a few weeks ago, I wrote a column criticizing the American Medical Association for its call to abolish boxing. As you might have expected, I have received letters from doctors telling me I'm misinformed and scientifically naive. One doctor even said I must have had terrible experiences with doctors to have written what I wrote.

That just shows how arrogant doctors are. It never would occur to them that I might have a defensible position. If I disagree with them, it's because I'm ignorant.

Doctors are used to being right. We come into their offices sick and generally not knowing what's wrong with us. We are in awe of their expertise and afraid for our well-being. We have a tendency to act like children in front of them. "If you can only make me well, Doc, I will love you for life." Doctors, who start out as regular human beings, come to expect us to worship them. They thrive on the power that comes from having knowledge about life and death.

Which brings us to their misguided stand against boxing. Doctors are offended by injuries in boxing, although they don't seem as mortified by the people who die skiing or bike riding or swimming every year. You rarely hear a peep out of them about the many injuries football players sustain—that includes kids in the peewee leagues and high school. Why the outrage over boxing?

Because many doctors are social snobs. They see people from ethnic minorities punching each other in a ring and they reach the conclusion that these poor, dumb blacks and Latinos must be protected from themselves because they don't know any better. The AMA is acting like a glorified SPCA, arrogantly trying to prevent cruelty to animals. They would never dare preach this way to football players, because most of them went to college. Nor would they come out against skiing, because many doctors love to ski.

Boxers know the risks of taking a right cross to the jaw better than doctors, and they take up the sport with a full understanding of its risks. A man should have the right to take a risk. Doctors may want to save us from adventure, but there still is honor in freely choosing to put yourself on the line. Risk is why race-car drivers speed around treacherous tracks. Danger is why mountain climbers continue to explore the mystery of Mount Everest. Yet doctors do not come out against auto racing or mountain climbing.

One physician wrote a letter to the Sporting Green saying the AMA's position against boxing is based on medical evidence. As I read the letter's twisted logic, I wondered if the AMA causes brain damage in doctors. "Skiing, bicycle riding and swimming kill more people each year (than boxing)," he writes. "Obviously, far more people engage in those activities than enter a boxing ring."

Does his position make sense to you? We should eliminate boxing, the sport with fewer negative consequences, but allow the real killer sports to survive. Amazing. If this doctor were really concerned with medical evidence, as he claims, he would attack all dangerous sports, not just boxing.

But he doesn't. The truth is, boxing offends the delicate sensibilities of doctors. They don't like the idea that two men *intentionally* try to hurt each other. They feel more comfortable when injuries are a byproduct of a sport—although ask any batter who has been beaned by a fastball if his broken skull was an innocent byproduct.

In other words, doctors are making a moral judgment, not a medical judgment, about which sports are acceptable. Every joker is entitled to ethical opinions, but doctors have no more expertise than you or I when it comes to right and wrong. If preaching excites them, let them become priests.

What if the AMA is successful in getting boxing banned? Will the sport disappear? No way. As long as man is man, he will want to see two guys of equal weight and ability solve their elemental little problem in a ring. If the sport becomes illegal, it will drift off to barges and back alleys, where men will fight in secret without proper supervision. And then you will see deaths and maiming like you never saw before.

Whom will the AMA blame then?

Lowell Cohn
The San Francisco Chronicle
December 27, 1984

Abbie Hoffman—Pol Pot in Style

Abbie Hoffman died. Old hippies and Yippies and followers of social reform all lamented his passing. The TV cameras interviewed bearded burn-out cases who all knew Hoffman. It was the end of an era, they all said.

No. The era had ended long ago. The era ended when Pol Pot butchered 2 million Cambodians and the same phony revolutionaries, the college kids whose parents had fat incomes and red convertibles, failed to say one word against the slaughter.

I've been itching to write some sort of nasty column about how my generation, the war babies born after WWII, grew up with a superiority complex and a sense of righteousness that was based on nothing more than ego. And how this same crowd ranted and raved about one injustice or another and then collectively closed its eyes when a New Holocaust took place smack dab in the middle of the generation's ego trip. It's a column I haven't been able to do.

When the war babies single-handedly beat back the escalation of the Vietnam war and caused Lyndon Johnson to leave office in disgrace (ironically leading to a rebirth of the Republican Party), it figured it was on a mission from God. The mission was to save the world. Unfortunately, this group had no methodology. In fact, the war babies were so shallow that their intellectual heroes turned out to be rock stars—the Beatles!

Rock stars as intellectual heroes has since become the model for every generation since the 60s. It's pathetic. Since the Beatles, we have seen a parade of nerdy singers and introverts with a message, a beat and a twanging guitar.

The Beatles were also goofballs. They wore weird clothes, followed cults, made faces into national TV cameras, said dumb things to serious questions. This became the model for behavior—Abbie Hoffman epitomized the techniques. He formed the wacky Youth International Party —members were called Yippies. He wrote "Steal This Book." He said dumb things, acted weird and lifted his shirt to show his chest on the David Susskind Show. It was a laugh riot and Hoffman was the king of gag masters.

Eventually, through a series of run-ins with the law, mostly over petty offenses blown out of proportion by a government that couldn't take a joke, Hoffman was under arrest. He took off and made the authorities look like fools by effortlessly hiding out for years while in the public eye posing as another person. What a wacky crazy guy. Hahahaha.

All the while Pol Pot was torturing millions of helpless Cambodians in the New Holocaust. It was fascinating how all that was ignored despite the reports of savagery coming out of Southeast Asia. While the same community a few years earlier railed against American racism practiced in Vietnam because of too many GIs calling the South Vietnam allies "gooks," not a word was said when millions of Cambodians were being systematically slaughtered. Here was the real racism of the rich war babies coming to the front. After all, who needs more Asians? Pol Pot wasn't like Hitler, these people aren't Jewish. So forget about them and let's protest the treatment of blacks in South Africa. Heck, one was beaten up the other day. And let's not forget Nicaragua. Keep U.S. troops out. We don't want another Vietnam, do we?

So the war babies continue to party to this day with Loni Hancock still fighting for People's Park in Berkeley. She now equates the park to Gettysburg. Sure it is, Loni—Gettysburg, Kan. What People's Park really represents is the net accomplishments of a generation of pot smoking, drug using, free-sexers who cared about nothing more than themselves. It's a weed patch for burn-out cases to flop. How glorious. The war babies promoted drug use, now cocaine terrorizes and corrupts the country. The war babies promoted indiscriminate sex and now AIDS haunts the land. The war babies promoted racial equality for all, as long as it wasn't in Asia.

I'm sorry about the death of Hoffman. I thought he was a funny guy—a performance artist of sorts. Unfortunately too many people used him and his mentors, The Beatles, as role models.

By the way, Pol Pot is still alive and expected to again take over Cambodia. Hey, but who cares?

John C. Dvorak

From Cradle to Commencement: Higher Education in the '90s

The grisly murders of college students in Gainesville, Florida, and new federal statutes governing the disclosure of crimes and the enforcement of drug and alcohol laws on college campuses symbolize the onset of a new and worrisome era in American higher education.

The murders and the *Student Right-to-Know and Campus Security Act*,* which requires schools receiving federal aid to report campus crime, focus public attention as much on the responsibility of colleges to provide adequate security for their students as on the crimes themselves. Similarly, the *Drug-Free Schools and Communities Act*,† which requires schools to enforce drug and alcohol laws or lose federal funds (including student financial aid), codifies increasing demands for educators to play greater parental and policing roles. While all three acts have caused us to reassess our expectations of colleges and universities, the statute governing drug and alcohol consumption by students portends the most lasting and harmful effect on higher education.

---

*The *Student Right-to-Know* and *Campus Security Acts*, signed into law in November 1990, require institutions to publish and make available to students such information as the graduation and placement rates for their degree-seeking students, as well as information concerning campus security which must include a statement on campus law enforcement and its relationship with outside law enforcement agencies.

†The *Drug-Free Schools and Communities Act*, which took effect on October 1, 1990, requires that institutions adopt and implement a program to prevent the unlawful possession, use, or distribution of illicit drugs and alcohol by students and employees on campus. Compliance with this act and the one described above is necessary for institutions to receive federal funds.

Authentic education is a critical and subversive activity. It should develop in students certain faculties for evaluating and transcending the unreflective opinions of the day. In good Socratic fashion, genuine education inspires students to question conventional wisdom—their relation to their personal past, their upbringing, and even their family's values. This function of liberal education is under assault at the dawn of a new decade, and, ironically, the primary threat emanates from well-intentioned parents whose expectations of colleges have changed.

When I address a new freshman class, I see before me a society of young women and men who are mature, moral, free agents in the world. Having voluntarily chosen to join a community where the pursuit of knowledge and the assumption of individual responsibility reign supreme, they must now learn to balance their newfound freedom with a heightened sense of responsibility for their lives. They are entering a new world that is no mere extension of high school, but a radical break from the past. No parental substitute awaits them at college.

That image is being shattered today by a variety of developments and trends that have gained momentum over the past decade. Economic insecurity has fueled a rise in careerism and an intellectual myopia among students that strikes at the heart of liberal learning. The rising cost of education has created an unfortunate consumerist attitude in students and parents alike, as more and more of them have come to view education as a commodity to be bought and sold. The devaluation of the intrinsic worth of education is an inevitable result of this contractual, market-confined view of the college experience.

Most importantly, legal, social, and cultural pressures have resurrected the principle of *in loco parentis* with a vengeance. Not only are parents, lawmakers, courts, and even students increasingly expecting colleges to act as guardians, but parents have come to play a more significant role in managing their children's college lives.

Today we can speak of a new principle: *in loco co-parentis*. Parents are demanding and assuming more active involvement in the college education of their children, and colleges are forced (often grudgingly) to comply. Alumni offices are offering more outreach to parents, colleges are expanding parent orientation programs, and institutional positions are being created to address parents' concerns and interests.

The reasons why parents have adopted a new and more interventionist stance are understandable: fear of crime, drugs and alcohol, AIDS, economic insecurity, soaring tuition costs, and even the perceived immaturity and irresponsibility of their own children. This new pressure on colleges, however, seriously subverts their mission.

The Gainesville murders have lent a new fever pitch to cries that colleges take greater responsibility for the security of their students. The new *Student Right-to-Know and Campus Security Act*, which becomes effective September 1, was born of the same perspective. The

Drug-Free Schools and Communities Act, however, raises current *in loco parentis* expectations to even greater heights by transforming colleges into extensions of law enforcement. All three factors signal the potential demise of colleges as academic communities and their advent as parents and police.

For more than a decade college personnel have been bolstering efforts to combat the personally destructive and socially disruptive effects of drug and alcohol use and abuse. Most of our responses to these troubles have taken the form of intensified educational programs and enhanced counseling efforts. After all, education is what we do best. We have generally assumed that students understood the laws governing alcohol consumption, and that it was their responsibility to choose to obey the law or to suffer the legal consequences.

Now, however, Congress (inspired by former drug czar William Bennett) has decided that colleges themselves should enforce those laws, a situation which promises far-reaching consequences for student-college relations. In their commendable efforts to combat illegal and harmful drug and alcohol use, Bennett, President Bush, Congress and supportive parents are overlooking an important point. As colleges and universities begin to assume a stronger parenting and policing role, the power of their educational, ethical, and liberating role for students will be undermined. More efficient management and control of students' social lives will lead inevitably to the retardation of their moral, psychological, and emotional growth.

In the 1990s, educators will have an opportunity to inspire and ennoble a new generation of students who are acutely aware of entering a new decade. Their generation has been labeled by educators and the media alike as greedy, self-absorbed, narcissistic, ego-consumed, and cynical. We have even heard from Republicans like David Gergen and Kevin Phillips that the '90s threaten to become an age of indifference. Yet, the members of this so-called "who cares?" generation are surrounded by cultural images that could empower them to make the '90s a decade of difference. They have watched the Berlin Wall crumble, Nelson Mandela emerge victorious from years of government efforts to crush his spirit, the mass democratic upheavals of people in Eastern Europe, and even a lone, anonymous Chinese student standing defenseless in front of a line of tanks in Tienanmen Square—as if to say, "I won't take it anymore."

These are images that can inspire our students to believe in their own significance and in a caring future. Signs abound that they are compassionate and committed to improving their social and political surroundings. The challenge of liberal education is to provide them with the skills and to inspire in them the moral vision needed to take advantage of the fertile opportunities that lie ahead.

The choices confronting higher education are clear. Either we continue to emphasize the intellectual education, personal guidance, and moral inspiration necessary for students to become mature, responsible, free agents in the community (while providing them a secure and healthy learning environment), or we succumb to the mounting pressures to provided extended day-care service during the college years.

Although ill-equipped for the roles of parent or police force, colleges can no doubt rise to that challenge. The price, however, will be high, and all of us (parents included) need to be aware of it. For the cost of child care that extends from the cradle to college commencement will surely include delayed adolescence, retarded moral and social development, the demise of authentic education, and a college-educated population unprepared for the responsibilities of democratic participation. Our society can ill afford to pay that price.

Scott A. Warren

KEY TERMS

Fallacy	Description	Example
Appeal to Authority (2 forms)	**1.** Appeals to an authority who is not an expert on the issue under discussion.	Abortion to save the mother is irrelevant because a pediatric surgeon has never seen a case in which such a dilemma has risen.
Snob Appeal	**2.** Appeals to people's desire for prestige and exclusivity.	Pamilla's not for everyone. The best never is.
Appeal to Fear	Implicitly threatens the audience.	Will there be a *job* waiting when *you* leave college?
Appeal to Pity	Attempts to win sympathy.	Professor Hall, I must get an A in your course. If you don't give me an A, I won't be able to go to law school.
Begging the Question (3 forms)	**1.** Offers no actual support; may restate as a premise the conclusion in different words.	Students like rock music because it is the most enjoyable music around.
Loaded question	**2.** Asks a question that contains an assumption that must be proven.	Have you started to pay your fair share of taxes yet?

Question begging epithet	**3.** Uses a single word to assert a claim that must be proven.	Reactionary, negligent, warmonger, deadbeat.
Equivocation	Shifts the meaning of a term within a single argument.	Pro-life advocates stress that the unborn child has a right to life. But doesn't the woman have a right to her own life?
False analogy	Compares 2 or more things which are not in essence similar and suggests that since they share certain characteristics, they share others as well.	I don't want to die falling off a rock. But you can kill yourself falling in the bathtub too.
False cause [Latin name: *post hoc, ergo propter hoc*]	Claims a causal relationship between events solely on the basis of a chronological relationship.	I joined the Confederacy for two weeks. Then I deserted. The Confederacy fell.
False dilemma	Presents two and only two alternatives for consideration when other possibilities exist.	Either you are in favor of recalling the mayor, or you are a supporter of her political platform.
Hasty Generalization	Generalizes from a sample which is too small or in some other way unrepresentative of the target population.	Students in Professor Hall's eight o'clock freshman composition class are often late. Today's college students are irresponsible and unreliable.
Personal attack [Latin name: *ad hominem*] (2 forms)	**1.** Attacks the person presenting the argument rather than the argument itself.	Because she is extremely wealthy, our mayor cannot properly represent this city.
Tu quoque ("you also")	**2.** Discredits an argument because the behavior of the person proposing it does not conform to the position he's supporting.	A teenager to his father: Don't tell me not to drink. You drink all the time.
Poisoning the well	Makes an assertion which will intimidate the audience and therefore discourage an open discussion.	Every patriotic American supports the war in the Gulf.

Slippery slope	Claims that an action should be avoided because it will lead to a series of extremely undesirable consequences.	The Handgun Initiative would create a huge bureaucracy equal to that in Russia. And we all know that bureaucracy in Russia kills people by locking them up in gulags. Are you ready for gulags in the U. S.?
Special pleading	Judges and labels the same act differently depending on the person or group who performs the act.	The supplying of weapons to Central America by the Russians was an act of aggression. Our military aid to the region, however, helped the Freedom Fighters in their quest for peace.
Straw man	Creates and then attacks a distorted version of the opposition's argument.	The democratic candidate wants the federal government to house everyone, feed everyone, care for everyone's children, and provide medical care for everyone. And he's going to take 50 percent of every dime you make to do it.

Chapter
10

Language and Meaning

"When I use a word," Humpty Dumpty said in rather a scornful tone, "it means just what I choose it to mean—neither more nor less."

— Lewis Carroll, *Alice Through the Looking Glass*

*I*n Chapter 9, we note how fallacious arguments can be built on the misuse of language; you will remember circular definitions in begging the question and the danger of equivocation, subtle shifts in the meaning of a given term within the same argument.

Now we'd like to concentrate on the precise use of language, on paying close attention to how we choose our words. As Francis Bacon put it four hundred years ago, "Men imagine that their minds have the command of language, but it often happens that language bears rule over their minds." Language itself, he suggests, can shape—even control—our thoughts. Poet W. H. Auden agrees: "Language is the mother, not the handmaiden, of thought; words will tell you things you never thought or felt before." Thus it is enormously important that we know the meaning of the words we use and that when we write, our readers, to the degree possible, share our understanding of words. To achieve this clarity in our writing, we must, when necessary, define our terms and prefer, usually, the concrete to the abstract.

Cicero, the Roman orator, claimed that every discourse should begin with a definition in order to make clear what the subject under consideration is. French philosopher Voltaire wrote, "If you would argue with me, first define your terms." And in more recent times, Ellen Willis, writing in *Rolling Stone*, admonishes us to "Find out who controls the definitions, and you have a pretty good clue who controls everything else."

Why is definition so crucial?

LOGICAL DEFINITION

To answer that question, let's examine the following sentences:

1. Was Ronald Reagan an effective president?
2. Does money mean success?
3. Was the movie "Basic Instinct" obscene?
4. Is television addictive?
5. Is alcoholism an illness?
6. Should we encourage entrepreneurs?

Remembering our discussion in Chapter 4, you will note that each sentence is a question at issue. Examine these questions more closely, and you will notice that each contains at least one key term which is open to interpretation. For example, what does it mean to be an "effective" president? If you were to write a paper based on this question at issue, you would first have to define "effective," to list the criteria for such a presidency before applying them to Ronald Reagan.

You need to define, to stipulate, to pin down precise meaning for terms such as these. To supply useful definitions, where do you begin? A good dictionary is the best *initial* source. Following the tradition of classical rhetoric laid down by Plato and Aristotle, first place the term in its general *class* and then narrow the definition by determining the **distinguishing characteristics**, the ways in which it differs from other terms in the same class.

Such a rigorous process is hardly necessary for a concrete term such as "fork," which belongs to the class of eating utensils and is distinguished from other members of its class, other eating utensils, by its shape, a handle at one end with two or more pointed prongs at the other. But abstract terms such as "success" and "obscene" must be carefully defined.

A definition of key terms in questions two and three above would look like this:

TERM	CLASS	DISTINGUISHING CHARACTERISTICS
Success	(is) a favorable result	(which) implies economic and social achievement in one's chosen professional field.
Obscene	(is) a negative quality	(which) offends prevailing notions of modesty or decency

Note that the distinguishing characteristics are still subject to interpretation, to individual assessment. Another writer could define success in terms of personal relationships or contributions to the community rather than professional achievement. And, of course, stipulating the precise meaning of "obscene" is a task which has long bedeviled our courts and has continued to do so with cases such as the sexually explicit music of "2 Live Crew" and the provocative photographs of Robert Mapplethorpe.

GUINDON

John White is my idea of an intellectual. He buys Playboy magazine, cuts out the interviews and hangs them all over his bedroom.

EXERCISE 10A

Defining Key Terms

For the remaining three questions at issue above (4–6), identify terms that require clarification and stipulate a definition. Place each term first in its general class and then narrow your definition with distinguishing characteristics as we have done above. You may find it interesting to compare your definitions with those of classmates.

DEFINITION AND THE SOCIAL SCIENCES

In a study on child abuse and health which we cite in Chapter 8, the researchers first had to define child abuse before they could determine its effect on women's health. They separated child abuse into three categories—emotional, physical, and sexual. Then they defined each category.

emotional abuse: repeated rejection or serious physical threats from parents, tension in the home more than 25 percent of the time, and frequent violent fighting among parents.

physical abuse: strong blows from an adult or forced eating of caustic substances; firm slaps were excluded.

sexual abuse: any nonvoluntary sexual activity with a person at least five years older.

Researchers interviewed 700 women from a private gynecological practice and tabulated their responses according to these categories. Without clear-cut definitions to guide them, social scientists would be left with subjective impressions rather than quantifiable results.

DEFINITION AND PERCEPTION

Our definitions can also reveal how we see people—as individuals and collectively. While delivering a lecture, feminist Gloria Steinem cited traditional definitions of the following terms, definitions which have played crucial roles in determining how women and men view themselves and others.

work: something men do, go to; as distinguished from housework and childcare, which is what women do

art: what white men produce

crafts: what women and ethnic minorities do

We can hope that these definitions are changing. And indeed, we have historical precedent for scientific definitions shifting to conform to new ways of thinking. In the nineteenth century, alcoholism was defined as criminal behavior. When the term was redefined as an illness after World War I, considerable progress in treatment became possible. Conversely, when the American Psychological Association recently stopped classifying homosexuality as an illness, the homosexual community was understandably gratified by the revision of a definition it found unjust and damaging to its members.

More recently, the term *addiction* (and related language) has undergone a metamorphosis in response, perhaps, to the expanding drug culture. *Boston Globe* columnist Ellen Goodman voices concern about the way in which a precise term traditionally applied to specific chemical dependencies has grown diffuse in meaning, allowing people to excuse their own behavior and the behavior of others.

A friend found with her hand in the fudge sauce admits sheepishly, "I'm addicted to chocolate." A casual eavesdropper can hear about a woman who is addicted to married men, or a man who is addicted to 20-year-olds. A bore at the party is a compulsive talker. A woman who lives at the mall is a compulsive shopper. A wife talking of her husband's endless office hours says, "He is a workaholic."

Goodman objects to this imprecise use of the term because it "undermines the sense that average people are in control of their own lives." She reminds us, through examples, of the word's precise meaning: "Addictions are real. Ask a smoker. Ask a drinker. Ask someone with tracks up his arm."

Language evolves over time. It's a natural process. But when expanded meaning results in loss of precision, we do well to examine, as Goodman does, the causes and effects of the revised meaning.

LANGUAGE: AN ABSTRACT SYSTEM OF SYMBOLS

As you have noticed from the preceding discussion, abstract words can present particular difficulties when it comes to stipulating precise meaning. But language itself, whether it refers to an abstract concept or a concrete object, is an abstract system of symbols. The word is not the thing itself, but a *symbol* or *signifier* used to represent the thing we refer to, which is the *signified*. For example, the word "cat" is a symbol or signifier for the animal itself, the signified.

"Cat"

THE SYMBOL or SIGNIFIER
(the word)

THE SIGNIFIED
(the thing being referred to)

But meaning is made only when the signified is processed through the mind of someone using or receiving the words. This process serves as an endlessly destabilizing force. Whenever a speaker, writer, listener, or reader encounters a word, a lifetime of associations renders the word, and thus the image it conjures up, distinct for each individual.

As literary theorist Stanley Fish points out, meaning is dependent not only on the individual but also on the context, situation, and interpretive community. To illustrate this point, let's look at the word "host." It means one thing if we are at a party and something else entirely if we are at church. Hence, the context or situation determines our understanding of "host."

If, however, you are not a member of any religion or of a religion which practices the ritual of communion, then you may understand the meaning of "host" *only* as the giver of a party. You are not part of the interpretive community, in this case a religious community, which understands "host" as a consecrated wafer, a religious symbol.

As you can see, language remains perpetually contingent, and thus as a means of communication, slippery. Even when the signified is *concrete*, individual experience and perception will always deny the word complete stability; the range of possible images will still be vast. Take the word "table." Nothing of the essence of table is part of the word "table." Although most words in English (or any modern language) have roots and a history in older languages, the assignation of a particular meaning to a given term remains essentially arbitrary. While all English speakers share a *general* understanding of the word "table," each user or receiver of this word, without having considerably more detail, will create a different picture.

If the symbolic representation of a *concrete*, visible object such as a table is as unstable as our discussion suggests, think how much more problematic *abstract* terms must be. Were we to substitute the abstraction "freedom" for the concrete "table," the range of interpretations would be considerably more diverse and much more challenging to convey to others. Visual pictures, which arise when concrete objects are signaled, don't come to mind as readily when we refer to abstractions, a distinction which required us to define the abstract terms in the questions at issue above and led Shakespeare to explain why poets give "to airy nothing a local habitation and a name."

Semanticist S. I. Hayakawa discusses the idea of an abstraction ladder in which language starts on the ground, so to speak, with an object available to our sense perception, and moves up to concepts abstracted from, derived from, the concrete source—for example, from a specific cow to livestock to farm assets to assets. He stresses that our powers of abstraction are indispensable. "The ability to climb to higher and higher levels of abstraction is a distinctively human trait without which none of our philosophical or scientific insights would be possible." But he cautions against staying at too high a level of abstraction.

> The kind of "thinking" we must be extremely wary of is that which *never* leaves the higher verbal levels of abstraction, the kind that never points *down* the abstraction ladder to lower levels of abstraction and from there to the extensional world:
>
> "What do you mean by *democracy*?"
>
> "Democracy means the preservation of human *rights*."
>
> "What do you mean by *rights*?"
>
> "By rights I mean those privileges God grants to all of us—I mean man's inherent privileges."
>
> "Such as?"
>
> "Liberty, for example."
>
> "What do you mean by *liberty*?"
>
> "Religious and political freedom."

"And what does that mean?"

"Religious and political freedom is what we enjoy under a democracy."

The writer never moves down to the essential lower levels on the abstraction ladder, and a discourse consisting only of abstractions, devoid of concrete details and examples, is necessarily vague, often difficult for the reader to understand, and, in this definition of democracy, circular.

The Importance of Specificity

To avoid the confusion that unclarified abstractions can generate, Hayakawa suggests pointing down "to extensional levels wherever necessary; in writing and speaking, this means giving *specific examples* of what we are talking about," grounding our arguments in experience.

Compare the empty, circular definition of democracy Hayakawa quotes above with the concrete illustrations that illuminate E. B. White's celebrated World War II definition of the same term.

July 3, 1943

> We received a letter from the Writers' War Board the other day asking for a statement on "The Meaning of Democracy." It presumably is our duty to comply with such a request, and it is certainly our pleasure. Surely the Board knows what democracy is. It is the line that forms on the right. It is the don't in don't shove. It is the hole in the stuffed shirt through which the sawdust slowly trickles; it is the dent in the high hat. Democracy is the recurrent suspicion that more than half of the people are right more than half of the time. It is the feeling of privacy in the voting booths, the feeling of communion in the libraries, the feeling of vitality everywhere. Democracy is a letter to the Editor. Democracy is the score at the beginning of the ninth. It is an idea that hasn't been disproved yet, a song the words of which have not gone bad. It's the mustard on the hot dog and the cream in the rationed coffee. Democracy is a request from a War Board, in the middle of a morning in the middle of a war, wanting to know what democracy is.

Such specificity is what writer Annie Dillard values when she says, "This is what life is all about: salamanders, fiddle tunes, you and me and things ... the fiz into particulars" (*Teaching a Stone to Talk*). And what novelist Vladimir Nabokov prizes when he asks us to "Caress the details, the divine details" (*Lectures on Literature*).

The Manipulation of Language

Sometimes abstractions are used, consciously or unconsciously, to confuse, distort, conceal, or evade, in short, to manipulate others—a practice Hemingway comments on in *A Farewell to Arms*, his World War I novel.

I was always embarrassed by the words sacred, glorious, and sacrifice and the expression in vain. We had heard them, sometimes standing in the rain almost out of earshot, so that only the shouted words came through, and had read them, on proclamations that were slapped up by billposters over other proclamations, now for a long time, and I had seen nothing sacred, and the things that were glorious had no glory and the sacrifices were like the stockyards at Chicago if nothing was done with the meat except to bury it. There were many words that you could not stand to hear and finally only the names of places had dignity. Certain numbers were the same way and certain dates and these with the names of the places were all you could say and have them mean anything. Abstract words such as glory, honor, courage, or hallow were obscene beside the concrete names of villages, the numbers of roads, the names of rivers, the numbers of regiments and the dates.

Hemingway eloquently indicates the power of concrete nouns to generate precise meaning readily visualized. Politicians, on the other hand, particularly in a dictatorship, often thrive on the willful manipulation of abstract language.

Prior to the political reorganization of the Soviet Union, *The New York Times* described a special edition of an Oxford University dictionary which the Soviets prepared for their students of English. Note the distinctions between the original used by British students and the Soviet edition.

British: *socialism* …"a theory or policy of social organization which advocates the ownership and control of the means of production, capital, land property, etc. by the community as a whole, and their administration or distribution in the interests of all"….

capitalism …"the condition of possessing capital or using it for production; a system of society based on this; dominance of private capital"….

Soviet: *socialism* …"a social and economic system which is replacing capitalism"….

capitalism …"an economic and social system based on private ownership of the means of production operated for private profit, and on the exploitation of man by man"….

Such manipulation of language is not limited to the Soviet Union. Writing on the complex environmental issue of wetlands, Anthony Lewis of *The New York Times* pointed out that President Bush found it necessary to shift his definition of that term. During his 1988 campaign, Bush declared that "All existing wetlands, no matter how small, should be preserved." But when pressured by real estate, oil, and mining interests to open protected wetlands to development and exploration, the president expediently redefined the word, a definition which left at least 10 million acres of wetlands unprotected.

These examples lend fresh meaning to our opening claims of power for those who control the definitions.

In the 1940s British writer George Orwell addressed the political significance of language in his celebrated essay, "Politics and the English Language," claiming that "political speech and writing are largely the defence of the indefensibles . . . . Defenceless villages are bombarded from the air, the inhabitants driven out into the countryside, the cattle machine-gunned, the huts set on fire with incendiary bullets: this is called *pacification*." In his novel *1984*, he satirizes the official use of deceptive language, coining, among other terms, the words "doublethink" and "newspeak."

In more recent times, we have had our own share of befuddling language, dubbed psychobabble, spacespeak, doublespeak, gobbledygook. Sometimes a euphemism is justified as a means of sparing feelings—someone passed away rather than died, or a large woman is referred to as mature in size. And the specialized lingo of a particular discipline may be necessary even though it appears as needless jargon to a lay person. Later in this chapter a writer refers to the terms metonymy and synecdoche—both useful to rhetoricians, but obscure to others.

But we must be wary of language which camouflages precise meaning. Note how language dulls reality in the following examples:

The "peacemaker" for the MX missile

"offshore" for foreign

"unlawful or arbitrary deprivation of life" for killing

"revenue enhancement" for taxes

"negative growth" for economic recession

"collateral damage" for civilian losses

One institution which is especially guilty of manipulating language for its own purposes is advertising. Recent legislation by the Food and Drug Administration—the Nutrition Labeling and Education Act—seeks to put an end to the blatant misuse of language which many food manufacturers are guilty of. Miles Orvell, a professor of English at Temple University, writes an essay applauding the FDA's removal of Citrus Hill "Fresh Choice" orange juice and Ragu's "Fresh Italian" pasta sauce from store shelves for their false claims of "freshness." He applauds this act as a consumer and as an English teacher. "In challenging the claims of food manufacturers, the F.D.A. is reconnecting label and contents, word and thing." Orvell is tired, as are many people, of food manufacturers who claim as Humpty Dumpty does that "When *I* use a word, it means just what I choose it to mean."

WRITING ASSIGNMENT 18

Composing an Extended Definition of an Abstract Term

THE LOCKHORNS

"IT'S NOT GOSSIP....IT'S ORAL HISTORY!"

Step 1

Choose a word from the list of abstract terms below, think about its implications for a few minutes, and then start writing a definition that captures its meaning and significance for you. (If a term other than one of those on the list comes to mind and interests you, substitute it, but clear it with your instructor first.) Using a freewriting approach, keep going for about 20 minutes. If time and your instructor permit, do this in class; you will find the combination of spontaneity and structure imposed by writing during class to be an aid to composing. You can't get up to make a phone call or clean the refrigerator.

education	liberation
sportsmanship	leadership
originality	imagination
machismo	character
courage	sexual harassment
defeat	marriage
maturity	soul
leisure	generosity
creativity	intelligence
progress	burn-out
trend	heroism
rationality	responsibility

Volunteers can enlighten (and entertain) the class by reading these drafts aloud.

Step 2

With more time for reflection and revision, take the spontaneous draft you have written and, in a page or two, expand and edit your definition. In the process of defining your term, analyze and clarify what it means to you, arriving at, or at least implying, a significant point. You may find yourself actually arguing a point, although in this assignment argument is not a requirement. As the discussion in this chapter has emphasized, you must include specific detail to animate your abstraction.

Step 3

If time permits, multiple definitions of the same term can be read to the class for comparison and discussion.

Here are some possible strategies for writing an extended definition; do not feel compelled to use them all.

- stipulate your precise meaning (see logical definition above), but don't include a dictionary definition unless you plan to use it or disagree with it.

- provide examples of the term

- explain the function or purpose of the term

- explore etymology (origin and history of a word). The most fruitful source for such explorations is *The Oxford English Dictionary*, a multivolume work available in most college libraries, and a dictionary well worth your acquaintance. Use the history of a term to help make a point.

- examine the connotations of the term

- discuss what it is not (Use this sparingly.)

- draw analogies (Here you will want to be precise; be sure the analogy really fits.)

A few cautions:

- define or illustrate more complex words with more familiar ones

- stick to one sense of the word unless you clarify an intended distinction

- avoid circularity

Look ahead in this chapter for helpful sentence hints:

- *appositives* for inserting short definitions, identifications, and concrete examples into your sentences

- clear *"focus"*

Audience The instructor and other members of the class.

Purpose To make an abstraction concrete.

Extended definitions: Student examples Several of our students have contributed their efforts on this topic. Here is a sampling.

Two different approaches to the same term:

Radical

The word "radical" has been defined in *The Oxford-English Dictionary* as "going to the root or origin, touching or acting upon what is essential and fundamental." Thus, a radical reform is said to be a fundamental, "thorough reform." In a political sense, an advocate of "radical reform" was described as "one who holds the most advanced views of political reform on democratic lines, and thus belongs to the extreme section of the Liberal party." While this may have been a commonly accepted usage of the term in England at the time, the word "radical" has drifted away from its original specific meaning to a rather vague term for anyone who appears to be trying to disrupt the status quo.

In the late 1800s and early 1900s, socialists, Communists, and anarchists alike were popularly categorized by the general American public with the term "radical." With the controversy surrounding the political goals of these different activists, "a radical" was at the very least a controversial figure. More often than not, the word "radical" brought to mind some sort of disruptive character, a nonspecific image of an extremist, most probably from the far left. On the political spectrum the "radical" is still viewed as an individual on the extreme left, opposite the "right" or "conservative" parties. "Conservatives" holding radically different views and goals are not normally termed "radicals"; they are merely part of the "ultraright."

The term "radical" today is used less as a description of political intent and more as a critique of overall manner and appearance. While many of the "radicals" in the 1960s did indeed advocate numerous political reforms, the general public was more impressed by their personal character and style of advocacy. It is not surprising that when asked to define "a radical," most individuals conjure up a vague image of some young person wearing ragged clothes and long hair. It is a pity that in this society, where progressive change is so essential, the term "radical" has been imbued with so much negativity, so many connotations which really have nothing to do with political reform.

Radical

A radical is an algebraic symbol which tells a person to carry out a certain mathematical operation. The end result of this operation will tell a person the root or origin of a number or problem.

Recently, while in Los Angeles, I overheard someone describe a car as radical. I immediately thought to myself, something is wrong here. Radicals do not have engines. They may contain a number, like 32, underneath their top line, but never a stock Chevy 302 engine. It simply would not fit. When I asked this person why he called the car a radical, he replied, "Because the car is different and unusual." Once again, I thought to myself, he has made a mistake. Radicals are quite common. In fact, they are an essential part of most algebraic theories. I had to infer that this man knew nothing about algebra. If he did, he would have realized that radicals are not different or unusual at all, and would not have called the car one.

While I was in New York this past summer, I happened to see a group of people carrying signs of protest in front of the United Nations Building. As I watched them, a man came over to me, pointed at the group and muttered, "Radicals." I thought to myself, man are you ever wrong. Radicals do not carry signs saying, "Feed the Poor." They may carry a number, like 2, in their top right hand corner, but this number only means to find the root of a problem. It does not mean, "Feed the Poor."

These two events show that there is a great deal of misunderstanding throughout the country in regards to what a radical is. At their simplest level, radicals tell us to find the root of a problem. At their most complex level, they tell us the same thing.

A student's definition in which the approach reflects the word itself:

Fun

What's fun? In the black community fun means trippin'.[1] For example, the fellas pitchin' pennies, shootin' dice, playin' three-card Molly[2] on the back of the bus, or playin' stick ball in the streets from the time they are five until they are 25. Little girls and big girls playin' Double Dutch,[3]

---

[1]trippin'—enjoying yourself

[2]three-card Molly—a card game involving three different-colored cards

[3]double dutch—a jump rope game involving two ropes swung in opposite directions. The jumping technique involves intricate rhythm and style and is often accompanied by a song or a chant recited by the child.

jumpin' ropes and singin' to the rhythm of their feet. Blastin' the ghetto box to the latest beat and watching the brothuhs break. Bustin' open the fire hydrants on a hot day in order to cool off by runnin' through the water. Listenin' to the dudes standing on the street corner rappin' to a sistuh as she strolls down the street. "Hey, Mamma, what it is! You sho' is lookin' mighty fine today! How 'bout slidin' by my pad for a bit?" Gettin' happy in church and callin' out, "Lordy, Lordy! Lordy have mercy! Yes, Lord! Help me Lord!" Helpin' Mamma wash the collard greens and sweet potatoes, stirrin' the corn bread and slicin' the fatback[4] for Sunday supper after church. The whole family sittin' on the stoop in the evening listenin' to grandmamma tell stories 'bout the ol' days while fussin' about the young folk. All of this comes down to trippin', enjoying one's self, and havin' fun in the hood.[5]

STIPULATING PERSONAL MEANING: INVENTING NEW WORDS TO FILL A NEED

Through the centuries, people have been defining what they consider themselves to be, using the term "man" in a number of inventive ways.

Plato First, he put man in the class "biped" and differentiated him from others in the class by describing him as "a featherless biped." When his rival, Diogenes, produced a plucked chicken, Plato had to add "having broad nails" as a further distinguishing characteristic.

Shakespeare "What a piece of work is a man! How noble in reason! how infinite in faculty! in form, in moving, how express and admirable! in action how like an angel! in apprehension how like a god! the beauty of the world! the paragon of animals! And yet, to me what is this quintessence of dust? Man delights not me; no, nor woman neither." (*Hamlet*, II.ii.316)

Ambrose Bierce "An animal so lost in rapturous contemplation of what he thinks he is as to overlook what he indubitably ought to be. His chief occupation is extermination of other animals and his own species, which, however, multiplies with such insistent rapidity as to infest the whole habitable earth and Canada." (*Devil's Dictionary*)

"Womanist"

Contemporary American writer Alice Walker sought to rectify some of the linguistic imbalance in gender representation when she coined the term

---

[4]fatback—discarded meat in the back of a butcher shop

[5]hood—the African-American community or neighborhood

womanist for her collection of nonfiction, *In Search of Our Mothers' Gardens, Womanist Prose by Alice Walker*. Why, we might ask, did she need to invent such a word? We can assume that she experienced a condition for which there was no term, so she created one. To stipulate the meaning of her neologism (a newly coined word or phrase), she opens the book with a series of definitions.

> *Womanist:*   1. From womanish. (Opp. of "girlish," i.e., frivolous, irresponsible, not serious.)   A black feminist or feminist of color. From the black folk expression of mothers to female children, "You acting womanish," i.e., like a woman. Usually referring to outrageous, audacious, courageous or *willful* behavior. Wanting to know more and in greater depth than is considered "good" for one. Interested in grown-up doings. Acting grown up. Being grown up. Interchangeable with another black folk expression: "You trying to be grown." Responsible. In charge. *Serious*.
>
> 2. Also: A woman who loves other women, sexually and/or nonsexually. Appreciates and prefers women's culture, women's emotional flexibility (values tears as natural counter-balance of laughter), and women's strength. Sometimes loves individual men, sexually and/or nonsexually. Committed to survival and wholeness of entire people, male *and* female. Not a separatist, except periodically, for health. Traditionally universalist, as in: "Mama, why are we brown, pink, and yellow, and our cousins are white, beige, and black?" Ans.: Well, you know the colored race is just like a flower garden, with every color flower represented." Traditionally capable, as in: "Mama, I'm walking to Canada and I'm taking you and a bunch of other slaves with me." Reply: "It wouldn't be the first time."
>
> 3. Loves music. Loves dance. Loves the moon. *Loves* the Spirit. Loves love and food and roundness. Loves struggle. *Loves* the Folk. Loves herself. *Regardless*.
>
> 4. Womanist is to feminist as purple to lavender.

"Sniglets"

Writer and performer Rich Hall created the word *sniglet* for "any word that doesn't appear in the dictionary, but should." Two examples from his collection:

n. The speed at which one tries to reach the phone before the answering machine comes on.

TELEVELOCITY
(teh leh veh la' sih tee)

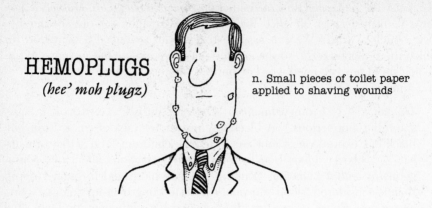

HEMOPLUGS
(hee' moh plugz)

n. Small pieces of toilet paper
applied to shaving wounds

 WRITING ASSIGNMENT 19

Creating a New Word

Now it's your turn to create a new word, to identify a meaning in need of a name. Give the word an extended definition so that those in your class can see how to use it and why our culture needs such an addition to the language.

APPLICATION TO WRITING

Appositives—A Strategy for Defining and Identifying Terms within the Sentence

Abstract terms need defining so that our readers understand what we mean. One might agree in theory but question in practice how a writer defines terms without derailing the organization of the paper or paragraph. Often, the answer is to use **appositives**—noun phrases placed beside nouns to elaborate on their meaning.

Here is Joan Didion, contemporary American essayist, giving us a vivid picture of the Los Angeles climate:

> In fact the climate is characterized by infrequent but violent extremes: two periods of torrential subtropical rains which continue for weeks and wash out the hills and send subdivisions sliding down toward the sea; about twenty scattered days a year of the Santa Ana, which, with its incendiary dryness, invariably means fire.

Didion has added details and combined ideas into one sentence by using appositives. In each case, the appositive (underlined) modifies the noun "extremes," explains or defines what the extremes are, all within one sentence.

Appositives usually follow the nouns they modify, but some writers introduce a sentence with an appositive: <u>An expression of frustrated rage,</u> punk rock tries to be outrageous in order to provoke strong reactions.

The phrase, "an expression of frustrated rage" modifies "punk rock." Such additions allow a writer to include essential information or background details that may not warrant separate sentences. The effect is streamlined thought in fluent prose, as the following examples in Exercise 10B illustrate.

EXERCISE 10B

Recognizing Appositives

In the three passages that follow, identify the appositives and the nouns they modify by underlining the appositives and circling the nouns.

*1. A descriptive passage with examples

The Evertons are introduced to a second national peculiarity, one they will soon recognize on the streets of Ibarra and in towns and cities beyond. It is something they will see everywhere—a disregard for danger, a companionship with death. By the end of a year they will know it well: the antic bravado, the fatal games, the coffin shop beside the cantina, the sugar skulls on the frosted cake.

— Harriet Doerr, *Stones for Ibarra*

2. Identification

Cotton Mather was an exception, one who so fully accepted and magnified the outlook of his locality that he has entered folklore as the archetypal Puritan, not only a villainous figure in the pages of Hawthorne, William Carlos Williams and Robert Lowell, but an object of parody even to his fellow townsmen in 18th-century Boston.

— Larzer Ziff, *New York Times Book Review*

3. Definition

As Baranczak points out, Milosz [Nobel Prize-winning poet] rejects symbols in favor of metonymy and synecdoche, those figures of speech which represent a whole by a thing allied to it or by a part of it.

— Helen Vendler in *The New Yorker*

Punctuation of Appositives

Punctuation choices are simple and logical. In most cases, the appositive phrase is set off from the noun it modifies with commas. If you want greater emphasis, you can do as Harriet Doerr did and use a dash: "It is something they will see everywhere—a disregard for danger, a companionship with death."

Or choose a colon (appropriate only when the appositive ends a sentence) for an even sharper break as Joan Didion did:

> In fact the climate is characterized by infrequent but violent extremes: two periods of torrential subtropical rains which continue for weeks and wash out the hills and send subdivisions sliding down toward the sea; about twenty scattered days a year of the Santa Ana, which, with its incendiary dryness, invariably means fire.

This passage also illustrates the way in which Didion varies punctuation to control all the information in this long sentence, providing logical markers for the reader: the colon sets off the appositive series; the semicolon marks the major division in the series, separating these points from the lesser pauses marked by commas.

Punctuation rules in English are surprisingly relaxed; punctuation is there simply to organize patterns of thought and guide the reader through the meaning of our sentences. It is in this role that punctuation provides a vital service.

EXERCISE 10C

Creating Appositives

Most of you already use appositives to some extent in your writing whether you recognize them or not. But a little conscious practice may expand your knowledge of this useful device. Combine the following sets of sentences by reducing one or more sentences to appositives. You may find more than one way to combine them.

Example:
Unilateral disarmament was considered dangerous and impractical. It was a policy that would require only one side to reduce its arms.

becomes

Unilateral disarmament, a policy that would require only one side to reduce its arms, was considered dangerous and impractical.

or

Unilateral disarmament, a policy that was considered dangerous and impractical, would require only one side to reduce its arms.

    *1. New York has long been the destination of America's adventurous young. It is a city of danger and opportunity.

    2. Punk was a return to the roots of rock 'n' roll. It was a revolt against the predictability of disco.

*3. People have very different ideas about the meaning of poverty. It is a condition that to some suggests insufficient income, to others laziness, and to still others a state of unwarranted discomfort.

4. Writing ability can have far-reaching effects on a college graduate's future accomplishments. Writing ability is the capacity to generate and organize relevant ideas, compose coherent sentences, choose precise diction, control mechanics.

5. They regarded the dictator with a mixture of fear and awe. These feelings were not conducive to an attitude of respect and trust toward their government.

6. According to Oliver North's testimony during the lengthy Senate hearings in 1987, he was simply following orders as any military man is trained to do. These orders came from his superiors in the National Security Council and the CIA.

7. When the Soviets sent troops into Vilnius, Vytautas Landsbergis isolated himself and members of his government in a fortified parliament building. Vilnius is the capital of Lithuania and Landsbergis was the Lithuanian president.

8. Lisa read only spare modern novels. She liked ones with quirky characters, subtle structure, and ambiguous turns in plot, if they had plots at all.

9. During the 1980s, psychiatrists expanded the definition of the term "addiction." It is a word whose meaning has undergone revision to cover a broader range of compulsive behaviors. These compulsions now include sex, television viewing, designer clothes, shopping. These extend to a whole spectrum of dependencies.

10. Concrete has spread over wider and wider areas of the American landscape. It has covered not just the weed patches, deserted lots, infertile acres but whole pastures, hillsides, and portions of the sea and sky.

Finally, write a sentence about your major, your job, or another interest, being sure to include a related technical term. Then add an appositive which defines or illustrates the term.

SENTENCE FOCUS—TECHNIQUES FOR AN EFFECTIVE STYLE

He draweth out the thread of his verbosity finer than the staple of his argument.

— Shakespeare, *Love's Labor's Lost*

We are all familiar with the confusion and obfuscation of much official prose today—political, bureaucratic, academic. Some of this muddled language may be deliberate, to conceal meaning, but often it is inadvertent, a result of writers surrendering to the abstractness of language, of fuzzy language overwhelming complex ideas. Unfocused writing is easy to write but usually difficult, often painful, to read. *The New Yorker* printed this one:

> Agreement on the overall objective of decision usefulness was a prerequisite to the establishment of a conceptual framework. Now, at least, we know where we are headed. (The Week in Review, newsletter of Deloitte Haskins & Sells)

After this, do we know where they are going?

Compare the following memo from the Internal Revenue Service and a possible revision.

> Advice has been requested concerning tax deductions for research expenses, including traveling expenses, incurred by college and university professors. (original)

> College and university professors have requested advice about tax deductions for their research expenses, including traveling expenses. (possible revision)

Which version is clearer, easier to read? We assume that the majority of readers will prefer the second. What are the differences? The possible revision is shorter by two words. But is this the only distinction? Make your evaluation before reading on.

Concrete Subjects

Look at the grammatical subjects in the two sentences—"advice" in the first, "professors" in the second—and notice what kind of nouns they are. One is an *abstract noun*, the other a *concrete noun*. Because the sentence subject tends to reflect what a passage is about, the subject is where the focus of a sentence usually sits. A concrete noun, capable of action and of a visual picture, can also focus a reader's attention more closely. And when that concrete noun is a person or people, readers are particularly inclined to follow the precise progression of ideas in a sentence. Hence, "professors" as the subject of the second sentence is preferable to the "advice" of the original.

Linguist Robin Lakoff comments on President George Bush's habit of using the very abstract noun "thing" as the subject of his sentences.

> His habit of substituting "thing" when he can't find a word is interesting. He'd refer to the "vision thing" or the "vice-presidential thing." By adding "thing" he takes meaning out of the noun [the subject] that you would ordinarily be highlighting. Ordinarily you'd be focusing on "vision," or "Vice President," but adding "thing" bleeds the meaning out of it. It's quite shocking that he's taking a word like "vision," which should be powerful and evocative, and he's trivializing it. When he called Dan Quayle to ask him to join the ticket, he said he wanted to talk to him about "this vice-presidential thing."

Active and Passive Verbs

Now look at the verbs. In the original sentence on tax deduction, the verb is "has been requested" while in the revision the verb is "has requested." The first is **passive voice**, the second, **active voice**. The basic distinction is that *with a passive verb, the subject is acted upon; the subject is not doing anything in the sentence—it is passive.* "Advice" is being requested, not, obviously, doing the requesting. *When the verb is active, its subject is performing the action of the sentence,* and thus the reader can see a subject doing something. The "professors" are doing the requesting.

We must wade through the original IRS memo to understand the point, whereas in the possible revision we see from the beginning that professors are requesting advice, people are doing something.

Sentences written in the passive are easy to spot because they always follow a grammatical pattern:

> subject + a form of the verb "to be" (am, is, are, was, were) + the past participle of the verb (usually with an *-ed* ending) + an expressed or implied "by" phrase, which contains the agent of the verb.

(subject)	(to be)	(past participle)	(optional "by" phrase)
Mistakes	were	made	(by the Governor).

The following two sentences say essentially the same thing, but note how the change in the form of the sentence shifts the emphasis from the concrete subject, "J. Robert Oppenheimer," to the abstract, "elemental danger."

Active J. Robert Oppenheimer, one of the creators of the atom bomb, <u>felt</u> the elemental danger loosed on the earth.

Passive The elemental danger loosed on the earth <u>was felt</u> by J. Robert Oppenheimer, one of the creators of the atom bomb.

Which version do you prefer? Why?

Aiming for direct, assertive prose, careful writers usually prefer active verbs. But on occasion, when one wants to emphasize someone or something not performing the action in a sentence, the passive is useful. Social scientists, for example, must often focus on the content of their research rather than on themselves as researchers. Under such circumstances, the passive serves a useful purpose.

> This research <u>was undertaken</u> with a grant from the National Science Foundation.

There is a less honorable use of the passive however, one politicians have a tendency to rely on—that is, to evade responsibility. William Safire in his *New York Times* column, "On Language," comments on this predilection, focusing on former White House chief of staff John Sununu, who, when asked at a press conference about the use of government funds for personal expenses, replied, "Obviously, some mistakes were made."

Safire notes that "The passive voice acknowledges the errors, but it avoids the blame entirely . . . . When deniability is impossible, dissociation is the way, and the [passive voice] allows the actor to separate himself from the act."

EXERCISE 10D

Evaluating Writing Style

Read the following paragraphs taken from an essay in which a student evaluates an editorial.

In his argument against the passage of Proposition 11, the fallacy of personal attack is committed frequently. First, the supporters of the bill are associated with communism, referring to them as "A lot of nice people who have given up on the Soviet Union and Red China . . . . " And there is name calling such as "reformers" and "pushers."

It is also the case that the opposition's argument is distorted. Their position is not to protect the environment from litter by requiring a deposit on beer and soft drink cans and bottles, but to "improve personal manners in public places" and "settle the hash of those who throw empty beer cans out of car windows." There is also the characterization of their policy as being "Damn-the-money. Full-speed-ahead," in an effort to discredit them.

1. How would you characterize the prose in this passage? Do you find it easy or difficult to read?
2. Identify the subjects and verbs, noting whether subjects are abstract or concrete, and whether verbs are active or passive.

After discussing these issues with classmates, read the revised passage below and evaluate the improvements. What makes it easier to read and understand than the original version?

In his argument against Proposition 11, columnist Abe Mellinkoff frequently commits the fallacy of personal attack. First, he associates the supporters of the bill with communism, referring to them as "A lot of nice people who have given up on the Soviet Union and Red China . . ." Then he refers to them as "reformers" and "pushers."

Mellinkoff also distorts the opposition's argument. They are not interested in protecting the environment from litter by requiring a deposit on beer and soft drink containers, but in improving "personal manners in public places" and in settling "the hash of those who throw empty beer cans out of car windows." He also characterizes their policy as "Damn-the-money. Full-speed-ahead," in an effort to discredit them.

More Ways to Tighten Sentences

Beyond the issues of concrete subjects and active verbs, we can note four additional features to be alert for when considering sharp focus.

The logical progression of focus

Central to good paragraph focus is the logical progression of ideas within a paragraph. In the first paragraph above, we find consistent subjects, "Mellinkoff" and the pronoun "he," reflecting the pattern of emphasis. But in the second paragraph, the second sentence opens with "They," still concrete, but referring to the opposition mentioned at the close of the preceding sentence. The focus has shifted, and the new subject reflects this movement from the "old" information, "Melinkoff," to the "new" point of focus, "opposition." Such a flow of information helps the reader to follow a coherent line of reasoning.

Expletives—"there is" and "it is"

The empty expletive phrases ("there is" and "it is") found in the first version have been deleted in the revision above, replaced by concrete subjects. The expletives are useful when a writer means that something exists:

> There are several reasons for recycling.

But when you can use a concrete noun paired with a more vigorous verb, the prose will be tighter. If you are unconvinced on the "there" issue, read the following paragraph from an essay on Writing Assignment 5 (Chapter 2).

> Children and the ability to have them are equally important to the society of the Small People. There is only one word for sex in their language and it translates as "to plant a wise one." To me this implies the final product is more important than the act of "planting a wise one." There is also a great emphasis put on childhood. There are seven terms used to describe stages of life from birth to puberty. There is only one word describing life after puberty.

This paragraph conveys the existence of the terms but very little additional reasoning. Focus is not the only weakness here, but note how easy it is to avoid vigorous, active prose once you let the "there disease" take over. Let's fix the focus of one such sentence.

> There is also a great emphasis put on childhood. (original)

> They emphasize childhood. (revision)

Overuse of "to be"

Beware of the verb "to be" (am, is, are, was, were). It is, of course, an important verb, but again, it states existence (being) only, and you often want your prose to be more expressive than that. Here's another reason to use passive verbs sparingly; they always, by definition, contain a form of the verb "to be." The same applies to "there are" sentences.

Dangling modifiers

Experienced writers often turn verbs into **verbal modifiers** (participles— verb forms ending in -*ing*—such as running, buying, and avoiding), increasing sentence fluency and combining ideas to express logical relationships.

> She thought critically about the issue. She recognized that her opponents had a good argument. (original)

> Thinking critically about the issue, she recognized that her opponents had a good argument. (revision)

Such modifiers can enhance the fluency of your prose, but you need to be cautious about their logic. The person or object serving as the sentence subject must also work logically as the agent of the verbal modifier.

In the example above, "she" is logical as the agent of "thinking" as well as the subject of the verb "recognized."

But look at the second sentence from the weak passage on Proposition 11 above.

> First, the supporters of the bill are associated with communism, <u>referring</u> to them as "A lot of nice people who . . ."

Who is doing the "referring" in this sentence? Obviously not the subject, "supporters," since they are not referring to themselves. The agent of "referring" needs to be the author, Mellinkoff, who is conspicuous by his absence in this paragraph but needs to be present to take charge, to assume an active, visible role.

When the logical agent is missing from the sentence, the verbal modifier is said to dangle, hence the term **dangling modifier**.

A wrap-up on writing style

1. Focus your thoughts and your writing on precisely what you want to say. When logically possible, prefer concrete, consistent subjects. As ideas develop through a paragraph, your sentence subjects may also develop and change, reflecting the new information introduced in the previous sentence.

2. Unless you have compelling reasons for preferring the passive voice, choose active verbs which allow for more direct, vigorous expression of your ideas.

3. Unless you intend to express the existence of something, avoid the over-used, empty phrases "it is" and "there are," and in the process look for more vigorous verbs.

Keep in mind that often we clarify our sentences during the revising process, that we may expect a first draft to have several poorly focused sentences and paragraphs. Always trying to get it right the first time may damage the quality of your prose and interrupt the flow of your ideas.

EXERCISE 10E

Sharpening Sentence Focus

The following sentences derive from essays written in response to Writing Assignment 5 in Chapter 2. That assignment asks you to characterize a people, an undiscovered tribe, on the basis of a limited sample of their vocabulary. Hence, many of the sentences illustrate the relationship between an inference and the fact on which it is based. Revise these sentences with this logic in mind, and with focus and conciseness as your goals.

It may help to provide a name for the group of people referred to when none is given, but "they" can serve. You may be tempted to revise some "ands" and combine sentences as further aids to improving focus and logic, as well as spot and rewrite some dangling modifiers.

°**1.** They are literate, given that they have twenty terms for "book." There also may be several kinds of artwork they create, since they have nine words for "artist."

2. In the society where this language is spoken, there exist twenty terms for what is known to us as "book." This indicates there are plenty of publications and they are widely read.

°**3.** By learning that the civilization consisted of literate and intelligent people, a picture of an advanced educational system is drawn.

4. Agriculture, particularly growth, holds special importance for the Unknowns, and they use such vocabulary to describe sex, i.e., "to plant a wise one."

5. In having so many words to describe the culture of their society, it follows that the development and appreciation of various cultural forms constitute a very important facet of their lives.

6. Some other attributes of the "new" people are they are nonviolent, peaceful, and self-governing. I base these statements on the fact that in their language there are no words for war, nor violent conflicts. There are several words for "leader," all of which are plural.

7. Having developed a complex social order, cultural forms have emerged as indicated by words for artist and theater.

SUMMARY

Words at a high level of abstraction such as "success" and "obscene" must be defined.

Definitions can affect how people view themselves and others, "addiction" being only one example.

Language is an abstract system of symbols.

The assignation of a particular meaning to a given term remains essentially arbitrary.

Meaning is dependent to a large degree on the individual, the context, and the interpretative community.

Political systems and advertising often manipulate abstract language for their own purposes.

The power to abstract is what makes us human. Specific, concrete details are what flesh out our ideas so our readers can grasp, visualize, and retain meaning.

Rather than contradictory, these two imperatives—the abstract and the concrete—are best seen as complementary in both our writing and our thinking.

For a vigorous and concise writing style, writers prefer concrete subjects and active verbs, and use "there is" only to express existence.

KEY TERMS

Distinguishing characteristics in logical definition, the ways in which a term differs from other terms in the same class.

Appositives noun phrases placed beside nouns to elaborate on their meaning; useful for describing, identifying, and defining.

Passive voice a sentence construction in which the subject is acted upon, not doing anything in the sentence. Example: The constitutionality of the 1991 civil rights legislation was ruled on by the Supreme Court.

Active voice a sentence construction in which the subject performs the action of the sentence. Example: The Supreme Court ruled on the constitutionality of the 1991 civil rights legislation.

Verbal modifier participles—verb forms ending in -*ing*—used as sentence modifiers. Example: <u>Before resorting to violence</u>, we must thoroughly investigate all other means of resolution.

Dangling modifier a verbal modifier that lacks a logical agent in the clause it modifies. Example: <u>Before resorting to violence</u>, all other means of resolution must be thoroughly investigated.

"You've taught me how to think."

Appendix
I

Antigone

A legend can be more powerful than the truth—in the end it can become the truth.

—Leon Edel

As we have mentioned in previous chapters (Chapters 1, 5, and 7 in particular), an argument can manifest itself not only in expository presentation but also in art, in literary works of the imagination. The power of literature to explore the full range of issues confronting us as humans appears to be as old as the origin of written texts. Writers have been using literature as persuasion for thousands of years, and many a poet has relied on literature to express the ineffable, that which words, without narrative and metaphor, seem inadequate to convey.

Many works of literature could serve to reveal poetic approaches to argument, but few illustrate the point as well as *Antigone* by Sophocles, Greek playwright of the fifth century B.C. This provocative play presents a number of conflicting moral imperatives, each of which appears to have merit. These compelling complexities may explain why the Antigone legend as told by Sophocles has captured the Western imagination for almost 2,500 years.

Philosophers Hegel, Kierkegaard, and Heidegger have explored its meaning in lengthy works, adding their interpretations of *Antigone* to their philosophic meditations. Literary critic George Steiner has written an entire book on the multiple *Antigone*s. Few works of the imagination create such fertile territory for critical thinking. But before going further with our discussion of the play, we would like you to read it for yourself. As we point out in Chapter 10, texts are not static but are endlessly open to new interpretations, yours included. There are many well-regarded translations, but we recommend the inexpensive Penguin Classics edition of Sophocles, *Three Theban Plays,* as a good place to start. This will allow you to see *Antigone* in context with the two additional plays—*King Oedipus* and *Oedipus at Colonus*—that make up the Sophocles trilogy.

Either before or after reading the play, you will want to consult a reliable Greek mythology to understand the central myth and the many mythological allusions sprinkled throughout the play. You will find numerous examples in your library; Robert Graves' *Greek Myths* offers a very thorough if complex source, Edith Hamilton, a simpler narrative version. At the least, you will want to have a simple outline of the family tree available. Family and the tragic inherited guilt for the family sins each generation is fated to bear are central in Greek mythology.

What follows is a list of suggestions for possible ways to explore *Antigone* through discussion and writing.

1. To prepare for an opening discussion of *Antigone* as argument, write for 15 minutes on a and b below. Then write responses to c.
   a. Who do you think is right in the play, Antigone or Creon? Neither? Both? Why?
   b. What are the major dilemmas or conflicts for the central characters in the play? Around what key issues does their clash of wills revolve?
   c. For each of the following characters, state their positions and their reasons for holding these views. Using the text, cite as many specific references as possible to support your findings. You may decide to work in groups or on your own to assemble these lists and write out your answers.

   Antigone
   Creon
   Haemon
   Teiresias

   (a and b above could be revised and shaped into essays.)

2. For a lively session, the class may be divided into groups identifying with Antigone, Creon, Haemon, and Teiresias. Either appoint a person or ask for a volunteer in each group to assume the appropriate role and have these four representatives argue their positions, either using the text for recitation or paraphrasing the key arguments. Group members will help their "actors" prepare, and then serve as audience for the performance.

3. In more than one passage, Creon expresses his attitude toward women as part of his argument. Identify these passages in the text and comment on what they say about Creon and possibly about fifth century B.C. Athens or the earlier time referred to in the play. You can use these notes as the basis for class discussion or shape them into an essay.

4. To provide commentary on the action and background detail, Greek dramas depended on the chorus, usually composed of 15 members and written in a different metrical form from the other dialogue. In *Antigone*, this chorus is made up of Theban elders. Choose one choral

passage, look up unfamiliar references, and write an analysis of the role this passage serves in the play as a whole.

5. Select one passage that resonates for you, that suggests meanings larger than just the context in which it appears. Write a paper explaining how this passage enlarges your understanding of the play.

6. After reading Chapter 9 in *Ergo*, go through *Antigone* and identify and explain any logical fallacies you discover. Then analyze the relative strengths and weaknesses of both Antigone and Creon's arguments, making specific references to the text.

7. Choose one of the following quotations and write a paper discussing its relationship to the positions both Antigone and Creon take in the play.

The only obligation I have a right to assume is to do at any time what I think right.
—*Henry David Thoreau*

Whenever unjust laws exist, people—on the basis of conscience—have a right to disobey those laws.
—*Martin Luther King*

A person who lives according to the common laws of his society is freer than one who "obeys himself alone."
—*adapted from Spinoza*

8. Many of the themes in *Antigone* and the debates they promote are timeless. In our century, the two world wars, the strife in Northern Ireland, the Israeli–Palestinian conflict, the struggle for racial freedom in South Africa, for example, have inspired comparison to the clashes between private conscience and public welfare, the divided loyalties, and painful paradoxes found in *Antigone*. We even hear of sisters sprinkling dirt on the bodies of their slain brothers during World War II battles in Latvia and Greece—what George Steiner calls "the Antigone gesture." From the following list of twentieth century treatments of the Antigone myth, choose one to analyze closely for a paper. In what ways does your choice parallel and in what ways does it depart from Sophocles' play?

Jean Anouilh, *Antigone* (1944). This version, performed in occupied Paris during World War II, managed to please both French patriots and German occupying forces. Anouilh skillfully inserted enough ambiguity to allow both audiences to bring their different "readings" to the same performances.

Bertolt Brecht, *Antigone* (1948). Brecht staged a savage attack on Nazi Germany with Antigone representing the hope of the German people themselves rising up in protest.

Athol Fugard, *The Island* (1973). Two black convicts stage a pointed production of *Antigone* in prison.

Antigone seems to embrace contraries, to present a dialectical approach to many issues central to the human condition. Exploring them critically enhances critical thought and our capacity to read wisely, and writing in response to such questions extends our ability to write clearly and cogently.

Fiction, drama, poetry, as well as explicit written argument, can be examined critically to illuminate human experience. This section of *Ergo* provides strategies as a model for exploring any number of timeless works. Novelist and critic E. M. Forster, in *Two Cheers for Democracy*, expresses the concept well: "A work of art . . . is a unique product . . . . The work of art stands up by itself, and nothing else does. It achieves something which has often been promised by society, but always delusively. Ancient Athens made a mess—but the *Antigone* stands up."

Appendix
II

Research and Documenting Sources

RESEARCH

Think First

*B*efore rushing to the library, topic in hand, to begin your research, there are two important preliminary steps.

First of all, narrow your topic to a clear question at issue (see Chapter 4), since such a question will help you to focus your research efforts. With only a topic to guide you, you might become lost in an avalanche of material, taking voluminous notes, most of which will have no application to your final paper.

Look at the difference in scope between an issue and a related question at issue:

Issue: Israel and its Arab neighbors

Question at issue: Should the disputed territories, the West Bank and the Gaza Strip, be given to the Palestinians or remain under the control of the Israelis?

Imagine what it would be like to research the issue, and then imagine what it would like to research the question at issue. Which would be easier?

Sometimes, however, you will need to do a little investigating in the library before you are able to arrive at a question at issue. Or you may be led to revise your question at issue as your research leads you in unexpected directions. But generally, narrowing the focus of your research will pay substantial dividends in time and energy.

As well as establishing, if possible, a question at issue before beginning your research, you should also construct an argument both for and against the question at issue. This argument would consist of premises in their roughest form—not developed, not supported, not refined.

You have knowledge based on your experience, your reading. This may be general knowledge, but it will be sufficient to enable you to construct a preliminary argument.

There are two advantages to this approach:

1. You are not overwhelmed by the opinions of experts, feeling as if they have left you nothing to say.
2. Your research has a very focused, precise purpose as you look for support for your premises, discovering in the process gaps in your reasoning, and counterarguments which had not occurred to you.

How to Begin Your Research

Indexes

What follows is a list of useful indexes with which to begin your research. These indexes are kept in the reference section of your library.

The Reader's Guide to Periodical Literature: Lists articles from over 170 popular magazines.

Social Sciences Index: Covers approximately 260 publications in anthropology, economics, environmental studies, geography, law, criminology, political science, public administration, psychology, sociology.

Public Affairs Information Service Bulletin (PAIS): Lists articles from government publications dealing with diverse topics of public interest.

Editorial Research Reports: Contains weekly reports on issues of national significance. These reports include excerpts from editorials and a recommended reading list.

Statistical Abstract of the United States: Summarizes statistics of political, industrial, economic, and social institutions in the United States.

Facts on File: Digests from a number of metropolitan newspapers on the important events of the day.

Humanities Index: Indexes by author and subject 299 periodicals in the humanities.

Essay and General Literature Index: Lists essays in books and chapters from books which may relate to your topic even though the title might not indicate this. Emphasizes social sciences and the humanities, especially literary criticism.

You are also likely to find indexes for *The New York Times*, the *Los Angeles Times*, and other major newspapers, including those in your particular region. These are especially helpful if the topic concerns recent events.

Since this list represents only a small sampling of the hundreds of indexes available to you, you may want to ask a librarian to recommend an index for your topic. Librarians also know if a particular index is part of the library's data base and therefore accessible to a computer search.

Computers

At most college libraries, card catalogues are being replaced by computers. Such on-line catalogues make a researcher's job much easier and faster.

If you are searching for a particular book, all you have to do is type in the title or the author, and the computer will supply you with specific information about the book, including its call number and availability.

If, on the other hand, you have no particular work in mind, but only a topic, the history of the Middle East, for instance, type that into the computer and it will display a list of relevant texts.

Librarians

If you run into any difficulties with either the on-line catalogue or the numerous indexes, or if you simply don't know where to begin, don't hesitate to ask the librarians at the reference desk; they are there to assist you.

DOCUMENTATION

What Information Should be Documented?

1. All direct quotations.
2. All indirect quotations in which we summarize the thoughts of others without quoting them directly. For example:
   Semanticist S. I. Hayakawa notes that although poetry and advertising seem unrelated, they actually share many characteristics (162).
3. All facts and statistics that are not common knowledge. If we were to state that many modern marriages end in divorce, documentation would not be necessary since the assertion reflects common knowledge. But if we state that 25 percent of the high school seniors in this country have tried cocaine, we must provide documentation; our readers would want to know the source of this conclusion to evaluate for themselves its reliability.

How Should It Be Documented?

Though each discipline has its preferred style of documentation, the two most common styles are set forth in the Modern Language Association (MLA) and the American Psychological Association (APA) style guides. English and the humanities prefer the MLA while the social sciences prefer the APA.

Both guides rely on parenthetical documentation—author and page number identified in the text of the paper—with a list of cited works and all relevant publishing information at the end of the paper.

Although a teacher may require a certain style of documentation, most are more concerned about consistency than about which style the student uses.

What follows is a brief introduction to the MLA and the APA styles of documentation as they would apply to a quotation taken from a book by one author and to a quotation taken from a magazine article.

The MLA Style of Documentation

For a book by one author (MLA):

Introduce the material being cited with a signal phrase, usually the author's name, and use a parenthetical citation stating the page number of the sentence.

> S. I. Hayakawa points out that advertising and poetry are alike in that "they both strive to give meaning to the data of everyday experience" (162).

Readers can then turn to the list of works cited at the end of the paper to discover the title and publishing information which will be listed under the author's last name.

When the author is not identified in the text—when there is no signal phrase—the author is identified in the parenthetical citation.

> Consumers want to identify with the happy, attractive people featured in advertisements (Hayakawa 164).

Note that there is no punctuation between the author's name and the page reference.

For a magazine article (MLA):

Once again, you may identify the work and/or author in a signal phrase, placing the page number in a parenthetical citation.

> In "Reinventing Baltimore," author Tony Hiss tells us that, "A city [Baltimore] that was almost two-thirds white in 1960 is now almost three-fifths black" (41).

Or, in the absence of a signal phrase, you may identify both the author and the page number in a parenthetical citation.

> Baltimore, "almost two-thirds white in 1960 is now almost three-fifths black" (Hiss 41).

The list of works cited (MLA):

This list, to be titled "Works Cited," will be the final page of your paper and include all of the works cited in it. These works will be listed in alphabetical order according to the last name of the author. It will not include works which you read but did not cite.

For a book by one author (MLA):

> Hayakawa, S. I. *Language in Thought and Action*. Orlando: Harcourt Brace Jovanovich, 1990.

Note that the information comes in three units—author, title, publishing information—each separated by a period, and that the second line is indented five spaces under the first. You can find the publishing information on the reverse side of the title page of the book.

For a magazine article (MLA):

> Hiss, Tony. "Annals of Place: Reinventing Baltimore." *The New Yorker* 29 April 1991: 40-73.

The APA Style of Documentation

For a book by one author (APA):

Introduce the quotation using the author's name followed by the date of publication in parentheses. Place the page reference in parentheses at the end of the passage.

> Semanticist S. I. Hayakawa (1990) points out that advertising and poetry are alike in that "they both strive to give meaning to the data of everyday experience" (p. 162).

If paraphrasing rather than quoting directly, include the author's name in a signal phrase followed by the publication date in parentheses, similar to the example above.

Or, if the author is not identified in a signal phrase, place his/her name and the publication date in parentheses at the end of the sentence. Note that a page number is not required for a paraphrase.

> Consumers want to identify with the happy, attractive people featured in advertisements (Hayakawa, 1990).

For a magazine article (APA):

For a quotation taken from a magazine article, follow the same format required for a book by one author.

The list of works cited (APA):

In APA style, the alphabetical list of works cited is entitled "References," and conforms to the following guidelines:

1. List the authors by last names, and use initials instead of first names.
2. Place the date of publication in parentheses after the author's name.
3. Underline titles and subtitles, capitalizing only the first word of the title (and proper nouns as well).

For a book by one author (AFA):

> Hayakawa, S. I. (1990). *Language in thought and action*. Orlando: Harcourt Brace Jovanovich.

For a magazine article (APA):

> Hiss, T. (1991, April 29). Annals of place: reinventing Baltimore. *The New Yorker*, pp. 40-73.

This discussion of documentation is a brief overview of the choices and formats available to you. For a complete guide to documentation, refer to a contemporary English handbook or to the Modern Language Association or American Psychological Association style guides.

Incorporating the Ideas of Others Into Your Own Writing

If you want your paper to read smoothly, you must take care to integrate direct quotations and paraphrases of other people's ideas into the grammatical flow of your sentences. Don't just "drop" them with a thud into a paragraph. Rely, rather, on a ready supply of introductory phrases with which to slide them in gracefully—phrases like, "As Freud discovered," "Justice O'Connor notes," and "According to *The New York Times*."

Sometimes, in order to make a quotation fit in smoothly with our own writing, we must add a word or words. Such additions are placed in brackets. For example:

> Carson McCullers sets a strangely luminous night scene:

>> There was a party at the banquet table in the center, and green-white August moths had found their way in from the night and fluttered about the clear candle flames.

> She seems to make a point of the "green-white August moths [that] had found their way in from the night. . . ."

As well as introducing them smoothly into the syntax of your sentence, you must also pay attention to semantics. Don't assume that the relevance of the quotation is self-evident. Make its relationship to your reasoning explicit. Is it an example? an appeal to authority? premise support? a counterargument? Whatever the case, the purpose of the quotation—how it relates to the point you are making—should be made explicit.

Punctuation and Format of Quotations

Periods and commas are placed *inside* quotation marks unless the quotation is followed by a parenthetical citation, in which case the period follows the citation.

> "Writing, like life itself, is a voyage of discovery," said Henry Miller, author of *Tropic of Cancer*.

> "Thinking is the activity I love best, and writing to me is simply thinking through my fingers."

>> —*Isaac Asimov*

"The true relationship between a leader and his people is often revealed through small, spontaneous gestures" (Friedman 106).

Colons and semicolons go *outside* quotation marks.

Read Hemingway's "Hill Like White Elephants"; we'll discuss it at our next meeting.

Use single quotation marks ['] for quotations within quotations.

"In coping with the violence of their city, Beirutis also seemed to disprove Hobbes's prediction that life in the 'state of nature' would be 'solitary.'"

—*Thomas Friedman, From Beirut to Jerusalem*

If the quotation is more than three lines long, it should be indented and single spaced. No quotation marks are necessary.

Omitting Words from a Direct Quotation

Sometimes we don't want to include all of a quotation, but just certain sections of it which apply to the point we are making. In this case, we may eliminate a part or parts of the quotation by the use of *ellipsis*: three spaced periods which indicate the intentional omission of words.

1. Something left out at the beginning.

". . . writers should be read but not seen. Rarely are they a winsome sight."
—*Edna Ferber*

2. Something left out in the middle.

"Everything goes by the board: honor, pride, decency . . . to get the book written. If a writer has to rob his mother, he will not hesitate; the "Ode on a Grecian Urn" is worth any number of old ladies."
—*William Faulkner*

3. Something left out at the end.

"I'd like to have money. And I'd like to be a good writer. These two can come together. . . ." [Note: the first dot is the period which ends the sentence.]
—*Dorothy Parker*

Selected Answers

*I*n keeping with the spirit of successful critical thinking, we acknowledge that considerable variation will emerge as you address the exercises in the text. But where we think it will help you, we offer a limited selection of sample responses.

Chapter 2

EXERCISE 2B

Distinguishing Between Facts, Inferences, and Judgments

1. This is an inference based on a collection of unstated facts and assumptions. It is also a judgment, the term "should" expressing the writer's approval.
3. While the phrase "much larger" is vague and could be considered misleading or judgmental, the actual figures could be verified and compared. Thus the statement represents a fact, but a fact in need of clarification before it could serve as strong support in an argument.

Chapter 3

EXERCISE 3A

Reducing Simple Arguments to Standard Form

1. a. Hunting an endangered species is forbidden.
   b. The bald eagle is an endangered species.
   ∴ Hunting bald eagles is prohibited.

2. a. Abortion involves a woman's right to privacy and the question of when life begins.

    b. Anything that involves personal rights and the onset of life raises
    serious moral questions.

∴ Abortion raises important moral questions.

EXERCISE 3C

Diagramming Arguments

1. a. Always wear a helmet when bicycling in the city since b. motorists
often do not see you and so c. accidents are common.

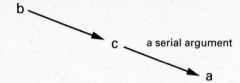

3. a. We all know that jogging is beneficial physically, but b. it also relieves
stress. c. This indicates that it is an effective remedy for depression.
Hence d. you should jog on a regular basis.

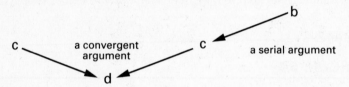

EXERCISE 3F

Identifying Hidden Assumptions

1. a. [Musicians don't understand business.]
   b. Maggie is a musician.
   ∴ She won't understand the business end of the partnership.

Chapter 5

EXERCISE 5A

Evaluating Premises in a Short Argument

1. a. Executives of several timber companies operating in Northern California have testified that more than 250,000 acres of virgin timber
are protected in state and national forests.

b. Such preserves are adequate for saving the old-growth redwoods.

∴. Further restrictions on logging are unnecessary.

2. and **3.** Premise (1) is a claim of fact by an authority. While the figures are verifiable and there are no immediate grounds for doubting them, the executives of timber companies could be suspect as authorities on this issue, given their vested interest in the outcome stated in the conclusion.

Premise (2) is a judgment, again possibly suspect in light of the sources, who stand to gain from such a judgment. For the argument to be acceptable, the timber company executives would need to provide considerably more support for their claim in premise (2) and also address the powerful counterarguments offered by environmental organizations opposed to the continued cutting of virgin timber. The timber industry would, in addition, need to explain its need for cutting virgin timber.

Chapter 6

EXERCISE 6B

Distinguishing Inductive from Deductive Reasoning

1. Inductive. The reasoning moves from specifics to a generalization. The conclusion—that Marie is out of town—does not necessarily follow. There are other possible explanations; she may be ill, or worse.
4. Deductive. The conclusion—that Philippe is devoted to his glass of red wine—follows of necessity from the premises. We can reach no other conclusion given the premises, and the reasoning moves from the general to the specific.

Chapter 7

EXERCISE 7A

Identifying Relationships Between Classes

1. Exclusion

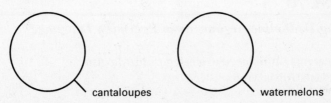
cantaloupes   watermelons

EXERCISE 7B

Determining the Validity of Categorical Syllogisms

1. Invalid

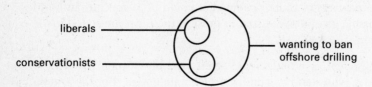

liberals
conservationists
wanting to ban offshore drilling

2. Valid

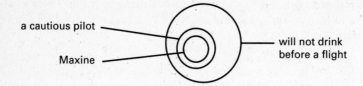

a cautious pilot
Maxine
will not drink before a flight

8. Invalid

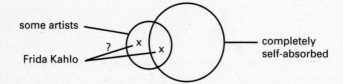

some artists
Frida Kahlo
completely self-absorbed

10. Valid

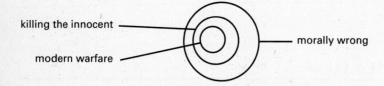

killing the innocent
modern warfare
morally wrong

EXERCISE 7C

Evaluating Deductive Arguments in Everyday Language

1. The argument reduced to a categorical syllogism:
   a. Plagiarism is wrong.

b. Paraphrasing the words of others without proper acknowledgment is the same as plagiarism.

∴ Paraphrasing the words of others without proper acknowledgment is wrong.

Circle diagrams to determine validity:

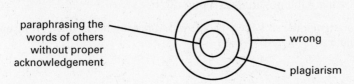

paraphrasing the words of others without proper acknowledgement — wrong

plagiarism

The argument is valid.

An evaluation of each premise according to the categories of acceptability:

The first premise—plagiarism is wrong—is a judgment, one that is part of our culture's shared belief system, and therefore, acceptable.

The second premise—paraphrasing the words of others without proper acknowledgment is the same as plagiarism—is also a judgment shared by the community, especially the academic community, and is therefore acceptable.

Final evaluation of the argument:

Since it is valid and the premises acceptable, the argument is sound.

EXERCISE 7D

Determining the Validity of Hypothetical Arguments

1. If a (opposition), then b (bad policy).
a (opposition).
∴ b (bad policy).

The antecedent is affirmed so the argument is valid.

3. If a (through window), then b (window unlocked).
b (window unlocked).
∴ a (through window).

The consequent is affirmed so the argument is invalid. An unlocked window is not the only way for a burglar to enter a house.

5. If a (respect opinion), then b (seek advice).
not b (don't seek advice).
∴ not a (don't respect opinion).

The consequent is denied so the argument is valid.

EXERCISE 7H

Editing the Illogical Series

1. This sentence suggests that "extra hours" and "[working] through many lunch hours" are separate classes when in fact one class is a member of the other. One possible revision:

In their attempt to excel, these people will work extra hours, often giving up their lunch hour.

EXERCISE 7I

Supplying Parallel Structure

2. She // rushed home, threw her assorted debris into a closet and prepared dinner for her guests.
6. There are two misfits—"economic" and "social"—adjectives in a list of nouns. The sentence can be corrected by replacing them with "economics" and "social status."

Chapter 8

EXERCISE 8B

Evaluating Inductive Arguments

1. The conclusion: all the containers of Sweet and Sour Yogurt filled that day are safe for consumption.

The target population: all the containers of Sweet and Sour Yogurt filled that day.

The projected property: safe for consumption.

The sample: one out of every thousand containers (about one every 15 minutes) filled that day.

Evaluation: the conclusion is justified since the method—random selection—and the frequency—one container every 15 minutes—lead to a representative sample.

4. Conclusion: TWA is more reliable than United.
The target population: all TWA and United flights.

The projected property: reliability of TWA and United flights.

The sample: 20 evenly spaced trips from November through April on United and 22 flights from May through October on TWA.

Evaluation: The sample is large enough, but not representative since the businessman flew United during the winter when we would expect there to be more late and canceled flights than in the summer and early fall when he flew with TWA.

Chapter 9

EXERCISE 9A

Identifying Fallacies

2. Slippery slope: This argument suggests a chain reaction which begins with allowing students to turn in papers after the due date and ends with all of America becoming "more ignorant," too large a consequence to result from a teacher's lenience.

9. Poisoning the well: Such an assertion puts the listener or reader on the defensive, forcing him to defend his patriotism and relieving the speaker or writer of the need to supply substantive premises in support of his conclusion that Americans should vote for the Republican party.

16. False cause: Superstition is often based on false cause reasoning. In this example, walking under the ladder occurred prior to his losing his wallet and receiving a speeding ticket, so he assumes on the basis of the sequence of events that the first event caused the other two.

27. Hasty generalization: He can't conclude on the basis of one incident that all hospitals care only about money, not about people. The sample is too small for such a conclusion.

33. Begging the question: This advertising slogan restates the conclusion— "that S & W vegetables are the best"—as a premise—"they use only premium quality." The two statements make essentially the same claim.

Chapter 10

EXERCISE 10B

Recognizing Appositives

1. Appositive #1: "one they will soon recognize on the streets of Ibarra and in towns and cities beyond."
The modified noun: "peculiarity"

Appositives #2 and #3: "a disregard for danger, a companionship with death."
The modified noun: "something"

Appositives #4, #5, #6, and #7: "the antic bravado, the fatal games, the coffin shop beside the cantina, the sugar skulls on the frosted cake."
The modified noun (or pronoun): "it"

EXERCISE 10C

Creating Appositives

1. New York, a city of danger and opportunity, has long been the destination of America's adventurous young.
3. People have very different ideas about the meaning of poverty, a condition that to some suggests insufficient income, to others laziness, and to still others a state of unwarranted discomfort.

EXERCISE 10E

Sharpening Sentence Focus

1. They are literate and produce several kinds of art, given that they have twenty terms for "book" and nine for "artist." [This revision eliminates the inappropriate "there is."]
3. By learning that the civilization consisted of literate and intelligent people, we can draw a picture of an advanced educational system. [The revision replaces the passive voice with the active voice by supplying the concrete subject "we," and also corrects the dangling modifier in the original.]

Credits

CARTOONS:

Frontispiece

Page ii, Drawing by Weber; © 1987 *The New Yorker Magazine, Inc.*

Chapter 1

Page 2, Reprinted with permission from *Detroit Free Press* and Richard Guindon.
Page 9, Drawing by Bernard Schoenbaum; © 1991 *The New Yorker Magazine, Inc.*

Chapter 2

Page 12, The Far Side cartoon by Gary Larson is reprinted by permission of Chronicle Features, San Francisco, CA.
Page 14, Copyright, 1990, Christian Science Monitor and World Monitor News Service. Distributed by the Los Angeles Times Syndicate.
Page 16, The Far Side cartoon by Gary Larson is reprinted by permission of Chronicle Features, San Francisco, CA.

Chapter 3

Page 27, Henrik Drescher
Page 32, Graphic by Dan Hubig © SAN FRANCISCO CHRONICLE Reprinted by permission.
Page 33, Copyright © 1991 by The New York Times Company. Reprinted by permission.

Chapter 4

Page 65, The "Quality Time" cartoon by Gail Machlis is reprinted courtesy of Chronicle Features, San Francisco, CA.
Page 66, Drawing by Koren; © 1988 The New Yorker Magazine, Inc.

Chapter 5

Page 93, Copyright © 1992 by The New York Times Company Reprinted by permission.

Chapter 7

Page 145, Henrik Drescher

Chapter 9

Page 157, The Far Side cartoon by Gary Larson is reprinted by permission of Chronicle Features, San Francisco, CA.
Page 159, DENNIS THE MENACE® used by permission of Hank Ketcham and © by North America Syndicate.
Page 161, Robert Gumpertz
Page 162, Drawing by Ed Fisher; © 1991 The New Yorker Magazine, Inc.
Page 164, Drawing by Ed Arno; © 1983 The New Yorker Magazine, Inc.
Page 166, Joseph Farris

Chapter 10

Page 185, Reprinted with permission from *Detroit Free Press* and Richard Guindon.

Page 192, Reprinted with special permission of King Features Syndicate, Inc.
Page 197, Arnie Ten
Page 198, Arnie Ten
Page 204, © 1990 *The Big Book of Hell* by Matt Groening. All Rights Reserved. Reprinted by permission of Pantheon Books, a division of Random House, NY.
Page 211, Drawing by Koren; © 1988 The New Yorker Magazine, Inc.

TEXT

Chapter 2

Page 15, "Commuter" from POEMS AND SKETCHES OF E. B. WHITE. Copyright 1925 by E. B. White. Reprinted by permission of HarperCollinsPublishers. **Pages 17–18,** "Totleigh Riddles" by John Cotton from THE TIMES LITERARY SUPPLEMENT, July 24, 1981. Reprinted by permission of the author. **Page 20,** Reprinted with the permission of Macmillan Publishing Company from THE ACTIVE READER by Michael J. Frisbie. Copyright © 1982 by Macmillan Publishing Company. **Pages 22–23,** "Hostess" by Donald Mangum. Reprinted by permission; © 1987 Donald Mangum. Originally in *The New Yorker.*

Chapter 3

Page 44, "Convicted" from NEWSWEEK, February 3, 1986. Copyright © 1986 Newsweek, Inc. All rights reserved. Reprinted by permission. **Page 45,** "Edward Kennedy Jr. discloses treatment for alcohol abuse" from THE HERALD SUN, July 12, 1991. Copyright © 1991 by The Associated Press. Reprinted by permission. **Page 47,** Two personal advertisements from THE SAN FRANCISCO FOCUS MAGAZINE, December 1991, page 160. Reprinted by permission of The San Francisco Focus Magazine.

Chapter 4

Pages 53–54, "The Writer" from *The Mind Reader,* copyright © 1971 by Richard Wilbur, reprinted by permission of Harcourt Brace Jovanovich, Inc.
Pages 69–71, "Capitol Punishment: Help or Hindrance to American Society," by Vickie Lee Christensen, © 1990.
Pages 71–74, "An Argument against the Colorization of Black-and-White Films," by Thomas Logan. Copyright © 1987 by Thomas Logan. Reprinted by permission.
Pages 74–76, "Free Needles Would Be a Help in S. F." by Randy Shilts from THE SAN FRANCISCO CHRONICLE, March 20, 1989. Copyright © 1989 by The San Francisco Chronicle. Reprinted by permission. **Page 77,** "They're Getting Older on Campus" from THE SAN FRANCISCO CHRONICLE, August 2, 1986. Copyright © 1986 by The San Francisco Chronicle. Reprinted by permission. **Pages 77–78,** "Ethnic Restriction At Lowell High" from THE SAN FRANCISCO CHRONICLE, July 24, 1988. Copyright © 1988 by The San Francisco Chronicle. Reprinted by permission. **Page 83,** "Breaking the Codes" from THE NEW REPUBLIC, July 8, 1991, pages 7 and 8. Copyright © 1991 by The New Republic. Reprinted by permission.

Chapter 5

Page 89, "Tree Facts" by Paul Sandberg from THE SAN FRANCISCO CHRONICLE, June 28, 1990. Copyright © 1990 by Paul Sandberg. Reprinted by permission of the author. **Pages 89–91,** "More 'Tree Facts'" by John B. Dewitt from THE SAN FRANCISCO CHRONICLE, July 3, 1990. Copyright © 1990 by John B. Dewitt. Reprinted by permission of the author. **Pages 94–95,** "New Way to Fight AIDS On Wrong Track" by Abe Mellinkoff from THE SAN FRANCISCO CHRONICLE, March 21, 1989. Copyright © 1989 by the San Francisco Chronicle. Reprinted by permission. **Pages 96–99** "The Invasion of the Nina, The Pinta, and the Santa Maria," by Alessandra Stanly from THE NEW YORK TIMES, June 2,

1991. Copyright © 1991 by the New York Times Company. Reprinted by permission. **Page 99,** From CAN'T WE MAKE MORAL JUDGEMENTS by Mary Midgley. Copyright © 1991 by St. Martin's Press, Inc. All rights reserved. Used with permission of St. Martin's Press, Inc. **Page 100,** "Old Poem" from LI PO AND TU FU by Li Po, translated by Arthur Cooper, page 141. Copyright © 1973 by Arthur Cooper. Reproduced by permission of Penguin Books Ltd. **Pages 100–101,** Poem #1129, "Tell all the Truth, but tell it slant..." by Emily Dickinson. Reprinted by permission of the publishers and the Trustees of Amherst College from THE POEMS OF EMILY DICKINSON, Thomas H. Johnson, ed., Cambridge, Mass.: The Belknap Press of Harvard University Press, Copyright © 1951, 1955, 1979, 1983 by the President and Fellows of Harvard College. **Pages 101–102,** From "A Defense of Abortion" by Judith Jarvis Thomson from PHILOSOPHY AND PUBLIC AFFAIRS, No. 1 (Fall 1971). Copyright © 1971 by Princeton University Press. Reprinted with permission of Princeton University Press.

Chapter 6

Page 105, Italo Calvino, translated by William Weaver, MR. PALOMAR. Orlando, FL.: Harcourt Brace Jovanovich, 1985, pages 108–109. **Pages 107–109,** Thomas Henry Huxley, AUTOBIOGRAPHY AND SELECTED ESSAYS. Boston, MA: Houghton Mifflin Company, 1909, pages 85–94. **Pages 109–112,** From ZEN AND THE ART OF MOTORCYCLE MAINTENANCE by Robert M. Pirsig, pages 99–103. Copyright © 1974 by Robert M. Pirsig. By permission of William Morrow & Company, Inc.

Chapter 7

Pages 130–131, Alexander W. Allison et al., THE NORTON ANTHOLOGY OF POETRY. New York, NY: W. W. Norton & Company, Inc., 1970, pages 370–371. **Pages 131–132,** "The Coy Mistress Replies" by Lysander Kemp from THE BELOIT POETRY JOURNAL, Winter 1954–1955. Reprinted by permission of The Beloit Poetry Journal. **Page 132,** "Dulce et Decorum Est" by Wilfred Owen: *The Collected Poems of Wilfred Owen.* Copyright © 1963 by Chatto & Windus, Ltd. Reprinted by permission of New Directions Publishing Corporation. **Page 137,** From "America Be On Guard" by Anthony Lewis from THE NEW YORK TIMES, November 18, 1991. "Copyright © 1991 by The New York Times Company. Reprinted by permission."

Chapter 8

Page 144, "Sexism Rampant" by Dominick Amarante from THE NATION, June 18, 1990. This article is reprinted from *The Nation* magazine/The Nation Company, Inc., © 1990. **Pages 144–145,** "Schulman Replies" by Grace Schulman from THE NATION, June 18, 1990. This article is reprinted from *The Nation* magazine/The Nation Company, Inc., © 1990. **Pages 147–148,** "Dispute Over Claims of Ibuprofen Dangers." Copyright © 1990 by United Press International. Reprinted by permission of United Press International. **Pages 148–151,** "What a Lovely Generalization!" by James Thurber. Copyright 1953 James Thurber. Copyright © 1981 Helen Thurber & Rosemary A. Thurber. From *Thurber Country* published by Simon & Schuster. **Pages 151–152,** Arthur Conan Doyle, "A Study in Scarlet." **Page 159,** Letter to the Editor by Bob Grimes from THE SAN FRANCISCO CHRONICLE, May 5, 1989.

Chapter 9

Pages 171–172, "How to Change Your Drinking Habits" by Abe Mellinkoff from THE SAN FRANCISCO CHRONICLE, October 1, 1982. Copyright © 1982 by The San Francisco Chronicle. Reprinted by permission. **Pages 173–174,** From "A Scholar and a Not-So-Gentle Woman—On Date Rape" by Camille Paglia from THE SAN FRANCISCO EXAMINER IMAGE MAGAZINE, July 7, 1991, page 11. Copyright © 1991 by the San Francisco Examiner. Reprinted by permission. **Pages 175–177,** "Abbie Hoffman—Pol Pot in style" by John C. Dvorak. Reprinted by permission of the author. **Pages 177–180,** "From Cradle to Commencement: Higher Education in the 90's" by Scott A. Warren from POMONA COLLEGE TODAY, Spring 1991, pages 10 and 11. Copyright © 1991 by Scott A. Warren. Reprinted by permission.

Chapter 10

Pages 186–187, From "The Borrowed Galanos" by Ellen Goodman. Copyright © 1988, The Boston Globe Newspaper Co./Washington Post Writers Group. Reprinted with permission. **Pages 188–189,** Excerpt from *Language in Thought and Action,* Fourth Edition by S. I. Hayakawa, copyright © 1978 by Harcourt Brace Jovanovich, Inc., reprinted by permission of the publisher. **Pages 189–190,** "Democracy" by E. B.

White from AN E. B. WHITE READER. Copyright © 1966 by E. B. White. Reprinted by permission. **Page 190,** From "Russians Redefine Oxford English," by Jo Thomas from THE NEW YORK TIMES, April 9, 1985. Copyright © 1985 by The New York Times Company. Reprinted by permission. **Page 190,** Ernest Hemingway, A FAREWELL TO ARMS. New York, NY: Charles Scribner's Sons, 1929, pages 177–178. **Pages 190–191**, Anthony Lewis, "Governing By Hypocrisy." THE NEW YORK TIMES, August 9, 1991. **Page 191,** "Politics and the English Language" by George Orwell, copyright 1946 by Sonia Brownell Orwell and renewed 1974 by Sonia Orwell, reprinted from his volume *Shooting an Elephant and Other Essays* by permission of Harcourt Brace Jovanovich, Inc. **Pages 196–197,** Excerpt from *In Search of Our Mothers' Gardens,* copyright © 1983 by Alice Walker, reprinted by permission of Harcourt Brace Jovanovich, Inc. **Page 202,** From "The Language Thing" by Timothy Beneke from THE EAST BAY EXPRESS, Volume 13, No. 37, page 12. Copyright © 1991 by Timothy Beneke. Reprinted by permission of the author.

Index